Clinical Mental Health Counseling

Clinical Mental Health Counseling

An Introduction to the Profession and Practice

Richard D. Parsons

West Chester University

cognella®
SAN DIEGO

Bassim Hamadeh, CEO and Publisher
Amy Smith, Senior Project Editor
Emely Villavicencio, Senior Graphic Designer
Stephanie Kohl, Licensing Coordinator
Natalie Piccotti, Director of Marketing
Kassie Graves, Vice President of Editorial
Jamie Giganti, Director of Academic Publishing

9781793548078

cognella® ACADEMIC PUBLISHING
3970 Sorrento Valley Blvd., Ste. 500, San Diego, CA 92121

BRIEF CONTENTS

DETAILED CONTENTS

SECTION IV Clinical Mental Health Counseling as Profession

PREFACE

Two things are clear. First, the need for mental health services is increasing dramatically. Second, the role and value of mental health counselors in service of those in need has achieved public and professional recognition.

The Need

A review of the latest statistics available from the National Institute of Mental Health Disorders, part of the National Institutes of Health (Johns Hopkins Medicine, n.d.), will confirm the need for counseling services. An estimated 26% of Americans ages 18 and older—about 1 in 4 adults—suffer from a diagnosable mental disorder in a given year. Consider the following data:

- Many people suffer from more than one mental disorder at a given time. In particular, depressive illnesses tend to co-occur with substance abuse and anxiety disorders.
- Approximately 9.5% of American adults ages 18 and older will suffer from a depressive illness (major depression, bipolar disorder, or dysthymia) each year.
- Approximately 18% of people ages 18 to 54 years in a given year have an anxiety disorder. Anxiety disorders include panic disorder, obsessive-compulsive disorder (OCD), posttraumatic stress disorder (PTSD), generalized anxiety disorder (GAD), and phobias (social phobia, agoraphobia, and specific phobia).

The pervasive, damaging effects of untreated mental illness are as concerning as the reality that these increased demands have placed a strain on our healthcare system's ability to meet this need.

Clinical Mental Health Counselors

The need for increased service and service providers has resulted in employment growth for mental health counselors. According to the Bureau of Labor Statistics (2020), the projected growth rate in mental health counselor employment in 2019 was 22%.

The need for clinical mental health counselors is clear, as is the increased interest among those seeking to enter the field. CACREP, for example, now includes 344 graduate programs providing CACREP-accredited training in clinical mental health counseling. For those entering the profession of clinical mental health counseling, their formation begins with an understanding of what makes their chosen profession unique and uniquely valuable.

This Text

Clinical Mental Health Counseling: An Introduction to the Profession and Practice is a text that provides the reader with an understanding of the evolution of the role and function of clinical mental health counseling and the value served by those within the profession. Beyond the presentation of material highlighting the role and function of ethical, effective practice, the text's primary focus is on fostering the development of the reader's professional identity as a clinical mental health counselor.

The chapters in Section I, "Foundations," review the history and foundation of this profession and highlight the factors that make mental health counseling unique among mental health professions. Chapters in Section II, "Clinical Mental Health in Practice," review the theories and models that guide mental health counselors' practice in case conceptualization and treatment formulation. Section III, "Clinical Mental Health Counseling in Context," presents chapters that review the various roles, settings, and populations served by the clinical mental health counselor. Chapters within the final section, Section IV, "Clinical Mental Health Counseling as Profession," discusses those elements that come together to make clinical mental health counseling a profession.

The text is developed to include best practices, current laws and regulations, and the impact of technology on practice delivery. Additionally, this book addresses the following CACREP competency standards.

TEXT FOCAL POINT	CACREP STANDARD
1. Comprehension of the history, philosophy, and current status of counseling and specifically the mental health counseling profession	• 2.F.1.a: History and philosophy of the counseling profession and its specialty areas • 2.F.1.f: Professional counseling organizations, including membership benefits, activities, services to members, and current issues • 2.F.1.g: Professional counseling credentialing, including certification, licensure, and accreditation practices and standards, and the effects of public policy on these issues • 5.C.1.a: History and development of clinical mental health counseling
2. Understanding the various roles and professional responsibilities assumed by counselors along with the nature of the interface with other mental health specialists	• 2.F.1.b: The multiple professional roles and functions of counselors across specialty areas, and their relationships with human service and integrated behavioral health care systems, including interagency and interorganizational collaboration and consultation
3. Understanding the unique role and function of clinical mental health counselors	• 5.C.2.a: Roles and settings of clinical mental health counselors • 5.C.2.c: Mental health service delivery modalities within the continuum of care, such as inpatient, outpatient, partial treatment and aftercare, and the mental health counseling services networks • 2,F.1.j: Technology's impact on the counseling profession • 2.F.1.h: Current labor market information relevant to opportunities for practice within the counseling profession • 2.F.1.k: Strategies for personal and professional self-evaluation and implications for practice
4. Professional standards, ethics, and legal standards affecting clinical mental health practice and professionals	• 5.C.2.k: Professional organizations, preparation standards, and credentials relevant to the practice of clinical mental health counseling • 2.F.1.d: The role and process of the professional counselor advocating on behalf of the profession • 2.F.1.i: Ethical standards of professional counseling organizations and credentialing bodies, and applications of ethical and legal considerations in professional counseling • 2.F.1.m: The role of counseling supervision in the profession

References

Johns Hopkins Medicine. (n.d.). *Mental health disorder statistics.* https://www.hopkinsmedicine.org/health/wellness-and-prevention/mental-health-disorder-statistics

U.S. Bureau of Labor Statistics. (2020). Substance abuse, behavioral disorder, and mental health counselors. *Occupational outlook handbook*. https://www.bls.gov/ooh/community-and-social-service/substance-abuse-behavioral-disorder-and-mental-health-counselors.htm

ACKNOWLEDGMENTS

Two things are clear. First, the need for mental health services is increasing dramatically. Second, the role and value of mental health counselors in service of those in need has achieved public and professional recognition.

The wonderfully competent people at Cognella Academic Publishing continue to be the best advocates and supporters for which an author could hope. While having a long affiliation with Cognella, I continue to be surprised, impressed, and awed by the level of support each member provides.

I would also like to acknowledge the professional expertise provided by Amy Smith, Senior Project Editor; and Tracy Buyan, Production Editor. A special thanks goes out to my friend and Vice President of Editorial, Kassie Graves. Her energy, creativity, and insight are truly inspiring. Her support is and has been essential to all our shared endeavors.

Finally—a special thank you to my wife, Ginny, for her gifts of understanding, support, and love.
RP/2021

SECTION I

Foundations

CHAPTER 1

Counseling—Unique Among the Helping Professions

So, I hear you are studying to be a counselor? Is that the same as a psychologist?

—R.J.

It might not occur at a family gathering, as was the case with the individual being queried by R. J., quoted above, but it is very likely that you will be asked to differentiate your calling to become a clinical mental health counselor from that of a clinical psychologist, social worker, or even a psychiatrist. Although it is easy to point to the specific degree earned, the organizational membership acquired, or even the state certification or licensed assigned, the real differentiation is found in the unique values and philosophical perspective collectively embraced by those called professional counselors.

As you continue to grow in your professional identity as a counselor, you will be able to articulate, value, and operate from a knowledge base, skill set, and philosophical perspective that distinguishes you and your profession from other helping professionals (Zhang & Parsons, 2016). This chapter will help you begin to identify all that makes the profession of counseling unique among the helping professions.

After completing this chapter, the reader will be able to:

- Describe the perspectives that differentiate professional counseling from other mental health professions.
- Identify the core, practice, and specialty competencies identified by CACREP.
- Describe the degree to which the reader owns and values the core perspectives of professional counseling.
- Describe the difference between certification and licensure.

Confusion Abounds

With apologies to William Shakespeare, one can wonder if this is simply "a rose, by any other name" remaining a rose? A therapist is a therapist, right?

Many laypeople are confused by the titles assigned to the various mental health professionals, be that *psychologist*, *psychiatrist*, or *counselor*. As a result, the public often assumes that they are synonymous and simply lumps them all into a collective called *therapist*. The helping profession is not a singular entity but comprises many related and sometimes overlapping, unique professions and professionals. The existence of clinical psychologists, psychiatrists, clinical social workers, and counselors, who in most circumstances appear to be often seeking the same goals and providing very similar services, may call to question the need for such variation of titles and professions. Is this merely a case of a difference in titles yet similar services? Or, is there something truly unique to each of these professions and the perspectives and values they bring to their service?

Those laying claim to the title of *clinical mental health counselor* are unique, not just in their academic preparation but in their philosophical view of the human condition and the values that guide their conceptualization of mental health and mental health services.

Counseling and Counselors: Distinct Profession and Professionals

As a mental health profession, counseling shares many similarities with other professions addressing mental health needs. The theories and research that serve as the foundation for our practice and the methods employed to facilitate change are applied by many others within the mental health professions. However, the core values and beliefs upon which counseling has developed set it apart from these other professions (Neukrug, 2011).

The core values that serve as underpinning for our profession can be identified within the definition of counseling proposed by the American Counseling Association (2010):

> Counseling is a professional relationship that empowers diverse individuals, families, and groups to accomplish mental health, wellness, education, and career goals.

Embedded within this definition are the pillars of the collective identity held by counselors, which distinguishes counselors from other helping professionals. Specifically, unique to the counseling profession is its emphasis on wellness, developmental perspective, prevention, and empowerment (McWhirter, 1991; Myers et al., 2001; Remley & Herlihy, 2020).

Developmental Perspective

Counselors have a "distinctive educational-developmental view of the helping process" (American Mental Health Counselors Association [AMHCA], 2010, p. 22). Professional counselors promote a developmental focus and ascribe many client problems to typical developmental milestones and transitions.

A developmental focus depicts the individual as a dynamic and fluid organism. As such, counselors view client challenges not as permanent conditions or maladies but, instead, as an invitation to growth. This view positions counselors to approach their work with clients more positively, viewing the client's difficulty as a reflection of a developmental block rather than an indication of severe pathology. This developmental perspective encourages counselors to see individuals as having the capacity to move forward, change, adapt, heal, and attain optimal mental health or wellness (Brady-Amoon, 2012).

The developmental perspective of professional counseling emphasizes the resiliency and strength of the client, which may lead to a greater belief in their efficacy and motivation to make life changes (Carney, 2007). Framing a challenge in a developmental context can facilitate a client's sense of empowerment, seeing the issue as something that is changeable (Vereen et al., 2014).

Wellness Perspective

Distinct from other mental health professionals, counselors emphasize a wellness perspective and paradigm, one that is clearly contrasted to the medical orientation of illness often employed in mental health services. This is not to suggest that clinical mental health counselors do not engage in therapy and remedial service, but rather that their approach moves beyond remediation and intervention to target development, growth, and prevention.

Counselors value helping each person achieve positive mental health (Remley & Herlihy, 2007). To this end, counselors focus on the client's strengths as opposed to seeing the client as being problematic or only having problems. Counselors believe in the value of counseling, not just for those experiencing blocks in their development but for all who seek to unfold their potential. As noted by Myers (1992):

> We do not believe that people must first be diagnosed with an illness before they can be treated with counseling services . . . all people can benefit from counseling, fully functioning people who experience everyday stress in their lives and those who are seriously mentally ill can benefit from a counseling philosophy that offers hope for a better tomorrow. (p. 138)

This focus on wellness and a view of pathology within the context of normal human development invites the professional counselor to employ psychoeducational and strengths-based methods of intervention in addition to the more traditional psychotherapy techniques.

Prevention

Like other helping professionals, counselors not only have the knowledge and skills to intervene at times when clients are experiencing difficulty but also philosophically value the provision of preventive care over just remediation (Remley & Herlihy, 2020). Counselors employ programs and strategies such as guidance curriculum, resiliency training, premarital communication training, and so on that are focused on helping clients develop the knowledge and skills that will help them prevent potential problems.

Empowerment

Counselors seek to assist those individuals and groups who feel powerless and marginalized to gain awareness of those external influences on their lives that create a sense of powerlessness and help them gain control over their lives (Puglia, 2008). This goal of promoting client personal power extends to the relationship between the counselor and the client. Counselors seek to promote client independence and, to that end, employ knowledge and skills that assist the client at the moment and help them develop the tools necessary to be more able to solve problems and navigate life's challenges on their own (Remley & Herlihy, 2007).

These core and distinguishing perspectives are intended to be more than words in a definition or textbook. Each of these perspectives represents a value held and cherished by those who identify as professional counselors—embracing these perspectives as personal and professional values will give shape to a counselor's service delivery and practice. As such, it is worthwhile to take time, now and throughout your professional development, to reflect upon these perspectives and identify the degree to which they guide your own professional decisions. Exercise 1.1 will help you begin this process of reviewing your values and valuing the core perspectives unique to counseling as a profession.

Exercise 1.1 Embracing a Counseling Perspective

Directions: Use the following scale to assess your level of ownership and personal valuing of each of the perspectives contributing to the uniqueness of counseling as a profession.

	Personal valuing: The degree to which you hold these perspectives as something to be genuinely valued and embodied in practice.				
	1	2	3	4	5
	Do not hold this as a valuable perspective.		I understand the concept but not sure I buy into its application.		I value the perspective, and I am actively working to assimilate it into my professional decision making.
Development					
Wellness					
Prevention					
Empowerment					

The Nature of Clinical Mental Health Counseling

Clinical mental health counselors are highly skilled professionals who combine traditional psychotherapy with a practical, problem-solving approach that creates a dynamic and efficient path for change and problem resolution. Perhaps the most immediate and observable distinction that can be made between a clinical mental health counselor and others within the helping professions can be found in their educational training.

As with many young and developing professions, those seeking training and education in clinical mental health counseling often experienced wide variation in the types of courses offered and the expanse of the curriculum provided. In response to this lack of standardization and consistency, the American Mental Health Counseling Association issued a call for increased specification and standardization of clinical mental health training programs. Currently, this specification and standardization can be found in the standards of training articulated by the Council for Accreditation of Counseling and Related Educational Programs (CACREP, 2016). Graduates of CACREP-accredited clinical mental health counseling programs have had 60 credit hours of specified coursework and supervised experience, including a total of 700 supervised clinical field hours. CACREP has identified the foundational, specialty, and practice experiences that are seen as essential to the preparation of clinical mental health counselors. Table 1.1 provides the listing of both content areas and specific competency standards to be addressed. You may find the listing of competencies to be useful markers to guide your continued professional development.

TABLE 1.1 CACREP Standards

Core Areas (All Counselors)

The eight common core areas represent the foundational knowledge required of all entry-level counselor education graduates. Therefore, counselor education programs must document where each of the lettered standards listed below is covered in the curriculum.

1. **Professional Counseling Orientation and Ethical Practice**
   a. history and philosophy of the counseling profession and its specialty areas
   b. the multiple professional roles and functions of counselors across specialty areas, and their relationships with human service and integrated behavioral health care systems, including interagency and interorganizational collaboration and consultation
   c. counselors' roles and responsibilities as members of interdisciplinary community outreach and emergency management response teams
   d. the role and process of the professional counselor advocating on behalf of the profession
   e. advocacy processes needed to address institutional and social barriers that impede access, equity, and success for clients
   f. professional counseling organizations, including membership benefits, activities, services to members, and current issues
   g. professional counseling credentialing, including certification, licensure, and accreditation practices and standards, and the effects of public policy on these issues
   h. current labor market information relevant to opportunities for practice within the counseling profession
   i. ethical standards of professional counseling organizations and credentialing bodies, and applications of ethical and legal considerations in professional counseling
   j. technology's impact on the counseling profession
   k. strategies for personal and professional self-evaluation and implications for practice
   l. self-care strategies appropriate to the counselor role
   m. the role of counseling supervision in the profession
2. **Social and Cultural Diversity**
   a. multicultural and pluralistic characteristics within and among diverse groups nationally and internationally
   b. theories and models of multicultural counseling, cultural identity development, and social justice and advocacy
   c. multicultural counseling competencies
   d. the impact of heritage, attitudes, beliefs, understandings, and acculturative experiences on an individual's views of others
   e. the effects of power and privilege for counselors and clients
   f. help-seeking behaviors of diverse clients
   g. the impact of spiritual beliefs on clients' and counselors' worldviews
   h. strategies for identifying and eliminating barriers, prejudices, and processes of intentional and unintentional oppression and discrimination
3. **Human Growth and Development**
   a. theories of individual and family development across the lifespan
   b. theories of learning
   c. theories of normal and abnormal personality development
   d. theories and etiology of addictions and addictive behaviors
   e. biological, neurological, and physiological factors that affect human development, functioning, and behavior
   f. systemic and environmental factors that affect human development, functioning, and behavior
   g. effects of crisis, disasters, and trauma on diverse individuals across the lifespan
   h. a general framework for understanding differing abilities and strategies for differentiated interventions
   i. ethical and culturally relevant strategies for promoting resilience and optimum development and wellness across the lifespan

4. **Career Development**
   a. theories and models of career development, counseling, and decision making
   b. approaches for conceptualizing the interrelationships among and between work, mental well-being, relationships, and other life roles and factors
   c. processes for identifying and using career, avocational, educational, occupational and labor market information resources, technology, and information systems
   d. approaches for assessing the conditions of the work environment on clients' life experiences
   e. strategies for assessing abilities, interests, values, personality and other factors that contribute to career development
   f. strategies for career development program planning, organization, implementation, administration, and evaluation
   g. strategies for advocating for diverse clients' career and educational development and employment opportunities in a global economy
   h. strategies for facilitating client skill development for career, educational, and life- work planning and management
   i. methods of identifying and using assessment tools and techniques relevant to career planning and decision making
   j. ethical and culturally relevant strategies for addressing career development
5. **Counseling and Helping Relationships**
   a. theories and models of counseling
   b. a systems approach to conceptualizing clients
   c. theories, models, and strategies for understanding and practicing consultation
   d. ethical and culturally relevant strategies for establishing and maintaining in-person and technology-assisted relationships
   e. the impact of technology on the counseling process
   f. counselor characteristics and behaviors that influence the counseling process
   g. essential interviewing, counseling, and case conceptualization skills
   h. developmentally relevant counseling treatment or intervention plans
   i. development of measurable outcomes for clients
   j. evidence-based counseling strategies and techniques for prevention and intervention
   k. strategies to promote client understanding of and access to a variety of community- based resources
   l. suicide prevention models and strategies
   m. crisis intervention, trauma-informed, and community-based strategies, such as Psychological First Aid
   n. processes for aiding students in developing a personal model of counseling
6. **Group Counseling and Group Work**
   a. theoretical foundations of group counseling and group work
   b. dynamics associated with group process and development
   c. therapeutic factors and how they contribute to group effectiveness
   d. characteristics and functions of effective group leaders
   e. approaches to group formation, including recruiting, screening, and selecting members
   f. types of groups and other considerations that affect conducting groups in varied settings
   g. ethical and culturally relevant strategies for designing and facilitating groups
   h. direct experiences in which students participate as group members in a small group activity, approved by the program, for a minimum of 10 clock hours over the course of one academic term
7. **Assessment and Testing**
   a. historical perspectives concerning the nature and meaning of assessment and testing in counseling
   b. methods of effectively preparing for and conducting initial assessment meetings
   c. procedures for assessing risk of aggression or danger to others, self-inflicted harm, or suicide
   d. procedures for identifying trauma and abuse and for reporting abuse
   e. use of assessments for diagnostic and intervention planning purposes
   f. basic concepts of standardized and non-standardized testing, norm-referenced and criterion-referenced assessments, and group and individual assessments
   g. statistical concepts, including scales of measurement, measures of central tendency, indices of variability, shapes and types of distributions, and correlations

(Continued)

(*Continued*)

h. reliability and validity in the use of assessments
i. use of assessments relevant to academic/educational, career, personal, and social development
j. use of environmental assessments and systematic behavioral observations
k. use of symptom checklists, and personality and psychological testing
l. use of assessment results to diagnose developmental, behavioral, and mental disorders
m. ethical and culturally relevant strategies for selecting, administering, and interpreting assessment and test results

8. **Research and Program Evaluation**
   a. the importance of research in advancing the counseling profession, including how to critique research to inform counseling practice
   b. identification of evidence-based counseling practices
   c. needs assessments
   d. development of outcome measures for counseling programs
   e. evaluation of counseling interventions and programs
   f. qualitative, quantitative, and mixed research methods
   g. designs used in research and program evaluation
   h. statistical methods used in conducting research and program evaluation
   i. analysis and use of data in counseling
   j. ethical and culturally relevant strategies for conducting, interpreting, and reporting the results of research and/or program evaluation

---

Professional Practice/Supervised Field Experience

Professional practice, which includes practicum and internship, provides for the application of theory and the development of counseling skills under supervision. These experiences will provide opportunities for students to counsel clients who represent the ethnic and demographic diversity of their community.

The following Standards apply to entry-level programs for which accreditation is being sought.

A. Students are covered by individual professional counseling liability insurance policies while enrolled in practicum and internship.
B. Supervision of practicum and internship students includes program-appropriate audio/video recordings and/or live supervision of students' interactions with clients.
C. Formative and summative evaluations of the student's counseling performance and ability to integrate and apply knowledge are conducted as part of the student's practicum and internship.
D. Students have the opportunity to become familiar with a variety of professional activities and resources, including technological resources, during their practicum and internship.
E. In addition to the development of individual counseling skills, during either the practicum or internship, students must lead or co-lead a counseling or psychoeducational group.

Practicum

F. Students complete supervised counseling practicum experiences that total a minimum of 100 clock hours over a full academic term that is a minimum of 10 weeks.
G. Practicum students complete at least 40 clock hours of direct service with actual clients that contributes to the development of counseling skills.
H. Practicum students have weekly interaction with supervisors that averages one hour per week of individual and/or triadic supervision throughout the practicum by (1) a counselor education program faculty member, (2) a student supervisor who is under the supervision of a counselor education program faculty member, or (3) a site supervisor who is working in consultation on a regular schedule with a counselor education program faculty member in accordance with the supervision agreement.
I. Practicum students participate in an average of 1 1/2 hours per week of group supervision on a regular schedule throughout the practicum. Group supervision must be provided by a counselor education program faculty member or a student supervisor who is under the supervision of a counselor education program faculty member.

Internship

J. After successful completion of the practicum, students complete 600 clock hours of supervised counseling internship in roles and settings with clients relevant to their specialty area.

K. Internship students complete at least 240 clock hours of direct service.
L. Internship students have weekly interaction with supervisors that averages one hour per week of individual and/or triadic supervision throughout the internship, provided by (1) the site supervisor, (2) counselor education program faculty, or (3) a student supervisor who is under the supervision of a counselor education program faculty member.
M. Internship students participate in an average of 1 1/2 hours per week of group supervision on a regular schedule throughout the internship. Group supervision must be provided by a counselor education program faculty member or a student supervisor who is under the supervision of a counselor education program faculty member.

Clinical Mental Health Counseling Specialty Requirements

Students who are preparing to specialize as clinical mental health counselors will demonstrate the knowledge and skills necessary to address a wide variety of circumstances within the context of clinical mental health counseling. Counselor education programs with a specialty area in clinical mental health counseling must document where each of the lettered standards listed below is covered in the curriculum.

1. **Foundations**
   a. history and development of clinical mental health counseling
   b. theories and models related to clinical mental health counseling
   c. principles, models, and documentation formats of biopsychosocial case conceptualization and treatment planning
   d. neurobiological and medical foundation and etiology of addiction and co-occurring disorders
   e. psychological tests and assessments specific to clinical mental health counseling
2. **Contextual Dimensions**
   a. roles and settings of clinical mental health counselors
   b. etiology, nomenclature, treatment, referral, and prevention of mental and emotional disorders
   c. mental health service delivery modalities within the continuum of care, such as inpatient, outpatient, partial treatment and aftercare, and the mental health counseling services networks
   d. diagnostic process, including differential diagnosis and the use of current diagnostic classification systems, including the *Diagnostic and Statistical Manual of Mental Disorders* (DSM) and the International Classification of Diseases (ICD)
   e. potential for substance use disorders to mimic and/or co-occur with a variety of neurological, medical, and psychological disorders
   f. impact of crisis and trauma on individuals with mental health diagnoses
   g. impact of biological and neurological mechanisms on mental health
   h. classifications, indications, and contraindications of commonly prescribed psychopharmacological medications for appropriate medical referral and consultation
   i. legislation and government policy relevant to clinical mental health counseling
   j. cultural factors relevant to clinical mental health counseling
   k. professional organizations, preparation standards, and credentials relevant to the practice of clinical mental health counseling
   l. legal and ethical considerations specific to clinical mental health counseling
   m. record keeping, third party reimbursement, and other practice and management issues in clinical mental health counseling
3. **Practice**
   a. intake interview, mental status evaluation, biopsychosocial history, mental health history, and psychological assessment for treatment planning and caseload management
   b. techniques and interventions for prevention and treatment of a broad range of mental health issues
   c. strategies for interfacing with the legal system regarding court-referred clients
   d. strategies for interfacing with integrated behavioral health care professionals
   e. strategies to advocate for persons with mental health issues

---

Source: CACREP, "Selections," *2016 CACREP Standards*. Copyright © 2016 by Council for Accreditation of Counseling & Related Educational Programs. Reprinted with permission.

As is clear from the competencies listed in Table 1.1, clinical mental health counselors have a foundational skill set distinct from those of other behavioral health disciplines. However, more central to their distinctiveness is the fact that at their core they are counselors and, as such, approach their practice from a holistic, preventive, strength-based, and wellness orientation (Seiler & Messina, 1976).

In addition to viewing each individual's level of functioning and lifestyle as a reflection of the interaction of biological, social, psycho-emotional, and spiritual factors, the clinical mental health counselor also appreciates the fact that clients are embedded in and thus influenced by their family, societal, historical, cultural and socioeconomic context (Pistole, 2001). As a result, the clinical mental health counselor's treatment plans often engage community resources and interdisciplinary service.

While remaining true to the core counseling values and perspectives, the clinical mental health counselor employs best practice and empirically supported interventions (see Chapter 6), synthesizing such remedial approaches with the underlying philosophy of restoring and strengthening development and mental health (Pistole, 2001). This training and orientation make the clinical mental health counselor well situated to lead the effort in integrating health care, providing high-quality care in a cost-effective manner.

Certifications and Licensure

In addition to core graduate training, many clinical mental health counselors seek additional credentialing to increase their expertise and professionalism (Neukrug, 2017). The acquisition of certifications or licensing serves as a mechanism not only to ensure ongoing professional development and increased competency but also to allow the counselor to expand the nature and focus of their practice.

Certification

Often counselors will seek specific certification credentials to enhance their expertise and bolster their resume. To obtain a particular certification, the counselor submits their credentials to an accredited professional group. One such group is the National Board for Certified Counselors (NBCC). Established by the American Counseling Association in 1982, the NBCC offers the National Certified Counselor credential (NCC), which gives testimony to the fact that the counselor has met national standards for education, training, and experience to practice as a counselor. Another certification often acquired by the mental health counselor is a *Certified Clinical Mental Health* Counselor (CCMHC) specialty. This certification requires that the candidate have NCC certification as offered through the NBCC. The possession of this certification attests to the fact that the counselor has met rigorous education, examination, supervision, experience and ethical requirements. As such, it offers the highest standards of practice in clinical mental health counseling. Certification, demonstrating that the counselor has specialized training and experience in a specialty is also available in areas such as substance abuse counseling, marriage and family counseling, school counseling, rehabilitation counseling, grief counseling, and pastoral/spiritual counseling, to name a few.

Licensing

Many clinical mental health counselors seek recognition from the state through the acquisition of a state license. States regulate the use of title and practice of a profession within their jurisdiction and limit their use to individuals with specific training and certification.

The title *licensed counselor* or *licensed professional counselor* can be employed only by those individuals who have met the set requirements for such licensing. Although the requirements vary from state to state, most states require the following:

- Earned a master's degree in counseling or a closely related mental health discipline.
- Completed a minimum of 2 years post-master's clinical work under the supervision of a licensed or certified mental health professional.
- Passed a state-developed or national licensure or certification examination.

Details on the licensure requirements across the states are available at the NBCC website (https://www.nbcc.org/search/stateboarddirectory). The information provided on this website will help you identify the specific contact information and processing requirements for any sate of interest.

Keystones

- Clinical mental health counselors are highly skilled professionals who combine traditional psychotherapy with a practical, problem-solving approach that creates a dynamic and efficient path for change and problem resolution.
- *Clinical mental health counselors* are unique not just in their academic preparation but also in their philosophical view of the human condition and the values that guide their conceptualization of mental health and mental health services.
- The core values and beliefs of counselors set them apart from other mental health professionals.
- Unique to the counseling profession is its emphasis on wellness, developmental perspective, prevention, and empowerment.
- Graduates of CACREP-accredited clinical mental health counseling programs have had 60 credit hours of specified coursework and supervised experience, including a total of 700 supervised clinical field hours. CACREP has identified the foundational, specialty, and practice experiences that are seen as essential to the preparation of clinical mental health counselors.
- CCMHC certification attests to the fact that the counselor has met rigorous education, examination, supervision, experience, and ethical requirements and, as such, offers the highest standards of practice in clinical mental health counseling.
- States regulate the use of the title of *licensed counselor* or *licensed professional counselor* and their practice within their jurisdiction and limit their use to individuals with specific training and certification.

Additional Resources

American Counseling Association. (2010). *20/20: Consensus definition of counseling.* https://www.counseling.org/about-us/about-aca/20-20-a-vision-for-the-future-of-counseling/consensus-definition-of-counseling

Granello, D., & Young, M. E. (2012). *Counseling today: Foundations of professional identity.* MyHelpingLab Series. Merrill.

Nassar-McMillan, S., & Niles, S. C. (2010). *Developing your identity as a professional counselor. Standards, settings, and specialties.* Brooks/Cole.

WebMD. (2019). *Guide to psychiatry and counseling.* https://www.webmd.com/mental-health/guide-to-psychiatry-and-counseling#4

References

American Counseling Association. (2010). *20/20: Consensus definition of counseling.* https://www.counseling.org/about-us/about-aca/20-20-a-vision-for-the-future-of-counseling/consensus-definition-of-counseling

American Mental Health Counselors Association. (2010). *Code of ethics.* http://www.amhca.org/assets/news/AMHCA_Code_of_Ethics_2010_w_pagination_cxd_51110.pdf

Brady-Amoon, P. (2012). Further extending the humanistic vision for the future of counseling: A response to Hansen. *The Journal of Humanistic Counseling, 51,* 184–196.

Carney, J. V. (2007). Humanistic wellness services for community mental health providers. *The Journal of Humanistic Counseling, Education and Development, 46,* 154–171.

Council for Accreditation of Counseling and Related Educational Programs. (2016). *2016 CACREP standards.* http://www.cacrep.org/wp-content/uploads/2017/08/2016-Standards-with-citations.pdf

McWhirter, E. H. (1991). Empowerment in counseling. *Journal of Counseling and Development, 69,* 222–227.

Myers, J. (1992). Wellness, prevention, development: The cornerstone of the profession. *Journal of Counseling & Development, 7,* 136.

Myers, J. E., Sweeney, T. J., & Witmer, J. M. (2001) Optimization of behavior: Promotion of wellness. In D. C. Locke, J. E. Myers, & E. L. Herr (Eds.), *The handbook of counseling* (pp. 641–652). Sage.

Neukrug, E. S. (2017). *A brief orientation to counseling: Professional identity, history, and standards* (2nd ed.). Cengage Learning.

Pistole, M. C. (2001). Mental health counseling: Identity and distinctiveness. *ERIC Digest.* https://www.counseling.org/resources/library/ERIC%20Digests/2001-09.pdf

Puglia, B. (2008). The professional identity of counseling students in master's level CACREP-accredited programs (Unpublished doctoral dissertation). Old Dominion University, Norfolk, VA.

Remley, T. P., & Herlihy, B. (2020). *Ethical, legal, and professional issues in counseling* (6th ed.). Pearson.

Seiler, G., & Messina, J. J. (1979). Toward professional identity: The dimension of mental health counseling in perspective. *American Mental Health Counselors Journal, 1,* 3–8.

Vereen, L. G., Hill, N. R., Sosa, G. A., & Kress, V. (2014). The synonymic nature of professional counseling and humanism: Presuppositions that guide our identities. *Journal of Humanistic Counseling, 53,* 191–202.

Zhang, N., & Parsons R. D. (2016). *Field experience: Transitioning from student to professional.* Sage.

CHAPTER 2

The History and Evolution of Clinical Mental Health Counseling

The events of today are influenced by the historical past and will influence the historical future.
—Leahey (1980, p. 14)

The emergence of clinical mental health counseling, as a profession, was not marked by a unitary dramatic event or at a singular point in time. What we now consider clinical mental health counseling took shape at the hands of a complex amalgam of historical, sociopolitical, and cultural forces. There were those who as pioneers and reformers helped shape the sciences of medicine, psychology, and psychiatry and in so doing laid the foundation for a new perspective, one that targeted prevention as well as intervention, developmental challenges, as well as crisis and valued the empowerment of those with whom they worked.

Understanding the seeds of our past and the strong foundation it provided will allow a fuller appreciation for the practice as it exists today and perhaps a glimpse into the future to be claimed. Reviewing the individuals, events, and circumstances that helped to breathe life into this new perspective, this relatively young profession of clinical mental health counseling, will not only further your understanding of the uniqueness of the clinical mental health counseling profession but may serve to stimulate your professional pride.

After completing this chapter, the reader will be able to:

- Describe the evolution of the perspective on mental illness from demonic possession to the current biopsychosocial view.
- Identify significant historical figures who contributed to the emergence of counseling as a profession.
- Describe the role of legislation in the development of clinical mental health counseling.

Mental Illness: The Emergence of a Humane and Scientific Perspective

Throughout history, there have been three general theories of the etiology (cause) of mental illness: supernatural, somatogenic, and psychogenic. Each of these perspectives hypothesized causation and directed the nature and form of care and treatment the individual received. It is essential to understand that each of these perspectives, while referenced to a particular historical period, did not build one upon the other in a linear fashion nor have they completely faded from our current practices.

A closer look at the history of mental illness and its treatment will demonstrate that these perspectives reemerge in importance during different periods and have even coexisted with another at times. The influence of each of these perspectives can be seen in our current practice of clinical mental health counseling (Farreras, 2020). It is not unusual to find a treatment plan that includes employment of medication or even the utilization of one's spiritual orientation.

The Supernatural: Demonic Possession

Evidence of the earliest conceptualization of the etiology of mental illness was that it was the result of some form of demonic possession (Restak, 2000). From this perspective of spiritual/demonic sources or causes, it is only logical that the treatment would be equally mystical—and most often brutal. This was undoubtedly the case with the use of trephination.

Trephination, a procedure used as early as 5000 BCE, entailed chipping or cracking a hole, or *trephine*, into the skull. The rationale was that the procedure would allow the evil spirit (or spirits) that inhabited the head of the mentally ill person to be released, thereby curing them of their affliction (Foerschner, 2010).

Surprisingly, reduction in symptoms was sometimes observed in some of those who survived the procedure. While we could speculate that such a "cure" was the result of a biochemical shakeup due to the head trauma, or perhaps an increased motivation to suppress one's symptoms, the existence of positive results (minimum) encouraged not only the continued use of trephination but refinement of the technique and the instruments employed. While no longer espoused as a method for releasing evil spirits, and no longer performed using stones or crude tools to crack holes in the person's skull, this process of removing a section of a person's skull and underlying dura mater continues to be employed as a technique useful in relieving intracranial pressure and treat health problems associated with intracranial diseases such as epileptic seizures, migraines, and some mental disorders (Irving, 2013).

Trephination was but one of the "treatments" that emerged from this demonic view of mental health. Other magico-religious approaches, including exorcisms, incantations, and various mystical rituals, were also used to drive out the evil spirit all in hopes of "curing" the suffering individual (Alexander & Sheldon, 1966).

The Biological: A Somatogenic Perspective

Hippocrates, the father of medicine (460–377 BCE), attempted to separate superstition from medicine. Hippocrates insisted that abnormal behavior had natural causes in the human body. He posited that abnormal behavior was the result of an imbalance in one of the four essential bodily fluids, or humors—blood, yellow bile, black bile, and phlegm—and therefore should be treated like other physical-based maladies (Kleisiaris et al., 2014). Even though Hippocrates turned his attention toward more natural interventions to bring the body back in balance, including emetics, laxatives, and bleeding (through the use of leeches or cupping), a sense of mental illness as supernatural continued, and spiritual remedies persisted.

The ineffectiveness of these early approaches to treatment of mental illness resulted in the increased warehousing of individuals with mental illness or their abandonment to the streets. From the 16th century on, asylums began to appear throughout the world to accommodate the burgeoning number of mentally ill individuals. During these early years, asylums were merely reformed penal institutions where the mentally ill were abandoned by relatives or sentenced by the law and faced a life of inhumane treatment. These were not facilities aimed at helping the mentally ill achieve any sense of normalcy (Farreras, 2020).

The most infamous asylum, Saint Mary of Bethlehem, was located in London, England. This monastery-turned-asylum began admitting the mentally ill in 1547 after Henry VIII announced its transformation. The institution soon earned the nickname "Bedlam" as its horrific conditions and practices were revealed. Violent patients were put on display like sideshow freaks for the public to peek at for the price of one penny; gentler patients were put out on the streets to beg for charity (Farreras, 2020).

Conditions began to improve in the mid to late 1800s. One of the most significant asylum reforms was introduced in Paris by Philippe Pinel. In 1792, Pinel took charge of La Bicetre and tested his hypothesis that mentally ill patients would improve if they were treated with kindness and consideration. Filth, noise, and abuse were eliminated. Patients were unchained, provided with sunny rooms, allowed to exercise freely on the asylum grounds, and were no longer treated like animals (Micale, 1985).

The same types of humanizing reforms were undertaken around this time by an English Quaker, William Tuke. Founded in 1796, the York Retreat in York, England, was run by Tuke and other Quakers who stressed the importance of treating all people with respect and compassion, even the mentally ill. In keeping faithful to this ideal, the York Retreat was a pleasant country house, modeled on a domestic lifestyle that allowed patients to live, work, and rest in a warm and religious environment that emphasized mildness, reason, and humanity (Porter, 2002).

This humanitarian movement, referred to as *moral treatment* (Linhorst, 2006), spread across the Atlantic to the United States in the early 1800s (Farreras, 2020). Moral treatment, applied to asylum care, focused on the mentally ill individual's spiritual and moral development and the rehabilitation of their character to lessen their mental ailments. These goals were sought through encouraging the patient to engage in manual labor and spiritual discussion, always accompanied by humane treatment (Fancher, 1995).

This interest in the development of the individual's social, psychological, and occupational needs as a form of treatment began to fade with the discovery of the neurological causes of paresis (i.e., syphilis of the brain). With this discovery, attention turned back to a biological perspective on both case conceptualization and treatment of mental illness. As a result of this shift, the inclusion of psychotropic drugs into the treatment regimen began to flourish (Kring et al., 2015).

The somatogenic model remains viable today and has resulted in a burgeoning of the pharmaceutical industry. The introduction of lithium in 1949 by the Australian psychiatrist J. F. J. Cade to control mania was soon followed by the introduction of a series of mood-stabilizing drugs. Chlorpromazine (commonly known as Thorazine), discovered in France in 1952, was the first antipsychotic medication. Valium became the world's most prescribed tranquilizer in the 1960s, and Prozac, introduced in 1987, became the most prescribed antidepressant (Porter, 2002; Ramachandraiah et al., 2009).

Current use of psychotropic drugs, such as antidepressants, sedatives (anxiolytics and hypnotics), and antipsychotics, is considerable (Svensson et al., 2019). While psychotropic medications can be a useful tool in treating mental health issues, some suggest their effectiveness is best attained when used in concert with counseling or psychotherapy (see Chapter 8).

Research (Sammons & McGuinness, 2015) has shown that, in many cases, a combination of psychotropic medications and psychotherapy gives patients the best result. Medications can help alleviate the symptoms of depression and anxiety more quickly, thus giving the person a chance to improve their symptoms while undergoing psychotherapy at the same time. Clinical mental health counselors are trained to identify conditions in which medical intervention has value and thus most often employ a biopsychosocial model when addressing the human condition (see Chapter 5).

Focusing on the Psychological: A Psychogenic Perspective

Freud, an Austrian neurologist and psychiatrist, developed a body of personality, psychopathology, and psychoanalysis theories that emphasized the utility of talking cures or therapies. Although Freud had many critics who considered his ideas pseudoscience, psychoanalysis was a very popular method of treating mental illness from the early to mid-1900s. It served to stimulate further consideration of the psychological nature of mental illness. Psychoanalysis was the dominant psychogenic model for treating mental illness during the first half of the 20th century. It also can be said to have served as the stimulus to the creation of more than 400 alternative models and theories of the human condition and treatment of mental illness (Magnavita, 2006) (see Chapter 3).

Attempts at Unification

Each of these perspectives directed practitioners to focus on one domain of the human condition to understand the cause for a person's distress and the strategies needed for treatment. To find some commonality, at least in terms of shared language, a classification system for identifying that which was deemed mental illness would need to be created. The hope of such a classification system was that by identifying patterns of symptoms (i.e., syndromes), specific causes and contributing factors could be identified and would thus result in the creation of specific treatment protocols.

In 1952, the American Psychiatric Association (APA) published the first *Diagnostic and Statistical Manual of Mental Disorders* (DSM). The DSM, which has gone through numerous revisions, marked the start of the current mental illness diagnosis and classification system. The latest version, DSM, 5th edition (DSM-5), was published in 2013 to reflect the latest research and knowledge about mental disorders (see Chapter 4).

Moving Beyond Pathology to Wellness

It could be argued that the foundations for clinical mental health counseling stretch back to ancient Greece and Rome (Krumbultz & Koblin, 2003). However, the evolution and emergence of modern-day counseling might more accurately be placed in the early 1900s.

In the early 1900s, counseling had not yet developed into the treatment of mental health issues and was more focused on education. The initial indication of the emergence of a new profession, counseling, came in response to the social impact of industrialization and rapid urbanization of America at the turn of the 20th century (Whiteley, 1984). The exploding population, especially within cities, created conditions of political corruption and social inequities. It was in this environment that those concerned with child and adult welfare, education and guidance, and immigration management stepped forward, setting the stage for the emergence of counseling as a profession (Smith, 2012).

Thus, while having roots in both the medical and psychological models of the human condition, this new profession of counseling and the pioneers that led in its development introduced a new educational-developmental service model. This model recognized and addressed the normative issues and crises experienced by individuals as they journeyed throughout their life span.

Frank Parsons (1854–1908), who is often referred to as the father of vocational guidance, was aware of the many challenges confronting our nation's newcomers and worked as an advocate for improving the lives of those adversely affected by the rapid industrialization of America (Aubrey, 1983). Consequently, he, with the support of local civic leaders, founded the Boston Vocational Bureau in 1908. The goal of the bureau was to help individuals match their interests and aptitudes with appropriate occupational choices and opportunities (Smith & Wekel, 2011). Through the processes of interviewing, counseling, and vocational assessments, those at the bureau would attempt to develop a clear understanding of the individuals with whom they worked, an understanding that included the person's aptitude, interests, values, ambitions, resources, strengths, and weaknesses (Protivnak, 2009). In May 1908, Parsons presented a report that described systematic guidance procedures. His landmark book, *Choosing a Vocation*, published in 1909, had an immediate impact in laying the seeds for the emergence of counseling as a profession, and the processes he developed for the bureau served as the foundation for today's specialization of career counseling (Savikas, 2011).

The significance of Parsons's work with regards to the development of counseling as a profession rests in the following three points.

1. His work targeted normative developmental issues, which reframed the value of counseling from pathology to healthy development.
2. By working with educators and vocational choice, he highlighted the value of prevention as a goal for counseling service.
3. His approach engaged the adolescent, their family, and teachers and, as a result, employed an ecological approach that is embraced by mental health counselors to this day.

Jesse B. Davis (1987–1955) was a high school counselor and pioneer in the establishment of school-based vocational guidance programs. Davis believed that assisting students with vocational choices would contribute to the American workforce and society and help with student character development.

As a principal of Central High School in Grand Rapids, Michigan, he implemented the first school-based systematic program. Davis's work was significant in the establishment of modern-day career counseling (Pope, 2009). Additionally, his commitment to vocational guidance led to the 1913 creation of the National Vocational Guidance Association, where he served as the organization's first secretary (Feller, 2014).

Edmund Griffith ("E. G.") Williamson (1900–1979) was a faculty member at the University of Minnesota, where he expanded on Parsons's work by creating a trait and factor theory of vocational counseling. His model integrated psychometric data in the process of career matching.

Trait and factor theory and the process that he employed has been identified as the first comprehensive counseling model. This trait and factor theory model (Williamson, 1939) guided counselors to engage the processes of (1) analysis (gathering data), (2) synthesis (collating information), (3) diagnosis (interpreting issues), (4) prognosis (estimating client career options), (5) counseling (collaborating with the client on direction), and (6) follow-up (providing support and addressing additional issues) (Williamson, 1939).

From Education and Career Guidance to Mental Health and Wellness

The awakening of the American public to the horrors of mental illness and the inadequacy of current "treatment" practices opened the door for counseling to expand its impact beyond educational institutions.

Clifford W. Beers (1876–1943), a financier in New York City, published an autobiographical account of his experience as a patient in mental institutions (Beers, 1908). His book *A Mind That Found Itself* described the horrific, degrading, and at times physical abuse he experienced while institutionalized for depression. His story captured the American public's attention, which, in turn, led to public outcry for treatment reforms for those identified with mental illness. Beers, who is recognized as the founder of the mental hygiene movement and the National Mental Health Association (1950), helped stimulate a more humane approach to mental health care (Guindon, 2011).

The process of "humanizing" those with mental illness was given further voice by ***Carl Rogers*** (1902–1987). It could be argued that the one individual exerting the most influence on the development of counseling as a profession distinct from psychiatry, social work, psychology, and even vocational guidance was Carl Rogers. His book *Counseling and Psychotherapy* (1942) challenged the assumptions and theories of Freud's psychoanalysis and advocated for new approaches and techniques to mental health service.

Rogers shifted focus from the client as one who is ill and needs the expertise of the professional to that of merely another human being at a point of life struggle where helpers should respect the autonomy of the client and believe in the client's own ability to address the issues they were experiencing and set a path for growth and wellness. The introduction of Rogers's nondirective (aka person-centered) approach to counseling infused humanistic principles into the profession and further supported the profession's emphasis on client health, wellness, and strength (Sommers-Flanagan & Sommers-Flanagan, 2012).

Rogers emphasized the essential and sufficient nature of the counseling relationship as the "therapeutic agent" promoting growth. He noted, "If I can provide a certain type of relationship, the other person will discover within himself the capacity to use the relationship for growth and change and personal development will occur" (Rogers, 1961, p. 33). With this orientation, counseling shifted the focus away from a counselor as an "expert" analyst and curer, as was embodied by Freud, to presenting the counselor as a facilitator of client health, wellness, and growth via the creation of an authentic human encounter in the counseling relationship (Schmidt, 1999).

The theory and approach espoused by Rogers has had a lasting impact on how clinical mental health counselors view their clients and the processes employed to facilitate growth. While the mental health counselor often uses directive interventions as part of their treatment plan, the valuing of the counseling relationship and the belief in the client's strength and resiliency remain central to their perspective.

Expanding Need and Opportunities for Service

Up into the 1960s, most students interested in a career in counseling pursued training as school-based counselors (Kottler & Brown, 2000). This almost exclusive focus on school counseling began to change with the passage of the Community Mental Health Centers Act in 1963.

Community Mental Health Centers Act of 1963

The Community Mental Health Centers Act of 1963 resulted in the creation of more than 2,000 mental health centers that not only provided direct service but also targeted preventive mental health services (Guindon, 2011; MacCluskie & Ingersoll, 2001; Scileppi et al., 2000). The increased need for services and the opportunity for service providers invited the employment of master's and doctoral-level counselors. This opportunity to move from the schools to the community and clinical settings strengthened counselors' community visibility and professional identities.

With this opening of community service as a venue for employment, many training programs began to adjust the curriculum to develop "community" and "mental health counselors" as distinct from school counselors (Hershenson & Berger, 2001; Lewis et al., 2003). The growth in educational programs created a need for oversight and the development of training standards. To this end, the Council for Accreditation of Counseling and Related Educational Programs was established in 1981.

CACREP's mission is to promote the professional competence of counseling and related practitioners through the development of preparation standards; the encouragement of excellence in program development; and the accreditation of professional preparation programs (CACREP, n.d.). The first standards for accreditation of programs in mental health counseling were established in 1988 (Smith & Robinson, 1966). Chapter 1 presented the 2016 standards (see Table 1.1), and these are scheduled to be reviewed and revised by 2023.

Organizing

A national association for all counselors was not founded until 1952. At a joint convention in Los Angeles, four independent associations, the National Vocational Guidance Association (NVGA), the National Association of Guidance and Counselor Trainers (NAGCT), the Student Personnel Association for Teacher Education (SPATE), and the American College Personnel Association, came together to form the American Personnel and Guidance Association (APGA). In 1983 the APGA changed its name to the American Association of Counseling and Development, and in 1992 it embraced its current title of the American Counseling Association (ACA).

The ACA, through its various iterations, developed numerous divisions to denote both the commonality among all counselors and yet the uniqueness of those with special interest and focus. In 1976, the American Mental Health Counseling Association was created to provide a "home" for counselors who were employed in nonschool settings. In 1978 the AMHCA became the 13th division of the APGA (now ACAO).

By the 1980s, it is was clear that mental health counseling as a profession had arrived. By articulating the unique scope of practice and standards for entry and guidelines for ethical practice, mental health counseling emerged as a unique profession (VanZandt, 1990). Growth of clinical mental health counseling nationwide has been significant, and as a result, members articulated a need for the establishment of a standalone association, one independent of the ACA. This independent organization of AMHCA was established in 2018 to meet the academic, internship supervision, and licensure requirements of clinical mental health counselors (Goodman, 2019).

The Future

As will be discussed more fully in Chapter 15, the future for mental health counseling is both bright and challenging. According to the U.S. Bureau of Labor Statistics (2020), employment opportunities for mental health counselors are expected to grow at a faster-than-average pace. This growth reflects increased demands and increased awareness of the value and effectiveness of mental health counseling services.

As a profession, our understanding of human development and those factors that can impede healthy development continues to grow. Research continues to provide practitioners with increasingly effective techniques for assisting those struggling with psychological and emotional challenges and strategies that can facilitate healthy development and thus serve a preventive value. While predicting the future is a fool's game, it appears reasonable to assume that the profession will continue to

Exercise 2.1 What It Means to Be a Mental Health Counselor

Directions: The following questions are meant to serve as a guide for a discussion with a counselor who is experiencing what it means to be a mental health counselor.

Sample Questions:

- Have the clients, and their concerns, changed throughout your career?
- Has your role, your duties, changed throughout your career?
- What is the most rewarding aspect of your career?
- What is the most frustrating, challenging part of being a mental health counselor?
- Are you a member of any professional organizations, such as the ACA or AMCHA? If so, what have you found to be a benefit of membership? If not, why not?
- If you could do it over, choose your career path, would you continue to commit to mental health counseling as a profession?
- If you had a crystal ball, how would you predict counseling will change in the next 15 years?

evolve in response to the changing needs of those we serve and the research and knowledge that will guide best practice.

An Invitation

Although an academic text can present the changing nature of clinical mental health counseling with its opportunities and challenges, the perspective from the ground may differ from that of the "ivory tower." Before moving on to the next chapter, you might find it beneficial to reach out to a mental health counselor licensed to provide clinical services to better understand "what is" and "what it means to be a mental health counselor" (see Exercise 2.1).

Keystones

- The view of mental illness has evolved from a focus on the mystical to the science-based practices of the 21st century.
- As a profession, counseling found its roots in the early work of those such as Frank Parsons who were interested in vocational guidance and education.
- The introduction of the Community Mental Health Act of 1963 not only resulted in counselors being introduced to clinical and community service but also stimulated efforts to develop standardized training in the area of mental health counseling.
- The 21st century promises to provide increased opportunities for clinical mental health counselors while similarly challenging them to develop the knowledge and expertise to ethically engage technology and provide services to special populations across varied cultures.

Additional Resources

American Association of State Counseling Boards: www.aascb.org
American Mental Health Counselors Association: www.amhca.org
Field, T. A. (2017). Clinical mental health counseling: A 40-year retrospective. *Journal of Mental Health Counseling, 39*(1), 1–11. https://doi.org/10.17744/mehc.39.1.01
Images from the History of Medicine: http://ihm.nlm.nih.gov/luna/servlet/view/all (search "mental illness")

References

Aubrey, B. F. (1983). The odyssey of counseling and images of the future. *Personnel and Guidance Journal, 62*(2), 78–82.
Beers, C. W. (1908). *A mind that found itself: An autobiography.* Sheffield Scientific School, Yale.
Bureau of Labor Statistics, U.S. Department of Labor. (2020). *Occupational outlook handbook.* https://www.bls.gov/ooh/community-and-social-service/substance-abuse-behavioral-disorder-and-mental-health-counselors.htm
Council for the Accreditation of Counseling and Related Educational Programs. (n.d.). *About CACREP.* https://www.cacrep.org/about-cacrep/
Fancher, R. T. (1955). *Cultures healing: Correcting the image of American mental health care.* W. H. Freeman.
Farreras, I. G. (2020). History of mental illness. In R. Biswas-Diener & E. Diener (Eds.), *Noba textbook series: Psychology.* DEF publishers. http://noba.to/65w3s7ex
Feller, R. (2014). *The first conference of the National Vocational Guidance Association: Roots of the National Career Development Association #2.* https://www.ncda.org/aws/NCDA/pt/sd/news_article/70380/_Parent/CC_layout_details/false
Foerschner, A. M. (2010). The history of mental illness: From skull drills to happy pills. *Inquiries, 2*(9). http://www.inquiriesjournal.com/articles/1673/the-history-of-mental-illness-from-skull-drills-to-happy-pills
Goodman, A. (2019). AMHCA and ACA Separate Associations. Retrieved from https://www.amhca.org/blogs/howard-goodman/2019/04/26/amhca-and-aca-separate-associations

Guindon, M. H. (2011). *A counseling primer: An introduction to the profession*. Routledge.
Hershenson, D. B., & Berger, G. P. (2001). The state of community counseling: A survey of directors of CACREP-accredited programs. *Journal of Counseling and Development, 79*, 188–193.
Irving, J. (2013). *Trephination*. https://www.ancient.eu/Trephination/
Kleisiaris, C. F., Sfakianakis, C., & Papathanasiou, I. V. (2014). Health care practices in ancient Greece: The Hippocratic ideal. *Journal of Medical Ethics and History of Medicine, 7*, 6.
Kottler, J. A., & Brown, R. W. (2000). *Introduction to therapeutic counseling: Voices from the field* (4th ed.). Brooks/Cole.
Kress, V. E., & Paylo, M. J. (2014). *Treating those with mental disorders: A comprehensive approach to case conceptualization and treatment*. Pearson.
Kring, A. M., Johnson, S. L., Davidson, G. C., & Neale, J. N. (2015). *Abnormal psychology* (13th ed.). Wiley.
Krumbultz, J. D., & Kolpin, T. G. (2003). *A brief history of school guidance and counseling in the United States*. http://education.stateuniversity.com/pages/2023/Guidance-Counseling-School.html
Leahey, T. H. (1980). *A history of psychology: Main currents in psychological thought*. Prentice Hall.
Lewis, J. A., Lewis, M. D., Daniels, J. A., & D'Andrea, M. J. (2003). Managing the community counseling program. In *Community counseling: Empowerment strategies for a diverse society* (3rd ed., pp. 298–326). Brooks/Cole.
Linhorst, D. M. (2006). *Empowering people with severe mental illness: A practical guide*. Oxford University Press.
MacCluskie, K. C., & Ingersoll, R. E. (2001). *Becoming a 21st century agency counselor*. Cengage.
MacDonald, M. (1981). *Mystical Bedlam: Madness, anxiety, and healing in seventeenth-century England*. Cambridge University Press.
Magnavita, J. J. (2006). In search of the unifying principles of psychotherapy: Conceptual, empirical, and clinical convergence. *American Psychologist, 61*(8), 882–892.
Micale, M. S. (1985). The Salpêtrière in the age of Charcot: An institutional perspective on medical history in the late nineteenth century. *Journal of Contemporary History, 20*, 703–731.
Pope, M. (2009). Jesse Butrick Davis (1871-1955): Pioneer of vocational guidance in the schools. *Career Development Quarterly, 57*(3), 248–258. doi:10.1002/j.2161-0045.2009.tb00110.x
Porter, R. (2002). *Madness: A brief history*. Oxford University Press.
Protivnak, J. J. (2009). Career development, key people in. In American Counseling Association (Ed.), *The ACA encyclopedia of counseling* (pp. 80–82). American Counseling Association.
Ramachandraiah, C. T., Subramaniam, N., & Tancer, M. (2009). The story of antipsychotics: Past and present. *Indian Journal of Psychiatry, 51*(4), 324–326.
Restak, R. (2000). *Mysteries of the mind*. National Geographic Society.
Robinson, G. P. (1995). Mental health counseling: Past, present, and future. *Journal of Counseling and Development, 74*, 158–161.
Rogers, C. (1961). *On Being a Person*. Houghton-Mifflin.
Rogers, C. R. (1942). *Counseling and psychotherapy: Newer concepts in practice*. Houghton Mifflin Company.
Savickas, M. L. (2011). Special section: The 100th anniversary of vocational guidance—introduction to the special section. *Career Development Quarterly, 57*(3), 194–288.
Schmidt, J. J. (1999). Two decades of CACREP and what do we know? *Counselor Education and Supervision, 39*, 34–46.
Scileppi, J. A., Teed, E. L., & Torres, R. D. (2000). *Community psychology: A common sense approach to mental health*. Prentice Hall.
Sammons, M. T., & McGuinness, K. M. (2015). Combining psychotropic medications and psychotherapy generally leads to improved outcomes and therefore reduces the overall cost of care. *The Tablet*, April. Retrieved from https://www.apadivisions.org/division-55/publications/tablet/2015/04/combininations
Smith, H. L. (2012). The historical development of community and clinical mental health counseling in the United States. *Turkish Psychological Counseling and Guidance Journal, 4*(37), 1–10.
Smith, H. B., & Robinson, G. P. (1996). Mental health counseling: Past, present, and future. In W. J. Weikel & A. J. Palmo (Eds.), *Foundations of mental health counseling* (2nd ed., pp. 38–50). Charles C Thomas.
Smith, H. B., & Weikel, W. J. (2011). Professional counseling comes of age: The first 35 years. In A. J. Palmo, W. J. Weikel, & D. P. Borsos (Eds.), *Foundations in mental health counseling* (4th ed., pp. 5–28). Charles C Thomas.
Sommers-Flanagan, J., & Sommers-Flanagan, R. (2012). *Counseling and psychotherapy theories in context and practice: Skills, strategies, and techniques* (2nd ed.). John Wiley & Sons.
Svensson, S. A., Hedenrud, T. M., & Wallerstedt, S. M. (2019). *Attitudes and behaviour towards psychotropic drug prescribing in Swedish primary care: A questionnaire study*. https://bmcfampract.biomedcentral.com/articles/10.1186/s12875-018-0885-4#citeas
VanZandt, C. E. (1990). Professionalism: A matter of personal initiatives. *Journal of Counseling and Development, 68*, 234–245.
Whiteley, J. M. (1984). Historical periods in the development of counseling psychology. *The Counseling Psychologist, 12*(1), 3–5.
Williamson, E. G. (1939). *How to counsel students: A manual of techniques for clinical counselors*. McGraw-Hill.

SECTION II

Clinical Mental Health Counseling in Practice

CHAPTER 3

Theories and Models Guiding Intentional Practice

My client was sharing so much information. I got overwhelmed—I didn't know where to go.
—Alphonso, graduate student in Mental Health Counseling

Graduate students often share a common theme: the feeling of simply being overwhelmed with the amount of information provided by their client. A counselor, having developed skills that foster the development of a working alliance and facilitate client disclosure, may find themselves stuck, unsure of what is relevant, what is tangential, and where to go next.

Without an organizational framework, "clinicians would be vulnerable, directionless creatures bombarded with literally hundreds of impressions and pieces of information in a single session" (Prochaska & Norcross, 2003, p. 5). The focus of this chapter is describing the models and theories that serve as the organizational frameworks guiding the intentional practice of a mental health counselor.

After completing this chapter, the reader will be able to:

- Describe the value of theory to a counselor's case conceptualization and reflection on practice.
- Describe the major theories employed within clinical mental health counseling.
- Describe the qualities associated with "good" theory.

Theory: Essential to Effective, Ethical Practice

Being competent as a professional counselor demands more than skill. It requires the acquisition and employment of mental structures that will help you organize information, make meaning of the data presented, and allow those data to guide practice decisions (Parsons & Zhang, 2014). Mental health counselors call upon theories to elucidate the nature of the human condition, clarify the causes and treatment of dysfunction, and provide insight into the elements of wellness. These theories become essential to the effective, intentional, and ethical practice of counseling.

Theories of counseling are the articulation of sets of interrelated principles that describe, explain, predict, and guide the counselor's actions in relevant situations. The National Cancer Institute's (2005) monograph *Theory at a Glance* distinguishes two types of theory, both of which hold relevance for the professional counselor: explanatory theory and change theory.

Explanatory theory helps one understand complex situations (Buchanan, 1994). Explanatory theories are useful to counselors in their attempt to understand the stories their clients share. A counseling theory that is explanatory in nature helps counselors to take the complexity and uniqueness of a client's presenting concerns and decompose this ill-structured problem into subproblems that can then be reconfigured in ways that allow for more meaningful resolution (Voss & Post, 1988). In contrast, a *change theory* guides the development of specific interventions. In this sense, one's theory facilitates the gathering and organization of client data, interpretation of those data, and, as will be demonstrated, selection and implementation of helping strategies (Magnuson et al., 2000).

The Utility of Theory to Practice

Theories employed in counseling are valuable in that they provide the counselor with the means to organize and make sense of the data collected, serve as a scaffold for making decisions about the direction to take, and allow for the monitoring of process and progress (Parsons & Zhang, 2014).

Organizing Data

As any practicing counselor can attest, the amount and type of information shared by a client can be a "bewildering array of random, disparate happenings without the aid of organizing conceptual theory to make sense of it all" (Hansen, 2006, p. 291). Theories help counselors discern that which is essential from that which is tangential. Such discernment provides the direction for the unfolding of the counseling process. Effective counselors call on theories to assist them in organizing clinical data, making complex processes coherent, and providing conceptual guidance for interventions (Hansen, 2006). The use of theories is essential to the development of a counselor's case conceptualization, one offering insight into the client's current situation and the elements needed for growth toward articulated goals (Day, 2007).

Support Intentionality in Session

At any point within the counseling relationship and dynamic, the counselor will be called to make decisions regarding the nature of the relationship, its direction, and the data being shared. In this process, the counselor will have a wide array of things they can do or say. Should a question be posed? If so, what? Is this the time to summarize, confront, interpret, or provide information? The theory or theories employed by the counselor will help them make discriminating judgments about the information being presented and provide a framework for directing counselor response. Counseling theory guides a counselor's procedural thinking—that is, viewing client data from the perspective of "If this occurs (within the client's story), then I will do this to achieve that" (Parsons & Zhang, 2014).

Monitoring Direction and Progress

Knowing where counseling is going as well as assessing the degree to which the process is both heading in the desired direction and is making appropriate progress is essential to effective, ethical practice. Counselors need to monitor and assess their effectiveness and progress throughout the counseling process. Theory can provide markers or criteria against which a counselor can assess the effectiveness of interventions at any point in the helping relationship (Parsons & Zhang, 2014), thus enacting the ethical mandate to monitor effectiveness (American Counseling Association [ACA], 2014, Section C.2.d).

An Abundance of Theories

Counselors have an abundance of theories from which to choose in guiding clinical practice. In 2015, *The SAGE Encyclopedia of Theory in Counseling and Psychotherapy* listed more than 300 different approaches to counseling practice (Neukrug, 2015). A full discussion of the various theories employed by mental health counselors is well beyond the scope of this text. Readers will find excellent resources for a detailed presentation of counseling theories at the end of this chapter.

The theories commonly employed by mental health counselors, along with their variants (see Table 3.1), have emerged from several general approaches, or "schools," of psychology, including psychodynamic, behavioral, humanistic, constructivist, and systemic.

Psychodynamic Theories

Although not the first articulation of a model of therapy, it could be argued that it was the work of Sigmund Freud (1856–1939), the founder of psychoanalysis, that clearly aroused the world's attention. His theories dominated the early 20th century and served as the foundation of many theories to follow. Freud's psychodynamic model and, by extension, psychoanalysis, serves as perhaps the first major force in the development of psychotherapy and thus ultimately counseling. This first force emphasized the deterministic nature of early childhood experience and the power of unconscious drives and instincts.

Those employing a psychodynamic model typically strive to help their clients become aware of unconscious material and facilitate their release of repressed thoughts and emotions. Some theories that are grounded in psychoanalytic theory include attachment therapy and object relations therapy.

Behavioral Theories

With their emphasis on observation, data collection, and the role of learning, behavioral theories stand in stark contrast to psychodynamic ones. Behavioral interventions are created after gathering and analyzing data reflecting the client's current behavior through a functional behavioral assessment. Interventions typically employ aspects of learning theory (e.g., respondent and operant conditioning; social modeling) and target conditions antecedent to the behavior and/or consequences that follow the behavior of concern. Processes such as shaping, alternative response training, extinction, and counterconditioning are often employed as treatment modalities. Behavioral therapy principles can be found in theories such as dialectical behavior therapy, cognitive-behavioral therapy, and multimodal therapy.

Humanistic Theories

Carol Rogers is often presented as the face of the third school of psychology, the humanistic orientation. This third force in psychology dismissed the negative view of Freud and the mechanistic view of the behaviorists and proposed a positive view of the nature of the human condition.

This humanistic approach is based on the intrinsic value of people and is focused on individual free will, personal growth, and self-actualization. Those fully embracing Rogers's humanistic approach tend to see themselves as a resource and facilitator. The general position is that meaningful change can occur if the counselor can bring genuineness, authenticity, empathic understanding, and unconditional valuing of the client to the encounter. These conditions are seen as both necessary and sufficient conditions for client growth. Existential and gestalt theories are founded on humanistic principles.

Constructivist Theories

A central tenet of constructivist theories is that there is no one objective view of the world; instead, each of us creates our version of reality, which stems from our unique life experiences. Constructivist theories are less a system of therapy and more a theory of knowledge. Constructivist theories emphasize the meaning that clients attribute to their sense of self, their relationships, the world, and the difficulties they may be encountering. From this perspective, clients are viewed as active agents in their own lives and ultimately can make choices beneficial to their well-being. Theories that embrace a constructivist paradigm include solution-focused brief therapy, narrative therapy, and feminist therapy.

Systemic Theories

Systemic theories emphasize the reality that we all function within and are affected by the various social systems in which we operate. Thus, these theories embrace a systemic perspective to address issues not from the perspective of the individual's inner psyche but rather from within their broader social, cultural, political, and economic contexts. Client functioning is best understood in relation to their roles within their social networks. Systemic therapy seeks to identify deeply entrenched patterns within an individual's relationships and to revise the dynamics of these social relationships and networks. Family therapy, couples therapy, and even to some degree feminist approaches to therapy reflect the principles of systemic theory.

TABLE 3.1 A Sampling of Contemporary Theories

THEORY/THERAPY	CORE CONCEPTS
Acceptance and commitment therapy	Acceptance involves allowing unwanted private experiences (thoughts, feelings, and urges) to come and go without struggling with them. Emphasizes contact with the present moment. Awareness of the here and now, experienced with openness, interest, and receptiveness (e.g., mindfulness). The observing self involves accessing a transcendent sense of self, a continuity of consciousness that is unchanging. Discovery of what is most important to oneself. Setting goals according to values and carrying them out responsibly in the service of a meaningful life.
Adlerian therapy	Focus is on the importance of an individual's personal convictions and private logic. Views individuals as holistic in that they behave, perceive, feel, become, and strive for meaning in their interpersonal relationships. Individuals have free will to make decisions based on idiosyncratic personal styles. Emphasis is on an individual's attempt to overcome basic inferiority and develop a sense of mastery. Process of encouragement supporting belief in personal potential. It is a growth model, emphasizing the development of social interest.

(*Continued*)

(*Continued*)

THEORY/THERAPY	CORE CONCEPTS
Behavioral therapy	Targets learned behaviors and environmental influences. Employs data (functional behavior assessment and analyses). Uses techniques consistent with learning theory (e.g., respondent and operant conditioning).
Cognitive therapy	Posits the essential connection between thoughts and feelings and behaviors. Targets identification and reformulation of dysfunctional/irrational thoughts and beliefs.
Cognitive-behavioral therapy	Combines principles of behavioral and cognitive psychology. Is problem focused/action oriented. Targets developing strategies to address goals, including the reduction of symptoms. Employs techniques to increase rational information processing and coping skills.
Dialectical behavior therapy	Based on the biosocial theory. Combines cognitive techniques for emotional regulation and reality testing concepts of distress tolerance, acceptance, and mindful awareness. Targets clients' increased emotional and cognitive regulation by identifying triggers that create reactions. Assesses skills for coping as applied to the sequence of events, thoughts, feeling, and behaviors.
Eye movement desensitization and reprocessing (EMDR)	Based on the belief that negative thoughts, feelings, and behaviors are the result of unprocessed memories. Targets theorized disruption to standard adaptive information processing caused by trauma. Attempts to facilitate the processing of unprocessed information being dysfunctionally held in memory networks.
Freudian psychotherapy	Based on the biological roots of behavior where instinctual forces drive a person's psyche. Focuses on unconscious drives, wishes, and instincts as the bases for human functioning. Targets the identification of unconscious conflicts and the cathartic release of repressed energy.
Feminist theory	Focuses on societal, cultural, and political causes and solutions to the adverse effects of disempowerment. Assists clients in recognizing forces of disempowerment with the goal of empowering self-direction. Emphasizes equality, including maintaining an egalitarian relationship between the counselor and client.
Gestalt therapy	Seeks to raise awareness of the client's here-and-now experience by focusing on the process of what is happening rather than the content of what is being shared. Promotes authenticity versus role play or being "phony." Believes in the power of the client's self-awareness as the basis to make changes and become more fully alive and free from "unfinished business."
Motivational interviewing	Focused on eliciting behavior changes by helping clients examine and resolve ambivalence. The counselor invokes client motivation to make positive changes.

THEORY/THERAPY	CORE CONCEPTS
Person-centered therapy	Values the innate positive quality of the client. Facilitates the client's self-acceptance and self-actualization. Posits that conditions such as counselor genuineness, authenticity, empathic understanding, and unconditional valuing of the client are necessary and sufficient conditions for client growth.
Solution-focused brief therapy	Based on social constructivism. Shifts focus from "problem-speak" to goal orientation. Identifying client goals and clarifying one small step that can be taken to advance toward the goal is central to the process. Sees clients as having the needed resources to be successful, thus focus is on identifying and using previous success rather than developing new resources.
Transtheoretical model of change	Targets stages of change, processes of change, and levels of change. Sees change as a process involving progress through specific stages from precontemplation (not ready) through action and termination. Targets specific interventions matched to the client's current stage of change to facilitate movement to the next stage.

Which Theory?

Although the growth and refinement in counseling and psychotherapy theory speak to the value of theory in the guidance of one's practice, it is clear that no one theory is "best," that is, having proven utility for all clients across all circumstances. As will be discussed in Chapter 6, some mental health providers suggest that theories and treatments should be selected based on their level of empirical support. The pool of such strategies is limited and not reflective of all theories or treatments that counselors have found effective within their practices. The simple truth is that not all treatments have been "researched." The fact that a particular theory lacks empirical support may speak more to the limitations of our research methodology than to the value of the theory. Thus, empirical support should not be the sole criteria upon which to select a theory of practice. When reviewing the literature in search of empirical support for a theory of choice, it is crucial for counselors to review the theories they employ against those criteria often used to define "good" theory.

Characteristics of a "Good" Theory

The tradition in science is to assess a theory against a set of standards or preferred qualities that collectively provide a measure of a theory's worth (Maddi, 1996). These include parsimony, precision, empirical validity, and utility:

- *Parsimony*: A "good" theory provides the simplest explanation, avoiding positing complex relationships when a simpler alternative exists. This principle suggests that, given an option, the theory that is simple, rather than unnecessarily complicated, is preferred.
- *Precision*: A "good" theory employs constructs and concepts that are clear and precise. The definitions of these constructs and concepts are clear and specific, as is the nature of the relationship between them (Monte & Sollod, 2009). This characteristic allows for empirical validation.

- *Empirical Validity/Testable*: The principle of testability simply suggests that a "good theory" provides concepts, constructs, and proposed explanations for the phenomenon that can be confirmed or disconfirmed by way of scientific empirical study. Testing counseling theories in order to assess their validity or truthfulness is a complicated process. The very nature of our counseling does not lend itself to the purity of a scientist's laboratory and controlled experimentation (Parsons, 2014).
- *Utility*: A theory should be of value to those practitioners seeking to employ it. For counselors, "good" theory moves beyond explanation to assisting in directing one's practice decisions (Parsons, 2014).

Beyond Theory: A Model of Mental Illness and Wellness

Most of the historical and traditional theories of counseling reflect a model that places mental illness and mental health as poles on one continuum, with psychopathology at one pole and mental health at the other. This one-dimensional perspective suggests that it is in the remediation of mental illness that one promotes mental health, that is, that mental health is simply a state absent of psychopathology. From this perspective, mental health is deemed an inferred by-product of "no mental illness" (Suldo & Shaffer, 2008). Therefore, this traditional perspective directs practitioners to identify and diagnose psychopathology and then employ treatment to relieve symptoms (Keyes & Lopez, 2002; Seligman, 2008).

Such a position is in contrast to the values held by a professional counselor who sees wellness as an independent state of growth and development. Unfortunately, accepting the implicit assumptions of this one-dimensional view can negatively affect the professional identities of counselors and the perceptions of those they serve. It is not unusual for those embracing this one-dimensional perspective to allocate those with severe and chronic emotional issues to treatment by a psychiatrist or clinical psychologist, assigning mental health counselors to the role of servicing those relatively "normal" clients facing normative crisis and issues (Gerig, 2018). This single-continuum model of mental health has been challenged: "The absence of disease may constitute a necessary, but not sufficient, criterion for mental health" (Jahoda, 1958, p. 15).

An alternative model, a dual-factor or two-dimensional model of mental health (Downie et al., 1990) posits that mental illness and mental health are related but distinct dimensions: One continuum indicates the presence or absence of mental health; the other continuum addresses the presence or absence of mental illness. Therefore, from such a dual-factor model, mental health is best viewed as a complete state, that is, not merely the absence of mental illness but also the presence of mental health. This dual-factor model is much more in line with and reflective of the values held by professional counselors and the profession's emphasis on prevention and promotion of wellness and the provision of intervention when and where needed.

Clinical mental health counselors are trained to work with those diagnosed with mental disorders. However, unique to the counseling profession are the values that direct counselors to move beyond providing interventions to those in need and to providing services that promote wellness, prevention, and empowerment to all people (see Chapter 1). Counselors believe that "all people can benefit from counseling, fully functioning people who experience everyday stress in their lives and those who are seriously mentally ill can benefit from a counseling philosophy that offers hope for a better tomorrow" (Myers, 1992, p. 138). Counselors approach their work with an eye toward addressing the issues of concerns while also moving the client toward more optimal, or "well," functioning.

Theories in Light of Wellness

One immediate implication of such a dual-continua model is that professional counselors need to consider theories in light of their value for directing intervention and treatment and their usefulness in the conceptualization and promotion of wellness.

Adlerian Theory

An illustration of the dual-continua value of some theories can be found when reviewing counselor employment of Adlerian theory in practice. Principles of Adlerian therapy have been incorporated within the Wheel of Wellness (WoW) (Myers et al., 2000) and the Indivisible Self (IS-Wel) model (Myers & Sweeney, 2005), two models that provide a framework for structuring interventions to enhance the well-being of persons struggling from a variety of issues (Myers & Sweeney, 2005, 2008). Working from these models, counselors create plans that improve the client's underdeveloped strengths and assets. This approach to "intervention" is based on the belief that change in one area of the client's level of capacity improves the client's overall functioning (Myers, 2003; Myers & Sweeney, 2005). The specifics of the wellness plan will vary as a function of the areas chosen for improvement. Additionally, when engaged in this phase, counselors take on the role of encourager and motivator to support client follow-through on selected wellness-promoting strategies.

Cognitive Theory

A similar expansion of a therapeutic model for the promotion of wellness can be seen in mindfulness-based cognitive therapy (MBCT). MBCT is an approach founded as an extension to cognitive theory. MBCT is beneficial when employed as a therapeutic intervention (for reviews, see Didonna, 2009). Specifically, the approach has research supporting its effectiveness in reducing depressive symptoms and residual anxiety (see Goldberg et al., 2019).

Beyond the therapeutic/remedial value of MBCT, its employment of mindfulness practice has been shown to promote mental and physical health and an individual's sense of well-being. Numerous benefits, including increased immune functioning (Grossman et al., 2004), reduction in psychological distress (Coffey & Hartman, 2008), and experience of overall well-being (Carmody & Baer, 2008) have been reported as a result of mindfulness practice. More specifically, mindfulness has been demonstrated to assist in each of the following areas of functioning.

- *Stress reduction.* Not only has mindfulness been shown to reduce stress (Hofmann et al., 2010), but it has also been demonstrated to increase positive affect (Farb et al., 2010). Studies have demonstrated the utility of mindfulness meditation in an individual's ability to apply emotional regulation strategies (Farb et al., 2010; Williams, 2010).
- *Working memory.* Improvements to working memory appear to be another benefit of mindfulness (Jha et al., 2010).

- *Focus.* Moore and Malinowski (2009) found that mindfulness meditation practice improves one's ability to focus attention and suppress distracting information.
- *Emotional reactivity.* Research (e.g., Ortner et al., 2007) supports the notion that mindfulness meditation decreases emotional reactivity.
- *Relationship satisfaction.* Several studies indicate that a person's ability to be mindful can help predict relationship satisfaction—that is, the ability to respond well to relationship stress and the skill in communicating one's emotions to a partner (Dekeyser et al., 2008).

Thus, MBCT and mindfulness not only have value for the treatment and remediation of mental disorders but also in the promotion of wellness.

The implication for mental health counselors is clear. When developing case conceptualizations and treatment plans, counselors need to not only consider the "goodness" of the theory and the scientific evidence supporting its use as a treatment approach but also consider the potential value of the theory or approach for offering relief from distress and promoting wellness.

Keystones

- Counseling theories help us articulate the assumptions, interpretations, and hypotheses we employ to understand what is happening with our clients and make predictions about what may happen in the future. An effective counselor employs theory to describe, explain, predict, and change behaviors.
- As explanatory theories, counseling theories help counselors take the complexity and uniqueness of a client's presenting concerns and decompose an ill-structured problem into subproblems that can then be reconfigured in ways that allow for more meaningful resolution.
- Effective counselors call on theories to assist them in organizing clinical data, making complex processes coherent, and providing conceptual guidance for interventions.
- Theories help counselors organize clinical data and connect seemingly disparate areas of knowledge and serve as a framework for case conceptualization and treatment planning.
- With hundreds of contemporary theories to choose from, it is useful for counselors to consider the evidence that supports the validity of theoretical constructs as well as the characteristics of the theory: parsimony, precision, and testability.
- The use of theory is not only practical but ethical: "use techniques/procedures/modalities that are grounded in theory and/or have an empirical or scientific foundation" (ACA, 2014, Principle C.7.a.).
- Given the professional values of the counseling profession, counselors need to consider theories and strategies in light of the degree to which they meet the characteristics of a "good" theory; that is, those that are supported by empirical research and have value for treatment of mental disorders and promotion of wellness.

Additional Resources

Capuzzi, D., & Stauffer, M. D. (Eds.). (2016). *Counseling and psychotherapy theories and interventions* (6th ed.). American Counseling Association.

Hansen, J. T. (2006, Summer). Counseling theories within a postmodernist epistemology: New roles for theories in counseling practice. *Journal of Counseling and Development, 84*, 291–297.

Mobley, J. A., & Gazda, G. M. (2011). *Creating a personal counseling theory. Vistas Online.* ACA Knowledge Center. https://www.counseling.org/docs/default-source/vistas/creating-a-personal-counseling-theory.pdf?sfvrsn=99d87e2c_14

Parsons, R. D. (2009). *Translating theory to practice.* Pearson.

Parsons, R. D., & Zhang, N. (2014). *Counseling theory: Guiding reflective practice.* Sage.

References

American Counseling Association. (2014). *ACA code of ethics.* Counseling.org https://www.counseling.org/Resources/aca-code-of-ethics.pdf

Buchanan, D. R. (1994). Reflections on the relationship between theory and practice. *Health Education Research, 9*, 273–283.

Carmody, J., & Baer, R. A. (2008). Relationships between mindfulness practice and levels of mindfulness, medical and psychological symptoms, and well-being in a mindfulness-based stress reduction program. *Journal of Behavioral Medicine, 31,* 23–33. https://doi.org/10.1007/s10865-007-9130-7

Coffey, K. A., & Hartman, M. (2008). Mechanisms of action in the inverse relationship between mindfulness and psychological distress. *Complementary Health Practice Review, 13,* 79–91. https://doi:10.1177/1533210108316307

Day, S. X. (2007). *Theory and design in counseling and psychotherapy* (2nd ed.). Houghton Mifflin.

Dekeyser, M., Raes, F., Leijssen, M. Leyson, S., & Dewulf, D. (2008). Mindfulness skills and interpersonal behavior. *Personality and Individual Differences, 44*, 1235–1245. https://doi.org/10.1016/j.paid.2007.11.018

Didonna, F. (Ed.). (2009). *Clinical handbook of mindfulness.* Springer.

Downie, R. S., Fyfe, C., & Tannahill, A. (1990). *Health promotion: Models and values.* Oxford University Press.

Farb, N. A. S., Anderson, A. K., Mayberg, H., Bean, J., McKeon, D., & Segal, Z. V. (2010). Minding one's emotions: Mindfulness training alters the neural expression of sadness. *Emotion, 10,* 25–33. https://doi.org/10.1037/a0017151.supp

Gerig, M. S. (2018). *Foundations for clinical mental health counseling: An introduction to the profession.* Pearson.

Goldberg, S. B., Tucker, R. P., Greene, P. A., Davidson, R. J., Kearney, D. J., & Simpson, T. L. (2019). Mindfulness-based cognitive therapy for the treatment of current depressive symptoms: A meta-analysis. *Cognitive Behaviour Therapy, 48*(6), 445–462, https://doi.org/10.1080/16506073.2018.1556330

Grossman, P., Niemann, L., Schmidt, S., & Walach, H. (2004). Mindfulness-based stress reduction and health benefits: A meta-analysis. *Journal of Psychosomatic Research, 57,* 35–43. https://doi.org/10.1016/S0022-3999(03)00573-7

Hansen, J. T. (2006, Summer). Counseling theories within a postmodernist epistemology: New roles for theories in counseling practice. *Journal of Counseling and Development, 84,* 291–297.

Hofmann, S. G., Sawyer, A. T., Witt, A. A., & Oh, D. (2010). The effect of mindfulness-based therapy on anxiety and depression: A meta-analytic review. *Journal of consulting and clinical psychology, 78*(2), 169–183. https://doi.org/10.1037/a0018555

Jahoda, M. (1958). *Current concepts of positive mental health.* Basic Books. doi:10.1037/11258-000

Jha, A. P., Stanley, E. A., Kiyonaga, A., Wong, L., & Gelfand, L. (2010). Examining the protective effects of mindfulness training on working memory capacity and affective experience. *Emotion, 10,* 54–64. https://doi.org/10.1037/a0018438

Keyes, C. L. M., & Lopez, S. J. (2002). Toward a science of mental health: Positive directions in diagnosis and interventions. In C. R. Snyder & S. J. Lopez (Eds.), *Handbook of positive psychology* (pp. 45–59). Oxford University Press.

Maddi, S. R. (1996). *Personality theories: A comparative analysis* (6th ed.). Brooks/Cole.

Magnuson, S., Norem, K., & Wilcoxon, A. (2000). Clinical supervision of prelicensed counselors: Recommendations for consideration and practice. *Journal of Mental Health Counseling, 22*(2), 176–188.

Monte, C. F., & Sollord, R. N. (2009). *Beneath the mask: An introduction to theories of personality* (8th ed.). John Wiley.

Moore, A., & Malinowski, P. (2009). Meditation, mindfulness, and cognitive flexibility. *Consciousness and Cognition, 18*, 176–186. https://doi.org/10.1016/j.concog.2008.12.008

Myers, J. (2003). Coping with caregiving stress: A wellness-oriented, strengths-based approach for family counselors. *The Family Journal: Counseling & Therapy for Couples & Families, 11*, 153–161.

Myers, J. E. (1992). Wellness, prevention, development: The cornerstone of the profession. *Journal of Counseling & Development, 71*(2), 136–139.

Myers, J. E., & Sweeney, T. J. (2005). The indivisible self: An evidence-based model of wellness (reprint). *Journal of Individual Psychology, 61*, 269–279.

Myers, J. E., Sweeney, T. J., & Witmer, M. (2000). The wheel of wellness, counseling for wellness: A holistic model for treatment planning. *Journal of Counseling and Development, 78*, 251–266.

National Cancer Institute. (2005, September). *Theory at a glance: A guide for health promotion practice* (2nd ed.). U.S. Department of Health and Human Services, National Institutes of Health. http://www.cancer.gov/cancertopics/cancerlibrary/theory.pdf

Neukrug, E. S. (Ed.). (2015). *The SAGE encyclopedia of theory in counseling and psychotherapy.* Sage.

Ortner, C. N. M., Kilner, S. J., & Zelazo, P. D. (2007). Mindfulness meditation and reduced emotional interference on a cognitive task. *Motivation and Emotion, 31,* 271–283. https://doi.org/10.1007/s11031-007-9076-7

Parsons, R. D. (2014). Theory and the reflective practitioner. In R. D. Parsons & N. Zhang (Eds.), *Counseling theory: Guiding reflective practice* (pp. 3–26). Sage.

Parsons, R. D., & Zhang, N. (2014). *Counseling theory: Guiding reflective practice.* Sage.

Prochaska, J. O., & Norcross, J. C. (2003). *Systems of psychotherapy: A transtheoretical analysis* (3rd ed.). Brooks/Cole.

Seligman, M. E. P. (2008). Positive health. *Applied Psychology: An International Review, 57,* 3–18. doi:10.1111/j.1464-0597.2008.00351.x

Suldo, S. M., & Shaffer, E. J. (2008). Looking beyond psychopathology: The dual-factor model of mental health in youth. *School Psychology Review, 37*(1), 52–68.

Voss, J. F., & Post, T. A. (1988). On the solving of ill-structured problems. In M. H. Chi, R. Glaser, & M. J. Farr (Eds.), *The nature of expertise* (pp. 261–285). Lawrence Erlbaum Associates.

Williams, J. M. G. (2010). Mindfulness and psychological process. *Emotion, 10,* 1–7. https://doi.org/10.1037/a0018360

Nosology
The DSM-5

CHAPTER 4

> Labels are for jelly beans, not people.
>
> —Nigel, addictions counselor

As professional counselors, trained to be empathic and respectful of the human condition, we are generally appalled by grouping, or pigeonholing, people into this or that category. Some may feel that such a process, one often reflected in the professional practice of diagnosing, is dehumanizing.

Allen Frances (2014) noted, "Hippocrates believed that it is more important to know the person who has the disease than the disease the person has" (p. 282). This sentiment would undoubtedly resonate with most, if not all, professional counselors. But Frances didn't stop with this observation. He continued, "We need to know what makes each person different and unique; on the other hand, we also need to group clients with similar problems as a way of choosing interventions and predicting the treatment course" (Frances, 2014, p. 282). While certainly straddling a line, Frances indirectly points out both the value and challenge of diagnostic taxonomies or nosologies in the practice of mental health counseling.

Although there are challenges to the foundational values and philosophy of professional counseling, and thus the use of diagnostic categories may signal a threat to the professional identity of counselors, such diagnostic categories, when valid, can be useful. At the ideal level, the use of a taxonomy or nosology to categorize that which challenges our clients should help counselors formulate case conceptualizations and decide on appropriate treatment plans. At a minimum, diagnostic labels can facilitate communication between professionals. On a very practical level, diagnostic categorization may be a requirement for counselors to receive third-party payment of services.

The current chapter will review the "what" and the "why" of mental health professional employment of taxonomy for diagnosing mental disorders. Two such nosologies currently employed in clinical mental health counseling, the *Diagnostic and Statistical Manual of Mental Disorders* (DSM-5) (American Psychiatric Association [APA], 2013) and the International Classification of Diseases (ICD-11) (World Health Organization [WHO], 2019), are reviewed.

After completing this chapter, the reader will be able to:

- Describe the three major sections of the American Psychiatric Association's *Diagnostic and Statistical Manual of Mental Disorders* (DSM-5).
- Explain the fundamental difference between the DSM-5 and the World Health Organization's International Classification of Diseases (ICD-11).
- Explain how the DSM-5 may pose challenges to the professional identity of counselors.

- Describe how the changes in the DSM-5 have brought it closer in line with the philosophy and perspective of professional counselors.

Nosologies: Their Place in Practice

Let's assume that a client comes to a counselor's office and presents with the following symptoms: loss of appetite; reduction in energy or desire to do anything; suicidal thoughts and feelings of reprisal; frequent, excessive crying; and feelings of hopelessness. Indeed, the client's behavioral, emotional, and cognitive profile—one depicting motivational immobility, sadness, and a sense of worthlessness, helplessness, and hopelessness—is tinted with their own unique experience of each and the sociocultural contexts within which these are experienced. But let's say that another client presents with their versions of the same behavioral, emotional, and cognitive symptoms. When symptoms consistently appear to cluster together, the cluster is deemed a syndrome and is provided a label or some form of classification (Calvo, 2014). Although the label, for example, *depression*, fails to capture the full, holistic experience and uniqueness of the client, it does provide an economical way of conveying information about the observed complex of symptoms.

The term *nosology* refers to the theory about the nature of medical conditions and the principles and rules of their classification (Jablensky, 2016). In science, classifying involves forming categories, or *taxa*, for ordering natural objects or entities and assigning names to these categories. Ideally, the categories should be jointly exhaustive to account for all possible entities and be mutually exclusive.

Nosological systems, be they in medicine or counseling, are intended to do more than simply provide a shorthand notion for lists of symptoms. The categories presented in these taxonomies are meant to identify syndromes as "distinct," having unique etiologies (causes) and prognoses (predictive courses and outcomes), and thus preferred treatment approaches.

While medicine has been able to craft a nosology (i.e., International Classification of Diseases [ICD-11]; WHO, 2019) that comes close to this ideal of taxonomies, reflecting a distinctiveness of cause–pattern and treatment for medical syndromes, this has not been the case for efforts to create a taxonomy of mental and behavioral disorders. The challenge, of course, is that the "objects" being classified in mental and behavioral disorders are not "natural" entities but explanatory constructs. As such, they fail to lend themselves to systematic, higher-level organization and classification (Jablensky, 2016).

Although there are significant limitations to the current models of classification employed in psychiatry and counseling, they have, even in their earliest forms, provided some order to what has been a chaotic field of study, and they facilitate communication among clinicians and researchers. The current edition of the *Diagnostic and Statistical Manual of Mental Disorders* (APA, 2013), a fifth iteration (DSM-5), while still less than perfect, has brought us closer to that which is desired.

Given their value to professional communication, their structure for understanding prevalence and treatment preference, and the fact that they are most often required for third-party reimbursement, it is safe to say that nosology is not something that will soon disappear (Avasthi et al., 2014).

DSM-5

The *Diagnostic and Statistical Manual for Mental Disorders* (APA, 2013), the principal taxonomy employed by clinical mental health counselors, was designed to assist professionals in assessing, diagnosing, and conceptualizing cases. DSM is "intended to serve as a practical, functional, and flexible guide for organizing information that can aid in the accurate diagnosis and treatment of mental disorders (APA, 2014, p. xii). Counselors engaging in diagnosis as an essential component of the counseling process will need to understand the diagnostic nosology and nomenclature, even if only to participate in interdisciplinary discussions and treatment decisions (Buckley, 2014).

The DSM-5 is divided into three major sections. Section I provides an introduction; a discussion of key concepts, such as the definition of a mental disorder; and guidelines for recording a diagnosis. Section I also incorporates two sets of ICD codes: ICD-9 and ICD-10. Additionally, this section includes harmonizing language with ICD-11, which was released after the DSM-5, in 2018, and is scheduled for universal employment in 2022 (WHO, 2019).

Section II of the DSM-5 is perhaps the core of the manual. It contains the diagnostic criteria and background for all the mental disorders and other conditions that can be coded. As implied by the title, the DSM-5 targets investigation of mental disorders. The DSM-5 defines a *mental disorder* as:

> a syndrome characterized by clinically significant disturbance in an individual's cognitive, emotion regulation or behavior that reflects a dysfunction in the psychological, biological, or developmental processes underlying mental functioning. Mental disorders are usually associated with significant distress or disability in social, occupation, or other important activities. An expectable or culturally approved response to a common stressor or loss, such as the death of a loved one, is not a mental disorder. Socially deviant behavior (e.g., political, religious, or sexual) and conflicts that are primarily between the individual and society are not mental disorders unless the deviance or conflict results from a dysfunctioning the individual, as described above. (APA, 2014, p. 20)

Table 4.1 lists the major categories of mental disorders found within this section.

TABLE 4.1 DSM-5 Classification

Neurodevelopmental disorders
Schizophrenia spectrum and other psychotic disorders
Bipolar and related disorders
Depressive disorders
Anxiety disorders
Obsessive-compulsive and related disorders
Trauma- and stressor-related disorders
Dissociative disorders
Somatic symptom and related disorders
Feeding and eating disorders
Elimination disorders
Sleep-wake disorders
Sexual dysfunctions

(*Continued*)

(*Continued*)
Gender dysphoria
Disruptive, impulse control, and conduct disorders
Substance-related and addictive disorders
Neurocognitive disorders
Personality disorders
Paraphilic disorders
Other mental disorders
Medication-induced movement disorders and other adverse effects of medication
Other conditions that may be a focus of clinical attention

Source: American Psychiatric Association. (2013). *Diagnostic and statistical manual of mental disorders* (5th ed.).

Of note, in this latest revision two factors guided the organization of this listing. First, the grouping is based on shared underlying vulnerabilities, risk factors, symptoms presentation, course, and response to treatment. Secondly, this edition of the DSM reflects a life-span perspective.

Shared Commonalities

Conditions are arranged so that those positioned next to each other share more commonalities than those placed further apart. For example, bipolar disorder follows the schizophrenia spectrum because they share several vulnerability factors. Next, internalizing disorders characterized by depression, anxiety, and somatic symptoms are listed in adjacent chapters because of common risk factors, treatment response, and comorbidity. Externalizing disorders, noted by their impulsivity, acting out, and substance use, are placed in the latter part of the manual (APA, 2013).

Life-Span Perspective

The structure of the DSM-5 reflects a life-span perspective, both across and within chapters. Neurodevelopmental disorders (e.g., autism spectrum disorder, attention-deficit/hyperactivity disorder [ADHD]) are listed first because they typically emerge early in life. Schizophrenia spectrum disorders also frequently have antecedents that manifest themselves in childhood. Next are disorders that usually appear in adolescence and early adulthood, such as bipolar disorders, depressive disorders, and anxiety disorders. In the middle and back of the manual are disorders that emerge in adulthood or late adulthood, such as personality disorders and neurocognitive disorders (e.g., dementia related to Alzheimer's disease) (APA, 2013).

The final section of the DSM-5, Section III, includes tools for enhancing the diagnostic process as well as a list of proposed mental disorders that require further study (e.g., internet gaming disorder) and an alternative system for diagnosing personality disorders. As will be discussed later within this chapter, Section III also provides guidance and support for the understanding of the cultural context of illness experienced by clients served (APA, 2013).

With this most recent iteration of the DSM, the APA has attempted to provide a more valid organizational structure grounded in research. In its current form, DSM-5 provides clinical utility by

- helping clinicians communicate clinical information to all stakeholders;
- assisting clinicians' treatment planning and implementation of effective interventions; and

- providing clinicians criteria for differentiating disorders from nonpathology for the purpose of determining who might benefit from disorder-based treatments (First, 2010).

It is also hoped that such a nosology will help clinicians uncover common etiological factors, which has been considered the holy grail of classification efforts (Insel et al., 2010; Stein et al., 2013).

The International Classification of Diseases

The International Classification of Diseases (ICD-11) is the 11th edition of a global categorization system for physical and mental illnesses published by the World Health Organization (WHO, 2019). The ICD-11 is a revised version of the ICD-10 and the first update to be developed and published in 2 decades. While including many of the same mental health disorders presented in DSM-5, this taxonomy is more extensive, covering health-related conditions not associated with mental disorders.

The new version of the ICD was officially presented at the World Health Assembly in May 2019 and will be used as the official reporting system by member states beginning January 1, 2022. The ICD-11 catalogs known human diseases, medical conditions, and mental health disorders used for insurance coding purposes, statistical tracking of illnesses, and a global health categorization tool that can be used across countries and in different languages.

In terms of mental health disorders, the ICD-11 has added the following disorders to the section detailing diagnoses (WHO, 2019):

- *Gaming disorder*: "A pattern of persistent or recurrent gaming behaviour ('digital gaming' or 'video-gaming')."
- *Compulsive sexual behavior disorder:* This is now classified as an impulse control disorder rather than an addictive disorder, characterized by a persistent pattern of failure to control intense, repetitive sexual impulses or urges.
- *Prolonged grief disorder*: Grief that extends beyond what most people would consider to be a reasonable or expected amount of time.
- *Complex PTSD*: Requires three symptoms of *posttraumatic stress disorder* (PTSD) (e.g., re-experiencing, avoiding reminders, and a heightened sense of threat/arousal), along with broader problems in emotion regulation, shame, guilt, and interpersonal conflict, such that it affects the person's entire life.
- *Attention deficit disorder*: Although included in DSM-5, this had not previously been included in the ICD-10.

Further, ICD-11 has deleted acute stress disorder, which is now classified as a reaction to trauma and a factor influencing health rather than a mental disorder, as is the case with the DSM-5.

The listing of mental disorders included in the ICD-11 is presented in Table 4.2.

TABLE 4.2 ICD-11 List of Mental Disorders

Neurodevelopmental disorders
Schizophrenia or other primary psychotic disorders
Catatonia
Mood disorders
Anxiety or fear-related disorders
Obsessive-compulsive or related disorders
Disorders specifically associated with stress
Dissociative disorders
Feeding or eating disorders
Elimination disorders
Disorders of bodily distress or bodily experience
Disorders due to substance use or addictive behaviours
Impulse control disorders
Disruptive behaviour or dissocial disorders
Personality disorders and related traits
Paraphilic disorders
Factitious disorders
Neurocognitive disorders
Mental or behavioural disorders associated with pregnancy, childbirth, and the puerperium

Source: World Health Organization. (2019). *The International Classification of Diseases (ICD-11)*. https://www.who.int/classifications/icd/en/

Whereas the DSM-5 is produced by the American Psychiatric Association and is generally employed by mental health providers in North America, the ICD-11 is global. Even though mental health professionals in the United States rely on the DSM, the DSM does not code its diagnoses, meaning that those mental health counselors seeking third-party payment will most likely turn to the ICM codes for insurance billing purposes. Also, the ICD-11 codes are HIPAA compliant; that is, they follow the Health Insurance Portability and Accountability Act (HIPAA), a U.S. law designed to protect health information.

DSM-5 and Counselor Professional Identity

Counselors approach their professional relationship with clients as one based on empowerment, rooted in diversity, and committed to accomplish mental health, wellness, education, and career goals (Kaplan et al., 2014). To achieve these goals, counselors often include diagnosis as an essential component of the counseling process.

Counselors are often required to employ the DSM-5 in their professional practice (Miller & Prosek, 2013). Although the DSM espouses that it is atheoretical (APA, 2013; Lilienfeld et al., 2013), and thus should cause no conflict to the professional values and philosophy that serves as the foundation for professional counseling, the continued, almost exclusive focus on biological factors and a pathophysiological model can challenge the professional identity of a mental health counselor.

This engagement with a pathophysiological model signals the "medicalization" of treating mental health issues with implications for selecting treatment modalities and the role of counselors as nonmedical professionals (see Chapter 8).

This movement toward strictly neurobiological interpretations of mental health is difficult to reconcile with the professional identity of counselors and scope of practice that "serves to promote wellness across the life-span . . . [including] preventing and treating mental disorders" (Kraus, 2013, p. 1). This is not to deny the powerful influence of one's neurobiology on mental health. Still, an exclusive focus on neurobiology undermines the value of a biosocial model that includes the contribution of learning, relationships, culture, self, and worldviews in the promotion of mental health and detracts from the humanistic roots of counseling (Montes, 2013).

Although there is a practical reality that directs mental health counselors to employ the DSM-5, it is essential to remember that at its roots the DSM-5 is a medical document that focuses on a disease approach to mental health. It is vital for counselors to integrate DSM-5 into their practice while maintaining their wellness orientation.

Counselors can move beyond an illness model even when employing the DSM-5 by focusing on a strength-based approach rather than limiting their focus to the diagnosis of deficiencies (Wright & Lopez, 2002). When employing the DSM-5, counselors can and must continue to engage their clients in the process of goal setting and continue to value the therapeutic alliance as an essential element to the achievement of these goals.

Differential Diagnosis, Case Conceptualization, and DSM-5

Assessing clients' symptoms to make a diagnosis is an important counseling skill. The data collected and the diagnoses derived are valuable in the process of case conceptualization (see Chapter 5) and treatment planning (see Chapters 5 and 6). DSM is not intended to be a simple template to be applied to each client in a quick and easy step of diagnosis. Case conceptualization is involved and, at a minimum, requires a careful clinical history with an identification of the social, psychological, and biological factors contributing to the onset and maintenance of the current condition. The DSM is not intended to be employed as a checklist of symptoms to be used as sole criteria for diagnoses. Clinical acumen and judgment are required: "The diagnostic criteria identify symptoms, behaviors, cognitive functions, personality traits, physical signs, syndrome combinations and durations that require clinical expertise to differentiate from normal life variations and transient response to stress" (APA, 2014, p. 5).

To assist in this process, the DSM-5 provides a section (Section III) of emerging measures and models. The approach, cross-cutting symptom measures, has been modeled on general medicine's review system. The concept is that mental disorders occur along dimensional continua rather than as strict categorical entities. With this perspective, it is possible for symptoms to cut across diagnostic boundaries. The DSM offers assessments that clinicians can use to quantify ratings that characterize patients in a simple, useful, and clinically meaningful way (Narrow & Kuhl, 2011).

In cross-cutting, symptom measures are operationalized at two levels. Level 1 consists of a 23-item (adults) or a 25-item (children/adolescents) measure of the presence and severity of symptoms over the past 2 weeks (Clarke et al., 2014). The items, except for suicide ideation, suicide attempts, and substance use in children/adolescents, are rated on a 5-point scale (i.e., 0 = none/never; 1 = slight/rare; 2 = mild/several days; 3 = moderate/more than half the days; and 4 = severe/almost daily), with higher scores indicating a greater frequency of occurrence or greater degree of severity. The suicide ideation, suicide attempts, and substance use items on the child/adolescent version of the scale are scored on a yes/no basis. Items scored as 2 or higher (i.e., mild/several days) or with a "yes" trigger the completion of a more detailed assessment (Clarke & Kuhle, 2014).

Level 2 cross-cutting symptom measures facilitate a more focused assessment of Level 1 domains flagged as concerning. Thus, a client who indicated experiencing mania on Level 1 might then be administered a more specific measure for mania, assessing the presence and severity of that symptom during the past 7 days.

Most proposed assessment measures are not included in the print version of the DSM-5. For example, the DSM-5 website currently includes many Level 2 cross-cutting symptom measures and disorder-specific severity measures intended to be used as dimensional assessments for some of the most frequently diagnosed concerns. Counselors can find more information about these tools and additional dimensional assessment tools by going to http://www.psychiatry.org/practice/dsm/dsm5/online-assessment-measures.

A significant change in the DSM-5 as contrasted to the previous iteration is the authors' attention to cultural context and the diverse ways individuals experience and describe distress. This is especially important to counselors given the ethical mandate of recognizing "that culture affects the manner in which clients' problems are defined and experienced. Clients' socioeconomic and cultural experiences are considered when diagnosing mental disorders" (ACA, 2014, E.5.b).

The DSM-5 includes an updated version of the Outline for Cultural Formulation. The DSM-5 also outlines an approach to assessment using the Cultural Formulation Interview (CFI), which has been field tested for diagnostic usefulness.

The Cultural Formulation Interview (CFI; APA, 2014, pp. 752–754) is a 15–20 minute, 16-item semistructured interview to assess the impact of culture on crucial aspects of the clinical presentation and treatment plan. The domains addressed include the following:

- The cultural definition of the problem
- Cultural perceptions of cause, context, and support
- Cultural factors affecting self-coping and past help-seeking
- Cultural factors affecting current help-seeking

In addition, the DSM-5 outlines a Cultural Formulation Interview (CFI)-Informant version. This assessment can be used to gather data from another person who is "knowledgeable about the clinical problems and life circumstances of the identified individual" (APA, 2014, p. 755). This would help in cases where the client was a child or perhaps a person who is cognitively impaired.

The APA has developed 12 additional modules, to be used as supplements to the CFI or independent of the CFI. These modules address topics or specific populations, such as immigrants and refugees; coping and help-seeking; and spiritual, religious, or moral traditions. The CFI and the supplemental modules can facilitate conversation about culture and provide a firm foundation for culturally sensitive counselors to build competence and better understand a client's worldview from a diagnostic perspective (Dailey et al., 2014).

Still Less Than Ideal

As suggested in the chapter introduction, many feel that using a classification system and the resulting application of a diagnostic label to clients is dehumanizing and stigmatizing. Even the term *mental illness* carries with it the implication that a person, perhaps one experiencing global anxiety, is "sick"! Most mental health professionals would not comfortably classify a client as "crazy" while at the same time thinking little about the implications of labeling them "sick."

Beyond the philosophical position that one should not label or pigeonhole people, there has been severe criticism about the utility and validity of DSM-5. In response to these concerns, the DSM-5 was submitted to field trials that focused on the feasibility and clinical utility of diagnosis. While these trials aroused additional criticism regarding the low reliability obtained, the designers argued that unlike the previous trials, the research was conducted with naturalistic patient samples from clinical settings and used nonexpert clinicians to rate the diagnoses through checklists rather than with standard diagnostic interviews (Regier et al., 2013). The focus was on clinical utility rather than scientific purity.

However, although remaining far from perfect, the current taxonomy appears to support clinicians by helping them communicate clinical information, differentiate disorder from nonpathology, and assist them in case conceptualization and treatment planning.

Keystones

- Nosological systems, be they in medicine or counseling, are intended to do more than simply provide a shorthand notion for lists of symptoms.
- The categories presented in these taxonomies are meant to identify syndromes as "distinct," having unique etiologies (causes) and prognoses (predictive courses and outcomes), and thus preferred treatment approaches.
- The *Diagnostic and Statistical Manual for Mental Disorders* (APA, 2013), the principal taxonomy employed by clinical mental health counselors, was designed to assist professionals in their assessment and conceptualization of cases.
- The International Classification of Diseases (ICD-11) is the 11th edition of a global categorization system for physical and mental illnesses published by the World Health Organization (WHO, 2019).
- Although including many of the same mental health disorders presented in DSM-5, the ICD taxonomy is more extensive, covering health-related conditions not associated with mental disorders.
- The *DSM* espouses that it is atheoretical (APA, 2013; Lilienfeld et al., 2013), but the continued, almost exclusive focus on biological factors and a pathophysiological model can challenge the professional identity of a mental health counselor.
- It is vital for counselors to integrate DSM-5 into their practice while maintaining their wellness orientation.

Additional Resources

APA Cultural Formulation Interview: www.psychiatry.org/File%20Library/Psychiatrists/Practice/DSM/APA_DSM5_Cultural-Formulation-Interview-Supplementary-Modules.pdf

APA Online Assessment Measures: www.psychiatry.org/psychiatrists/practice/dsm/educational-resources/assessment-measures

Buckley, M. R. (Ed.). (2014). Special issue: Counseling and the DSM-5. *The Professional Counselor, 4*(3), 159–284.

Seligman, L. (2004). *Diagnosis and treatment planning in counseling* (3rd ed). Springer Science + Business Media.

References

American Counseling Association. (2014). *2014 ACA code of ethics.*

American Psychiatric Association. (2014). *Online assessment measures.* http://www.psychiatry.org/practice/dsm/dsm5/online-assessment-measures

American Psychiatric Association. (2013). *Diagnostic and statistical manual of mental disorders* (5th ed.).

Avasthi, A., Sarkar, S., & Grover, S. (2014). Approaches to psychiatric nosology: A viewpoint. *Indian Journal of Psychiatry, 56*(3), 301–304. https://doi.org/10.4103/0019-5545.120560

Buckley, M. R. (2014). Back to basics: Using the DSM-5 to benefit clients. *The Professional Counselor, 4*(3), 159–165.

Calvo, F., Karras, B. T., Phillips, R., Kimball, A. M., & Wolf, F. (2003). Diagnoses, syndromes, and diseases: A knowledge representation problem. *Annual Symposium proceedings. AMIA Symposium, 2003,* 802.

Clarke, D. E., & Kuhl, E. A. (2014). DSM-5 cross-cutting symptom measures: a step towards the future of psychiatric care? *World Psychiatry: Official Journal of the World Psychiatric Association (WPA), 13*(3), 314–316. https://doi.org/10.1002/wps.20154

Clarke, D. E., Narrow, W. E., Regier, D. A., Kuramoto, S. J., Kupfer, D. J., Kuhl, E. A., Greiner, L., & Kraemer, H. C. (2014). DSM-5 field trials in the United States and Canada, Part I: Study design, sampling strategy, implementation, and analytic approaches. *American Journal of Psychiatry, 170,* 42–58.

Dailey, S. F., Gill, C. S., Karl, S. L., & Barrio Minton, C. A. (2014). *DSM-5 learning companion for counselors.* American Counseling Association.

First, M. B. (2010). Clinical utility in the revision of the diagnostic and statistical manual of mental disorders (DSM). *Professional Psychology: Research and Practice, 41,* 465–473.

Frances, A. (2014). DSM, psychotherapy, counseling, and the medicalization of mental illness: A commentary from Allen Frances. *The Professional Counselor, 4*(3), 282–284.

Insel, T., Cuthbert, B., Garvey, M., Heinssen, R., Pine, D. S., Quinn, K., Sanislow, C., & Wang, P. (2010). Research domain criteria (RDoC): Toward a new classification framework for research on mental disorders. *American Journal of Psychiatry, 167,* 748–751. https://doi.org/10.1176/appi.ajp.2010.09091379

Jablensky, A. (2016). Psychiatric classifications: validity and utility. *World Psychiatry: Official Journal of the World Psychiatric Association (WPA), 15*(1), 26–31. https://doi.org/10.1002/wps.20284

Jablensky, A., & Kendell, R. E. (2002). Criteria for assessing a classification in psychiatry. In M. Maj, W. Gaebel, J. J. López-Ibor, & N. Sartorius (Eds.), *Psychiatric diagnosis and classification* (pp. 1–24). Wiley.

Kaplan, D. M., Tarvydas, V. M., & Gladding, S. T. (2014). 20/20: A vision for the future of counseling: The new consensus definition of counseling. *Journal of Counseling & Development, 92,* 366–372. https://doi.org/10.1002/j.1556-6676.2014.00164.x

Kraus, K. (2013). *20/20 A vision for the future of counseling: Endorsement letter.* American Counseling Association. http://www.counseling.org/docs/david-kaplan's-files/endorsement-letter.docx?sfvrsn=2

Lilienfeld, S. O., Smith, S. F., & Watts, A. L. (2013). Issues in diagnosis: Conceptual issues and controversies. In W. E. Craighead, D. J. Miklowitz, & L. W. Craighead (Eds.), *Psychopathology history, diagnosis, and empirical foundations* (2nd ed., pp. 1–35). John Wiley & Sons.

Miller, R., & Prosek, E. A. (2013). Trends and implications of proposed changes to the DSM-5 for vulnerable populations. *Journal of Counseling & Development, 91,* 359–366. https://doi.org/10.1002/j.1566-6676.00106.x

Montes, S. (2013, November 1). Facing a rising tide of personality disorders. *Counseling Today, 56*(5), 33–39.

Narrow, W. E., & Kuhl, E. A. (2011). Dimensional approaches to psychiatric diagnosis in DSM-5. *Journal of Mental Health Policy and Economics, 14,* 115–123.

Regier, D. A., Narrow, W. E., Clarke, D. E., Kraemer H. C., Kuramoto, S. J., Kuhl, E. A., & Kupfer, D. J. (2013). DSM-5 field trials in the United States and Canada, Part II: Test-retest reliability of selected categorical diagnoses. *American Journal of Psychiatry, 170,* 59–70. https://doi.org/10.1176/appi.ajp.2012.12070999

Stein, D. J., Lund, C., & Nesse, R. M. (2013). Classification systems in psychiatry: Diagnosis and global mental health in the era of DSM-5 and ICD-11. *Current Opinion in Psychiatry, 26,* 493–497. https://doi.org/10.1097/YCO.0b013e3283642dfd

World Health Organization. (2019). *The International Classification of Diseases (ICD-11).* https://www.who.int/classifications/icd/en/

Wright, B. A., & Lopez, S. J. (2002). Widening the diagnostic focus: A case for including human strengths and environmental resources. In C. R. Snyder & S. J. Lopez (Eds.), *Handbook of positive psychology* (pp. 26–44). Oxford University Press.

Case Conceptualization

A Biopsychosocial Approach

CHAPTER 5

It's a bit overwhelming. Where do I begin?

—Malik, first-year graduate student

It is not unusual for those beginning their formation as clinical mental health counselors to sit with a client and simply feel overwhelmed with the information being disclosed. Counselors are trained to build a working alliance with their clients and facilitate the client's sharing of their story. Using questions, reflections, summarizations, and a variety of verbal and nonverbal encouragers, a counselor will gather extensive information about and from the client. But not all of the information collected is pertinent or relevant to the work being done. Counselors need to be able to understand that which is relevant from that which is redundant or even superfluous. Further, once the critical data are identified a counselor then turns their attention to understanding how all of this information goes together and sheds light on both the nature of the presenting concern and the direction and approach to treatment.

The counselor configures those data into a coherent and meaningful understanding of the client and the conditions giving life to the current situation. This "making sense" of the client's story is, in essence, case conceptualization.

There are many case conceptualization approaches, all reflecting specific theoretical orientations, such as a cognitive approach, a psychodynamic approach, or even a system approach. The current chapter discusses the general nature of case conceptualization and presents a holistic, comprehensive model, the biopsychosocial model of case formulation.

After completing this chapter, the reader will be able to:

- Explain what is meant by case conceptualization.
- Identify the four Ps, the targets for inclusion in case conceptualization regardless of theoretical orientation.
- Discuss the biopsychosocial model of case formulation.

Case Conceptualization

Case conceptualization, or case formulation, can be defined as a set of "hypotheses about the causes, precipitants, and maintaining influences of a person's psychological, interpersonal, and behavioral problems" (Eells, 2002, p. 815). As a hypothesis, a case formulation may include inferences about predisposing vulnerabilities reflecting childhood traumas, a pathogenic learning history, biological or genetic influences, sociocultural influences, currently operating contingencies of reinforcement, or maladaptive cognitive patterns and beliefs about the self and the world.

Case conceptualization is a process essential to counseling. It helps counselors understand their clients and begin to identify treatment goals, appropriate interventions, and potential problems that may arise (Levenson & Strupp, 2007). Case conceptualization is the process of making meaning of all that the client has shared, which will give direction to treatment planning.

As a hypothesis, a case formulation is also subject to revision as new information emerges, as tests of the working hypothesis indicate, and as a clinician views the patient through the lens of an alternative theoretical framework. A counselor's case conceptualization is not only an appropriately comprehensive, yet flexible, account of a client's presenting concerns, but it also serves as the scaffold supporting the counselor's decisions and chosen direction.

Effective case conceptualization demands the use of a complex set of skills, including the ability to (1) collect relevant client data, (2) integrate the data into a consistent view of the client's main issues, and (3) develop a coherent plan for change that follows logically from this conceptualization of the client's main issues (Neukrug & Schwiter, 2006). The data gathered should allow the counselor to understand the cognitive, behavioral, emotional, cultural, contextual, and sociopolitical aspects of the client's story. It is in understanding these aspects and their role in the client's overall level of functioning that a counselor will be able to produce viable treatment strategies (Loganbill & Stoltenberg, 1983; Sue & Sue, 2003).

Not an Easy Process

Case conceptualization can be a challenging process. The challenge is obtaining all of the essential elements, like pieces of a puzzle, and arranging these pieces in a picture of the client's concerns, goals, challenges, and resources. Just like the picture on the puzzle box provides a view of what the pieces should produce once assembled, a counselor's theory often provides a similar framework or scaffold.

A counselor's theoretical approach may act as a lens, filtering client data and guiding the integration of those data into a case conceptualization. The nature of a counselor's case formulation can vary widely depending on which theory of psychotherapy and psychopathology a counselor employs. Counselors operating from a psychodynamic framework may focus upon early childhood experiences and unconscious conflicts. A counselor applying a cognitive theory would attempt to identify maladaptive thoughts and cognitive distortions. A behavioral formulation would rely heavily on data collected, showing the conditions surrounding the appearance of the behaviors of concern. Counselors with a behavioral approach would be interested in descriptions of antecedent and consequential events that may elicit and/or reinforce problematic behaviors.

Using their particular model or theoretical framework, along with their professional experience and knowledge of the research, counselors will assemble the data, the puzzle pieces, into a coherent view of "what is" as well as perhaps "what was" and "what is desired." This integrated view, or case conceptualization, sets the framework for consideration of strategies and techniques needed to move the client toward the desired outcome.

As noted earlier, case formulation can be difficult. Exercise 5.1 invites you to employ your "theory" of the human condition, to review the data provided by one client, Christina, and identify what you feel is central to the issue presented.

Exercise 5.1 An Attempt at Case Conceptualization/Formulation

Directions: While you may be just beginning your studies and, therefore, not yet fully knowledgeable of the theories and research supporting the counseling process, your life experience has positioned you to hold to a perspective, a "theory," on the human condition. Review the following case data through the lens of your orientation and identify the factors that you feel are essential to understanding the nature of the problem and the direction that should be taken to assist this client.

Remember that you are developing working hypotheses, not absolute truths. You may find it helpful to compare your case formulation with that of a colleague or classmate.

Christina

Presenting Problem

Christina has not spoken to her mother for over 4 months. Christina's mother called her a slut during the summer when she dumped her boyfriend to date a married coworker. The relationship with that man lasted only a month, and Christina went back to her original boyfriend. Christina is currently experiencing stress related to her relationship with her mother. She is anxious about the upcoming Thanksgiving holiday, thinking that she may not attend what has been a long-standing family tradition of dinner at mom's. She is very concerned about how she will handle being in the same room with her mother after 4 months of not speaking to each other.

Client Data

Christina is 38 years old and has lived on her own since graduating from college at age 20. Several pharmaceutical companies actively recruited Christina following graduation due to her exemplary performance as a dual major in biology and chemistry and a minor in marketing. Christina graduated magna cum laude and initially took a job as a research scientist for a major pharmaceutical company. Since being hired, Christina has moved up through the ranks and now serves as vice president for East Coast sales.

Family Information

Christina's mother, a Kashmiri Hindu, came to the United States when Christina was 6 months old. She left her home in Kashmir as part of the Kashmiri exodus, which saw a massive displacement of Hindus from Kashmir. While there were threats and rumors that the Kashmiri Hindus were to be killed, the incident that served as the impetus for Christina's mother to leave was a vicious attack on her neighbor who had acid thrown on her because she went out into the marketplace without wearing a headscarf.

Client History

Christina is an attractive, bright woman who reached puberty at the age of 11. Her years in middle school and high school were marked by success in social contexts (e.g., being elected student council president), academics (e.g., receiving a 4-year presidential scholarship to an Ivy League university), and athletically (e.g., being selected as captain for both the girl's lacrosse and softball teams). In addition to these areas of notable success, Christina received a lot of male attention due to her early development. In middle school, her early physical development drew the attention of those within her class and those much older (high school) boys. Christina was not allowed to date until she turned 18 (her senior year). Prior to that, she missed out on school formal dances or proms and could only socialize in group settings.

Recent Developments

In an interview with the counselor, Christina alluded to the fact that she had a history, while in college, of participating in risky sexual behaviors (one-night stands, unprotected sex, promiscuity, etc.). She was hesitant to respond when the counselor attempted to gain more information, stating, "That was the past ... I'm different now, even though my mom doesn't think so."

In discussing her current relationship, she noted that she has been with her current boyfriend off and on for the past 3 years. She did note that she has had four secret affairs throughout the past 3 years, all with married men. She quickly added that these occurred only during times when she and her boyfriend were separated. Christina expressed a concern about whether she could ever settle down with one man or be committed to one monogamous relationship.

Client Goals

When asked by the counselor what she would hope to achieve as a result of coming to counseling, the client, quite unexpectedly, began to cry. This was a change from her previous anger and aggressive style and presentation. She responded, "I can't stand it that my mother is so disapproving of me. Why can't she love me? I'm not a bad child."

The Four Ps

While case conceptualizations will be unique, as defined by the client's uniqueness and the model employed by the counselor, most agree that a case conceptualization should include identification of the four Ps: predisposing, precipitating, perpetuating, and protective factors (Kendjelic & Eells, 2007).

Predisposing Factors

Predisposing factors are those factors that put a client at risk of developing a problem. These are the features that render a person vulnerable to the presenting symptoms. This can include medical and psychiatric history, family history, temperament genetics, and chronic social stressors.

Although predisposing risk factors increase the likelihood that a client may develop a particular mental health disorder, these factors are not absolute, nor do they guarantee the emergence of a disorder. For example, an individual with a long and extensive family history of alcoholism would be wise to monitor their behaviors regarding alcohol use, but alcoholism is a very complex disease, and every case is different. There are dozens of risk factors and causes, any of which can impact a specific individual. It is important to remember that none of the risk factors are determinative. Consider the impact of severe neglect and the lack of opportunity to develop stable attachments during childhood; these could place the individual at risk for developing reactive attachment disorder.

Precipitating Factors

Precipitating factors refer to a specific event or trigger to the onset of the current problem. These could include that which is occurring that has moved the client to seek counseling. Significant events such as increased stress, the experience of trauma or loss, or a substantial change in life circumstances can all serve as precipitating factors.

Perpetuating Factors

Perpetuating factors are those that maintain the problem once it has become established. Perpetuating factors not only make the client's condition endure but can make it progressively worse. Factors included in this category would be things like behavioral patterns, such as avoidance behaviors employed by clients experiencing anxiety; or cognitive patterns, such as attentional biases or tendency to employ catastrophic thinking for individuals who are depressed; or even biological patterns, such as hypersomnia for those experiencing depression.

Protective Factors

Protective factors are strengths of the client or those factors that reduce the severity of problems and promote healthy and adaptive functioning. Protective factors are those factors that can reduce or prevent a condition from occurring or, following treatment, reduce the possibility of reoccurrence. Protective factors would include client strengths, resilience, or supports that can mitigate the impact of their disorder. Interestingly, focus on the client's protective factors has been an element that has traditionally been underutilized in treatment planning (Kuyken et al., 2009). This is particularly important to clinical mental health counselors because they value a strengths-based approach to service delivery.

Biopsychosocial Model of Case Conceptualization

Case conceptualization can be approached from any theoretical orientation (e.g., cognitive-behavioral, psychodynamic, family systems, etc.). A comprehensive, holistic approach to case conceptualization, or case formulation, is the biopsychosocial model.

First introduced by George Engle in the 1980s, it has been described as working hypotheses explaining the biological, psychological, and sociocultural factors that have combined to create and maintain the presenting clinical problem (APA, 1996) (see Table 5.1).

TABLE 5.1 Examples of Factors Reviewed in Biopsychosocial Model

BIOLOGICAL	PSYCHOLOGICAL	SOCIAL
• Family medical history	• Emotional development	• Family constellation/dynamics
• Genetic/risk factors	• Coping strategies	• Peer relationships
• Physical development	• Self-esteem	• Interpersonal skills
• Constitution	• Resiliency	• Neighborhood (school)
• Intelligence	• Self-efficacy	• Ethnic influences
• Temperament	• Attitudes/beliefs/values	• Socioeconomic issues
• Chronic illness	• Patterns of behavior	• Culture(s)/norms/values
• Medical comorbidities	• Patterns of cognition	• Religion(s)/spiritual resources
• Illness	• Responses to stressors	
• Current medications	• Coping strategies	
• Substance use/abuse		

Biological Factors

Each of us enters this life with biological predispositions that manifest throughout our development as both assets and challenges. Historically, the forces of nature (biology) and nurture (environment) have been placed in opposition in explaining the development of an individual's intelligence, personality, or even mental disorders. Today, most hold the position that psychiatric disorders tend to result from the interaction of genetic dispositions with environmental stressors (i.e., the diathesis-stress model). For example, certain genes are known to trigger mental health disorders. One of these, the *DISC1* gene, has been associated with schizophrenia. However, not everyone with this gene develops schizophrenia. Environmental triggers and stressors can interact with this genetic predisposition in such a way as to make it more likely that the individual will suffer from schizophrenia.

Genes are biological factors that may play a role in the development of mental disorders, but they are not the only biological factors to be considered. Defects in or injuries to some regions of the brain have also been linked to some mental illnesses, as has prenatal damage, for example, lack of oxygen to the brain, which may be a factor in the development of certain conditions.

Some mental health disorders are caused by a chemical imbalance or dysfunction in the neural pathways facilitating these chemicals to disperse in the brain. Additionally, certain infections have been linked to brain damage and the development of mental illness or the worsening of its symptoms. For example, a condition known as pediatric autoimmune neuropsychiatric disorder (PANDA) associated with streptococcus (strep) bacteria has been linked to obsessive-compulsive disorder and other mental illnesses in children.

In reviewing a client's biological factors, a counselor will review the family health history, the client's current physical health, and any evidence of biological factors that may position the client to be prone to the development of disease, psychiatric disorders, or comorbidities. Counselors and clients working together identify those biological factors that can increase or decrease risks and play a role in the emergence of a mental disorder or psychological challenge.

Psychological Factors

The second component of the biopsychosocial model is the gathering of data reflecting the client's psychological profile. Understanding the client's self and world view and any experience with early loss, neglect, abuse, or trauma would be essential to a comprehensive case formulation. It would also be vital to include data reflecting the client's strengths and coping style and their levels of self-esteem and resiliency.

Social Factors

The final domain investigated in the biopsychosocial model of case formulation is the client's connectedness with their friends, family, and community, given that "Mental or psychological well-being is influenced not only by individual characteristics or attributes but also by the socioeconomic circumstances in which persons find themselves and the broader environment in which they live" (WHO, 2012). According to the World Health Organization, mental health is impacted by the social, economic, and physical environments in which people live, with social inequalities associated with increased risk of many common mental disorders (WHO, 2014).

Understanding the social contexts in which an individual lives, works, and plays is important for assessing the stress, the challenges, and the supportive resources present. Stressors emerging from living in poverty or the context of a dysfunctional family can trigger many clients' emotional and behavioral problems. Of particular importance for a comprehensive case conceptualization is an understanding of the client's culture, ethnic heritage, and religion/belief system (see Chapter 9).

Connecting the Biological, Psychological, and Social With the Four Ps

Counselors employing a biopsychosocial formulation of their case will review data reflecting the client's biological, psychological, and social profile in search of factors contributing to the predisposition, precipitation, perpetuation, and protection of the client in terms of the presenting concerns (see Table 5.2).

TABLE 5.2 The Four P Considerations of a Biopsychological Perspective

	PREDISPOSING FACTORS	PRECIPITATING FACTORS	PERPETUATING FACTORS	PROTECTIVE FACTORS
Biological Domain	• Birth temperament • Family history • Toxic exposure • History of trauma	• Medical illness • Substance use • Hormonal changes • Sleep deprivation	• Chronic illness • Cognitive deficits • Substance use • Lack of treatment	• Good health • Absence of family psychiatric history • No substance use • Resilient
Social Domain	• Low SES • Marginalization/discrimination • Childhood exposure to violence, conflict	• Social stressors • Loss of relationship • Interpersonal trauma	• Dysfunctional relationships • Hostile environment • Poor finances • Social isolation • Chronic relationship discord	• Supportive relationship/community • Spiritual beliefs • Health care support
Psychological Domain	• Attachment style • Low self-image • Negative/rigid cognitive style • Problem with emotional modulation	• Cognitive distortions • Emotional dysregulation • Unconscious conflicts	• Interpersonal conflicts • Chronic negative thoughts • Poor distress tolerance • Poor coping skills	• Positive sense of self • Good insight • Good coping skills • Reflective

Source: Adapted from Barker, P. (1995). *The child and adolescent psychiatry evaluation: Basic child psychiatry*. Blackwell Scientific, Inc.

Such a holistic approach will unearth not only variables contributing to the emergence and maintenance of the problem but will also provide targets and resources that can be called upon in the treatment planning. Case Illustration 5.1 provides an abbreviated view of the utility of this model.

In reviewing the data in Clinical Illustration 5.1, several factors that can and should be addressed in treatment planning can be identified. A counselor working directly with this client may employ cognitive strategies to help the client reframe his view of his physical challenges and their meaning to his value as a person. Such an approach may prove helpful in elevating his self-esteem. Another element that has emerged from this case formulation and could be incorporated in a treatment plan is the school's culture and environment, supporting bullying. A counselor may attempt to address this social contributor to the presenting concern by assisting the school in implementing antibullying intervention and prevention strategies. One final point for intervention addresses the significant changes that have occurred in the family and the stress accompanying those changes.

CASE ILLUSTRATION 5.1 Withdrawn

Presenting concern: LaSalle is an 8-year-old African American male who is in the third grade at an urban public school. The client is new to the school, recently transferring from another state. The move was the result of his grandfather's passing and the need to move out of the grandfather's house due to his mother's inability to pay the mortgage. The school has been in session for 5 weeks prior to his entrance. Teachers are reporting that LaSalle is not participating in class and is often seen sitting alone at lunch or standing alone at recess. His mother reported that he is isolating at home and is refusing to go to school. When asked, the client complains that he is being made fun of at school and "bullied."

Client Profile

- A family history of anxiety and depression. One uncle (father's brother) committed suicide.
- The client was born with a hearing defect.
- The client has undergone surgery to correct hearing deficit (cochlear implants).
- The client is mildly asthmatic and employs inhalers as needed.
- The grandfather, with whom the client lived, was killed in a car accident, resulting in the family moving to this new state and new school. The grandfather was the client's "hero" and pushed the values of schooling and hard work.
- Grandfather was a healthy male model, worked for the transit authority, and was an employed handyman (on weekends), loved to read.
- The family consists of a mother, who holds multiple minimum wage jobs and works 60 hours a week, a father, unemployed and a self-identified "drinker," and four siblings ages 9, 11, 14, and 15 (all females).
- School is located in an urban setting, transient population, limited resources.
- Community is lower SES, high crime and violence rates, with numerous active gangs.

	BIOLOGICAL	PSYCHOLOGICAL	SOCIAL
Predisposing	Genetic loading (family history of depression, anxiety, and potential substance abuse). Prenatal infection causing hearing loss.	He was verbally abused by his father and oldest sibling. When he was 1 to 3 years of age, his female siblings would dress him in girls' clothing and play with him as if he were a toy/doll.	Family financial difficulties, poverty. Ordinal position within the family as well as being the only male among his siblings.
Precipitating	The client experiences problems with a device worn outside his ear that is inconsistent in performance and sometimes causes discomfort (inflammation around the site).	Experienced severe loss with grandfather's death.	Teased and bullied at school.
Perpetuating	Infection and poor response to the medicine.	Low self-esteem and negative body image (hearing/asthma).	Absence of family support (father, alcohol; mother, unavailable due to work schedule). Father pushes for son's aggressive retaliation, "stop being a little girl!"
Protective	Available medical services (community medical clinic walking distance to the current residence).	Motivated (grandfather model of hard work); mother's concern and investment in helping and LaSalle's insight.	School teachers and the school counselor are aware and concerned about LaSalle's adjustment and the increasing incidence of bullying in the school.

In this case, a clinical mental health counselor would be of excellent service in providing family therapeutic support and assisting the family in connecting with community-based services.

Case Conceptualization Does Not Equal Diagnosis

Diagnosis is not the same as case conceptualization. Diagnosis entails the grouping of consistent symptoms seen within a population and categorizing that grouping into a distinct entity, a syndrome, which is then assigned a diagnostic label.

When a counselor is diagnosing, they will attempt to identify the presenting symptoms and compare those to the criteria found within a taxonomy such as the DSM-5 (see Chapter 4). For example, a client presenting with five of the nine symptomatic criteria listed in the DSM-5 for a major depressive episode would be diagnosed as depressed.

Case conceptualization goes beyond this shorthand labeling of the client's concerns, attempting to identify how these concerns reflect the client's biology, social context, and psychological factors. Case formulation reflects a more dimensional perspective in which problems are viewed as being on continua from normal to abnormal. Case formulation synthesizes the information into a theory as to how problems developed and how change might unfold.

Diagnosis and case formulation complement each other and should coexist. Diagnosis by itself does not encompass the complexity of the individual case. Generally, the diagnosis does not tell the clinician how two children with the same diagnosis, such as obsessive-compulsive disorder, differ in terms of strengths, vulnerabilities, precipitants of symptom exacerbations, the developmental impact of the symptoms, or the meaning of the symptoms to the child and family. Case formulation is seen as a vehicle to supplement and apply diagnosis to the specifics of an individual's life. Case formulation also serves as a vehicle for converting a diagnosis to a plan for treatment, especially the choice of type and timing of interventions (Eells, 1997).

From Case Conceptualization to Treatment Planning

The process of case conceptualization sets the stage for the formulation and implementation of a treatment plan (Jongsma et al., 2006). The data collected during the case conceptualization process serves as the springboard for the formulation and implementation of the treatment plan (Jongsma et al., 2006). The plan developed for implementation reflects the counselor's assessment of the client's adaptive functioning and readiness for change and the counselor's understanding of the research supporting treatment efficacy (Eells, 2007) (see Chapter 6).

Keystones

- Case conceptualization, or case formulation, can be defined as a set of "hypotheses about the causes, precipitants, and maintaining influences of a person's psychological, interpersonal, and behavioral problems" (Eells, 2002, p. 815).
- A case formulation may include inferences about predisposing vulnerabilities reflecting childhood traumas, a pathogenic learning history, biological or genetic influences, sociocultural

influences, currently operating contingencies of reinforcement, or maladaptive cognitive patterns and beliefs about the self and the world.

- Effective case conceptualization demands the use of a complex set of skills, including the ability to (1) collect relevant client data, (2) integrate these data into a consistent view of the client's main issues, and (3) develop a coherent plan for change that follows logically from this conceptualization of the client's main issues.
- The nature of a counselor's case formulation can vary widely depending on which theory of psychotherapy and psychopathology a counselor employs but typically includes data on the predisposing, precipitating, perpetuating, and protective factors.
- A comprehensive, holistic approach to case conceptualization, or case formulation, is the biopsychosocial model.
- Diagnosis is not the same as case conceptualization; case conceptualization goes beyond the labeling of the client or client's concern to attempting to identify how these concerns reflect the client's biology, social context, and psychological factors.
- The process of case conceptualization sets the stage for the formulation and implementation of a treatment plan.

Additional Resources

Campbell, W. H., & Rohrbaugh, R. M. (2006). *The biopsychosocial formulation manual: A guide for mental health professionals.* Routledge.

Kramer, U. (Ed.). (2019). *Case formulation for personality disorders.* Academic Press.

Sperry, L. (2020). *Case conceptualization.* Routledge.

Zubernis, L., & Snyder, M. (2016). *Case conceptualization and effective interventions: Assessing and treating mental, emotional, and behavioral disorders.* Sage.

References

American Psychiatric Association Commission on Psychotherapy. (1996). *Definition of the biopsychosocial formulation.* American Psychiatric Association.

Eells, T. D. (Ed.). (1997). *Handbook of psychotherapy case formulation.* Guilford Press.

Eells, T. D. (2002). Formulation. In M. Hersen & W. Sledge (Eds.), *The encyclopedia of psychotherapy* (pp. 815–822). Academic Press.

Eells, T. D. (Ed.). (2007). *Handbook of psychotherapy case formulation.* Guilford Press.

Jongsma, A. E., Peterson, L. M., & McInnis, W. P. (2006). *The adolescent psychotherapy treatment planner* (4th ed.). John Wiley.

Kendjelic, E. M., & Eells, T. D. (2007). Generic psychotherapy case formulation training improves formulation quality. *Psychotherapy: Theory, Research, Practice, Training, 44*(1), 66–77.

Kuyken, W., Padesky, C. A., & Dudley, R. (2009). *Collaborative case conceptualization: Working effectively with clients in cognitive-behavioral therapy.* Guilford Press.

Levenson, H., & Strupp, H. H. (2007). Cyclical maladaptive patterns: Case formulation in time-limited dynamic psychotherapy. In T. D. Eells (Ed.), *Handbook of psychotherapy case formulation* (2nd ed., pp. 164–197). Guilford Press.

Loganbill, C., & Stoltenberg, C. (1983). The case conceptualization format: A training device for practicum. *Counselor Education and Supervision, 22*, 235–241.

Neukrug, E., & Schwitzer, A. (2006). *Skills and tools for today's professional counselors and psychotherapists. From natural helping to professional counseling.* Brooks/Cole.

Sue, D. W., & Sue, D. (2003). *Counseling the culturally diverse: Theory and practice* (4th ed.). Wiley.

World Health Organization. (2012). *Risks to mental health: An overview of vulnerabilities and risk factors.* Background paper by WHO Secretariat for the development of a comprehensive Mental Health Action Plan.

World Health Organization. (2014). *Social determinants of mental health.* https://apps.who.int/iris/bitstream/handle/10665/112828/9789241506809_eng.pdf?sequence=1

Best Practice Applied

CHAPTER 6

I always liked that theory; I am comfortable with it.
—Rena, community mental health counselor

Those in training to become mental health counselors will be introduced to numerous theories, techniques, and interventions. Some of these may likely align with a student's self and world view. A student in training, or even a counselor in practice, may find some theory or technique "comfortable" when contrasted to another. The question is whether one's comfort level or personal liking for a theory or technique should be the criteria for its selection and employment when working with a specific client and a specific presenting concern.

The answer, of course, is no.

While some can argue, and rightfully so, that counseling is as much of an art as a science, the fiduciary responsibility we have for providing our clients with the best care possible suggests that even our artistry should have its foundation in the science of our profession. The counseling process is and should be fluid, flexible, and dynamic. The application of our professional knowledge should be shaped by each client's uniqueness and the multitude of circumstances that are encountered in any one session. But this flexibility and dynamism does not mean that one can simply "wing it." Numerous studies point to findings that clinical outcomes are superior when treatment with empirical support is employed (Cukrowicz et al., 2005).

It is the blending of our science with the need for our professional flexibility in its application that is the focus of this chapter. The current chapter reviews what is meant by "best practice" and the advantages and challenges of incorporating evidence-based practice (EBP) into your treatment planning.

After completing this chapter, the reader will be able to:

- Define evidence-based practice (EBP).
- Differentiate EBP from empirically supported treatment (EST).
- Describe the benefits and the challenges of employing EBP.

Evidence-Based Practice

At its core, evidence-based practice (EBP) reflects the conscientious, explicit, and judicious use of current best evidence in making decisions about the care of individual patients (Sackett et al.,

1996). While initially applied to those within the medical health field, the concept was expanded to include practicing psychologists in 2006. At that time, the American Psychological Association's Presidential Task Force on Evidence-Based Practice in Psychology defined evidence-based practice (EBP) as "the integration of the best available research with clinical expertise in the context of patient characteristics, culture, and preferences" (2006, p. 273).

Key to this definition is the articulation of three essential components, or what has been described as the three legs of the EBP stool (Yates, 2013). The first component, or leg, is that practice decisions are based on research and science. This is not meant to inhibit a counselor's flexibility in the application of that science; in fact, the second and third legs of the stool highlight the need to adjust to unique conditions of each counseling encounter. The second leg highlights the need for counselors to integrate the research data with their clinical expertise. The third leg calls for the application of the research in a way that reflects the understanding of and respect for the unique client "characteristics, culture and preferences" (APA Presidential Task Force on EBP, 2006, p. 273).

The 2006 policy developed by the American Psychological Association emphasizes the need for practitioners to integrate clinical expertise and specific clinical information about the client with the pertinent research evidence as to the basis for making clinical decisions, implementing treatment plans, fostering a therapeutic alliance, and achieving positive outcomes. EBP encompasses scientific and local evidence, such as diagnostic patient information; situational information, including cost and time constraints; and the provider's judgment and experience, to achieve the best outcome (Rousseau & Gunia, 2016).

The employment of EBP is not intended to hamstring or inordinately constrict the counselor's approach to providing the most effective service to any specific client. Is it not a mandate to blindly follow a manualized approach to treatment. EBP calls counselors to be able to deliver interventions that reflect well-researched treatment modalities as adapted to meet each client's unique needs and the specifics of the particular counseling relationship.

Several forces have spurred increased interest in counselors' employment of EBP. The current emphasis on accountability coming from professional organizations such as the American Counseling Association (ACA; Bradley et al., 2005) and the American Psychological Association (APA; Clay, 2001), the federal government's Center for Mental Health Services of SAMHSA (Chandler, 2009), and third-party payers provides a significant impetus to the employment of EBP. Government-sponsored health agencies have emphasized and often require the use of evidence-based treatment interventions. Behavioral science professionals using evidence-based practices are more likely to receive funding from state and federal agencies (Smith et al., 2014).

Additionally, the employment of EBP is responsive to the counselors' codes of ethics. The American Mental Health Counselors Association (AMHCA) directs its members to integrate research into practice, specifically: "Acknowledge how science and evidence-based practice may be leveraged to improve outcomes and increase collaboration in an integrated care setting" (2020, A.2.a.i.). This same sentiment is even more explicitly stated in the American Counseling Association's code of ethics, which directs counselors to "use techniques/procedures/modalities that are grounded in theory and/or have an empirical or scientific foundation" (ACA, 2014, C.7.a).

Perhaps a primary motive for adopting EBP is its inclusion of empirically supported treatments and the hope that such inclusion will increase counselor efficacy. Incorporating research inevitably promotes the development of guidelines, databases, and other clinical tools that can help clinicians make critical treatment decisions, particularly in community-based settings (Nelson et al., 2006). Evidence-based practice and treatments are associated with higher quality and more effective service (Springer, 2007) and the enhancement of the health and well-being of the public (APA Presidential Task Force on EBP, 2006).

EBP and Empirically Supported Treatments

While EBP calls for the employment of research as a foundation for treatment planning, there is often a misunderstanding that EBP is the same as empirically supported treatment (EST). EBP is not synonymous with EST.

EBP, more broadly, refers to a process of making data-informed clinical decisions (Bloom et al., 2009). As part of that decision making, a counselor may choose to employ an empirically supported treatment, one for which research has demonstrated its efficacy, but that is not a defining element of EBP.

EST is often emphasized in the employment of EBP. The American Counseling Association (Morkides, 2009) and the American Counseling Association Practice Research Network (Bradley et al., 2005) posit that it is critical for counselors' optimal function that they incorporate evidence-based interventions into their treatment planning. These positions reflect our understanding that interventions supported by research are more likely to be effective when compared to those interventions lacking research support (Massey et al., 2005).

While ESTs have been shown to improve client outcomes in more than one randomized clinical trial (Chambless & Ollendick, 2001), their employment in practice does not preclude the counselor's use of their clinical expertise to apply these treatments in a manner that addresses their clients' unique characteristics, cultures, and preferences (APA Presidential Task Force on EBP, 2006).

Empirically Supported Treatments

The majority of evidence-based therapies are cognitive-behavioral, whereas many practitioners employ existential-humanistic, interpersonal, psychodynamic, systemic, or integrative models (Emmelkamp et al., 2014). Smith et al. (2014) identified three theoretical approaches that have research supporting their utility for use with a variety of client conditions. The interventions identified were cognitive-behavioral therapy (CBT), person-centered counseling, and dialectal behavioral therapy (DBT).

Butler et al. (2006), for example, reported on a meta-analysis demonstrating the effectiveness of CBT with 16 different disorders over 332 clinical trials. Person-centered counseling has research support for its effectiveness with anxiety, depression, and adolescent and family counseling (Gibbard & Hanley, 2008; Karver et al., 2006). As for DBT, research supports its efficacy with treating borderline personality disorder, suicide, depression, bipolar disorder, and substance abuse (Bedics et al., 2012; Kliem et al., 2010; Lynch et al., 2003).

As might be expected, research on best practice and treatment efficacy continues. Various treatments are being assessed for efficacy and effectiveness. However, not every approach or technique described in the literature reaches the criteria for inclusion as an EST. Smith (2011) suggested that the following factors should be considered when determining what constitutes an evidence-based practice:

- Defining the evidence that one needs.
- Determining how much evidence is needed.
- Examining conditions necessary for the evidence to be valid.
- Assessing real-life issues when applying a practice or program.

Smith (2011) identified a set of criteria that could be employed in determining whether a protocol or treatment reached the threshold for being evidence based (see Table 6.1).

TABLE 6.1 Criteria for Identifying Evidence-Based Treatment

1. Has the research used **randomized clinical trials** demonstrating effectiveness?
2. **Has there been demonstrated effectiveness** using different samples and varied settings?
3. Are outcome, dependent variables, and treatment interventions **clearly defined**?
4. **Feasibility** of the practice or intervention. Has the intervention been administered according to procedures and standards that can be used by others?
5. **Assurances of fidelity**. Have interventions been implemented according to standard ethical practices, and are the procedures transparent?
6. Is the intervention **theoretically grounded**?
7. Have the practices or interventions been used with **diverse populations**?

Source: Adapted from R. L. Smith. (2011). *Achievement motivation training: An evidence-based approach to enhancing performance*. http://www.counseling.org/resources/library/vistas/2011-v-online/article_56.pdf

While the criteria for identifying a specific intervention or treatment as empirically supported continue to evolve, two resources that can help a counselor stay current with best practices are the *Journal of Counseling & Development* and the APA's Division 12 (the Society of Clinical Psychology) website.

In 2003, the *Journal of Counseling & Development* introduced a best practices section that updates counselors on the latest research evidence to support their counseling practices. Division 12, the Society of Clinical Psychology of the American Psychological Association, provides a website that offers information about effective treatments for psychological diagnoses (https://www.div12.org/psychological-treatments/). The searchable website provides basic descriptions for each psychological diagnosis and treatment. In addition, the website lists clinical resources and training opportunities.

Note that the absence of a particular treatment for any targeted diagnosis does not automatically mean that treatment is not viable. Other psychological treatments may also be effective in treating any of the disorders identified but may not have been evaluated for inclusion. Table 6.2 provides a sampling from the website of treatments associated with specific diagnostic presentations. Exercise 6.1 invites you to employ the website and other resources to identify research that might support your approach to the treatment of specific presenting concerns.

TABLE 6.2 Sample of Evidence-Based Interventions by Diagnosis

DIAGNOSIS	SUPPORTED INTERVENTIONS
Depression	Acceptance and commitment therapy for depression Cognitive therapy for depression Emotion-focused therapy for depression Rational emotive behavioral therapy for depression Short-term psychodynamic therapy for depression
Generalized anxiety	Cognitive and behavioral therapies for generalized anxiety disorder Mom Power: Promoting resilience in mothers and families
Mixed substance abuse/ dependence	Friends Care for Mixed Substance Abuse/Dependence Motivational interviewing Motivational enhancement therapy (MET) MET plus cognitive-behavioral therapy Prize-based contingency management
Obsessive-compulsive disorder	Exposure and response prevention Cognitive-behavioral therapy Acceptance and commitment therapy
Posttraumatic stress disorder (PTSD)	Cognitive processing therapy Eye movement desensitization and reprocessing for post-stress inoculation training
Specific Phobias	Exposure therapies

Exercise 6.1 Research Guiding Practice Decision

Directions: Review the list of presenting concerns or diagnoses listed in column A, and then in column B identify the theory or approach to treatment that you might employ. For example, in being presented with a client exhibiting a simple phobia, specifically a fear of puppies, what approach or strategy might you employ? Then, search the literature and attempt to find research that supports your approach. List that reference in column C, identifying the design of the study (e.g., Was it a randomized control-group study? Was it a small sample or single-subject study? Was it an anecdotal clinical report?). In column D, discuss your findings with your colleagues or classmates. You may also want to share findings for your future reference.

A. PRESENTING CONCERN	B. YOUR APPROACH	C. SUPPORTIVE RESEARCH	D. RESEARCH DESIGN
(Example) Obsessive-compulsive disorder	Some type of cognitive-behavioral approach.	Psychological treatment of obsessive-compulsive disorder: a meta-analysis. Rosa-Alcázar, A. I., Sánchez-Meca, J., Gómez-Conesa, A., & Marín-Martínez, F. (2008). *Clinical Psychology Review, 28*(8), 1310–1325.	Control group study using placebo and waiting list for comparison.
48-year-old veteran experiencing depression			

(*Continued*)

(*Continued*)

A. PRESENTING CONCERN	B. YOUR APPROACH	C. SUPPORTIVE RESEARCH	D. RESEARCH DESIGN
18-year-old female with an intense fear of puppies (simple phobia)			
52-year-old self-identified alcoholic			
29-year-old female experiencing PTSD after being attacked by a stranger			

Challenges to Employment of EBP

Even though counselors are called to use techniques grounded in theory and/or that have an empirical or scientific foundation (ACA, 2014, C.7.a. Scientific Basis for Treatment), the utilization of EBP can be impeded by several factors. A counselor's misunderstanding of the nature of EBP or a failure to have the appropriate training or support for the utilization of evidence-based procedures can result in the underutilization of EBP.

Misunderstanding of EBP

For some, the misperception that EBP demands the use of empirically supported treatments and their manualized treatment plans is the major hurdle. As noted, EBP and EST, while certainly working in concert, are not synonymous. Nor is the strict, rigid use of manualized treatment protocols essential to counselor employment of EBP.

Employment of an evidence-based approach to practice does not restrict the counselor's flexibility in treatment planning. The misunderstanding that EBP constricts the counselor's ability for professional judgments in line with the uniqueness of each client and counseling relationship is a hurdle to the employment of EPB. It must be reiterated that even when employing empirically supported treatments within an EBP model, the treatments are employed, incorporating the counselor's clinical expertise and judgment into the application of these strategies. The appropriate use of EBP incorporates clinical expertise, which, by definition, requires incorporating patient values, preferences, and individual circumstances as integral parts of decision making. Applying evidence-based principles ensures that providers use the best existing evidence as a starting framework, while simultaneously affording them the flexibility to individualize treatment (Cook et al., 2017).

As described by Kendall et al. (2008), this is a situation where practitioners follow basic treatment guidelines of evidence-based treatment with "flexibility within fidelity." The approach would allow counselors to be true to the model's core components rather than rigidly locking into the specifics of a manualized presentation of the treatment. The approach would allow for modification of treatments and even the use of treatments that fail to meet the criteria for inclusion as empirically supported treatment. The proviso, however, is for counselors to employ all treatment with careful monitoring and allow data to provide directions and modification of treatment plans.

Limited Generalizability

Another challenge to fully incorporating an evidence-based approach to practice is that some procedures that appear efficacious in a controlled environment do not work in real-world clinical settings (Southam-Gerow et al., 2009). Of special consideration for the mental health counselor who values wellness and prevention is that an evidence-based practice typically targets the amelioration of symptoms or disorders compared to the development of wellness.

Counselor Competence

For strategies, procedures, or techniques that have generalizability to the real-life counseling setting, a challenge may be that many counselors lack the training to employ them. The ethical responsibility for practicing within the known limits of one's competency is clear. The American Counseling Association (2014) directs its members to "practice only within the boundaries of their competence, based on their education, training, supervised experience, state and national professional credentials, and appropriate professional experience" (C.2.a). Similarly, the American Mental Health Counseling Association calls its members to both maintain knowledge of scientific information related to service (AMHCA, 2020, C.1.c) while providing "only those services and use only those techniques for which they are qualified by education, training, or experience" (AMHCA, 2020, C.1.b). Knowing what to do and being competent to do it are two different things.

With limited funding and resources available to support a counselor's professional development, the employment of the latest and greatest intervention may simply not be possible. This is particularly concerning because training in EBP, and the use of evidence-based interventions, not only ensures that counselors are up to date on the state of the profession but position them to provide the most effective service (Beidas et al., 2012).

Keystones

- Evidence-based practice (EBP) has been defined as "the integration of the best available research with clinical expertise in the context of patient characteristics, culture, and preferences" (APA Presidential Task Force on EBP, 2006, p. 273).
- Engagement in empirically based practice is more than a rational response to organizational mandates; it also represents adherence to a call for ethical practice. The ACA Code of Ethics states, "Counselors have a responsibility to the public to engage in counseling practices that are based on rigorous research methodologies" (ACA, 2014, Section C, Professional Responsibility).
- A significant misunderstanding about EBP is that some think it restricts the counselor's ability to use their experience and "local" knowledge to craft meaningful interventions and that it ties them to the rigid application of manualized treatment protocols.
- Kendall et al. (2008) suggest that a model of "flexibility within fidelity" should guide a practitioner's employment of EBP. This approach encourages practitioners to follow basic treatment guidelines of evidence-based treatments without rigid adherence, allowing for flexibility given the uniqueness of each counseling relationship.

Additional Resources

Bertolino, B. (2018). *Effective counseling and psychotherapy: An evidence-based approach*. Springer.

Brown, C. (2016). *The evidence-based practitioner: Applying research to meet client needs*. F.A. Davis.

SAMHSA Evidence-Based Practices Resource Center: https://www.samhsa.gov/ebp-resource-center

Sue, D., & Sue, D. M. (2008). *Foundations of counseling and psychotherapy: Evidence-based practices for a diverse society*. John Wiley & Sons.

References

American Counseling Association. (2014). *ACA code of ethics*. Author.

American Psychological Association, Presidential Task Force on Evidence-Based Practice in Psychology. (2006). Evidence-based practice in psychology. *American Psychologist, 61*, 271–285.

American Mental Health Counselors Association. (2020). *AMHCA code of ethics*. https://www.amhca.org/HigherLogic/System/DownloadDocumentFile.ashx?DocumentFileKey=24a27502-196e-b763-ff57-490a12f7edb1&forceDialog=0

Bedics, J. D., Atkins, D. C., Comtois, K. A., & Linehan, M. M. (2012). Treatment differences in the therapeutic relationship and introject during a 2-year randomized controlled trial of dialectical behavior therapy versus nonbehavioral psychotherapy experts for borderline personality disorder. *Journal of Consulting and Clinical Psychology, 80*(1), 66–77.

Beidas, R. S., Edmunds, J. M., Marcus, S. C., Kendall, P. C. (2012). Training and consultation to promote implementation of an empirically supported treatment: A randomized trial. *Psychiatric Services, 63*, 660–665.

Bloom, M., Fischer, J., & Orme, J. G. (1995). *Evaluating practice: Guidelines for the accountable professional* (2nd ed.). Prentice Hall.

Bradley, L. J., Sexton, T. L., & Smith, H. B. (2005). The American Counseling Association Practice Research Network (ACA-PRN): A new research tool. *Journal of Counseling & Development, 83*, 488–491.

Butler, A. C., Chapman, J. E., Forman, E. M., & Beck, A. T. (2006). The empirical status of cognitive-behavioral therapy: A review of meta-analyses. *Clinical Psychology Review, 26*(1), 17–31.

Chambless, D. L., & Ollendick, T. H. (2001). Empirically supported psychological interventions: Controversies and evidence. *Annual Review of Psychology, 52*, 685–716.

Chandler, D. (2009). Implementation of integrated dual disorders treatment in eight California programs. *American Journal of Psychiatric Rehabilitation, 12*, 330–351.

Clay, R. A. (2011). Treatment guidelines development now underway. *Monitor on Psychology, 42*, 18–19.

Cook, S. C., Schwartz, A. C., & Kaslow, N. J. (2017). Evidence-based psychotherapy: Advantages and challenges. *Neurotherapeutics, 14*(3), 537–545.

Cukrowicz, K. C., White, B. A., Reitzel, L. R., Burns, A. B., Driscoll, K. A., Kemper, T. S., & Joiner, T. E., Jr. (2005). Improved treatment outcomes associated with the shift to empirically supported treatment in graduate training clinic. *Professional Psychology: Research and Practice, 36*, 330–337.

Emmelkamp, P. M., Beckers, D. D., Muris, P., Cuijpers, P., Lutz, W., Andersson, G., Araya, R., Banos, R. R. M., Barkham, M., Berking, M., Berger, T., Botella, C., Carlbring, P., Colom, F., Essau, C., Hemans, D., Hofman, S. G., Kanppe, S., Ollendick, T. H., Raes, F., Rief, W., Riper, H., Van Der Oord, S., & Verliet, B. (2014). Advancing psychotherapy and evidence-based psychological interventions. *International Journal of Methods in Psychiatric Research, 23*(1), 58–91.

Ganju, V. (2003). Implementation of evidence-based practices in state mental health systems: Implication for research and effectiveness studies. *Schizophrenia Bulletin, 29*(1), 125–131.

Gibbard, S., & Hanley, T. (2008). A five-year evaluation of the effectiveness of person-centered counseling in routine clinical practice in primary care. *Counseling and Psychotherapy Research, 8*(4), 215–222.

Karver, M. S., Handelsman, J. B., Fields, S., & Bickman, L. (2006). Meta-analysis of therapeutic relationship variables in youth and family therapy: The evidence for different relationship variables in the child and adolescent treatment outcome literature. *Clinical Psychology Review, 26*, 50–65.

Kendall, P. C., Gosch, E., Furr, J. M., & Sood, E. (2008). Flexibility within fidelity. *Journal of the American Academy of Child and Adolescent Psychiatry, 47*, 987–993.

Kliem, S., Kröger, C., & Kosfelder, J. (2010). Dialectical behavior therapy for borderline personality disorder: A meta-analysis using mixed-effects modeling. *Journal of Consulting Clinical Psychology, 78*(6), 936–951.

Lynch, T. R., Morse, J. Q., Mendelson, T., & Robins, C. J. (2003). Dialectical behavior therapy for depressed older adults: A randomized pilot study. *American Journal of Geriatric Psychiatry, 11*, 33–45.

Massey, O. T., Armstrong, K., Boroughs, M., Henson, K., & McCash, L. (2005). Mental health services in schools: A qualitative analysis of challenges to implementation, operation, and sustainability. *Psychology in the Schools, 42*(4), 361–372.

Morkides, C. (2009, July). Measuring counselor success. *Counseling Today*. http://ct.counseling.org/2009/07/measuring-counselor-success/

Nelson T. D., Steele, R. G., & Mize, J. A. (2006). Practitioner attitudes towards evidence-based practice: Themes and challenges. *Administration and Policy in Mental Health, 6*(33), 398–409. https://doi.org/10.1007/s10488-006-0044-4

Rousseau, D. M., & Gunia, B. C. (2016). Evidence-based practice: the psychology of EBP implementation. *Annual Review of Psychology, 67*, 667–692. https://doi.org/10.1146/annurev-psych-122414-033336

Sackett, D. L., Rosenberg, W. M. C., Gray, J. A. M., & Richardson, W. S. (1996). Evidence-based medicine: What it is and what it isn't. *BMJ, 312*, 71–72.
Smith, R. L. (2011). *Achievement motivation training: An evidence-based approach to enhancing performance.* http://counseling-outfitters.com/vistas/vistas11/Article_56.pdf
Smith, R. L., Hunnicutt Hollenbaugh, M., & Arora, S. (2014). *Evidence-based practices and single-subject research designs in counseling.* https://www.counseling.org/knowledge-center/vistas/by-subject2/vistas-assessment/docs/default-source/vistas/article_36
Southam-Gerow, M. A., Hourigan, S. E., & Allin, R. B., Jr. (2009). Adapting evidence-based mental health treatments in community settings: Preliminary results from a partnership approach. *Behavior Modification, 33*(1), 82–103.
Spring, B. (2007). Evidence-based practice in clinical psychology: What it is, why it matters. What you need to know. *Journal of Clinical Psychology, 63*(7), 611–631.
Springer, D. (2007). The teaching of evidence-based practice in social work higher education—living by the Charlie Parker dictum: A response to papers by Shlonsky and Stern, and Soydan. *Research on Social Work Practice, 17*, 619–624.
Yates, C. (2013). Evidence-based practice: The components, history, and process. *Counseling Outcome Research and Evaluation, 4*, 41–45.

SECTION III

Clinical Mental Health Counseling in Context

CHAPTER 7

The Clinical Mental Health Counselor

Roles and Settings

Someday—private practice. For now, I want the supervision and benefits offered by the Elsen Clinic.
—Raul, graduating clinical mental health counselor

Raul, like many entering the mental health counseling profession, has thoughts of being in private practice someday. It is clear that he has thought about his choices and how each may serve him personally and professionally.

As implied with Raul's "someday" reference, the careers of most mental health counselors unfold over time. The opportunities available to mental health counselors span a wide variety of professional settings, with a multitude of titles, and the gift of many new and different experiences.

The current chapter reviews the contexts and roles in which one can find a professional mental health counselor.

After completing this chapter, the reader will be able to:

- Explain what is meant by the continuum of care.
- Describe the impact of the Community Mental Health Centers Act of 1963.
- Describe the roles and functions as well as the unique challenges encountered by clinical mental health counselors working in a variety of different settings.

Clinical Mental Health Counselors and the Continuum of Care

Mental health counseling is considered one of the core mental health professions in the United States (Colangelo, 2009). Much of the growth and interest in mental health counseling services was stimulated by the passage of the Community Mental Health Centers Act of 1963. The Community Mental Health Centers Act of 1963 mandated the development of a nationwide network of community-based mental health clinics. As prescribed within this bill, these clinics would all provide five essential services. Community-based clinics were to provide short-term inpatient counseling, outpatient counseling, emergency services, crisis stabilization, and consultation/education (Lourie, 2003).

The services outlined, if placed on a continuum of care, would range between those services targeting the most distressed clients and engaging the most intense forms of intervention and therapy to preventive programming and wellness services. The concept of a continuum of care also points to the fact that individuals, depending on internal and external faculties at any one time, can shift positions on the continuum, thus requiring more, less, or different forms of service.

This continuum of mental health care served as a paradigm for the detailing of mental health service delivery (Hoff & Adamowski, 1998). It opened the doors of employment to nonmedical providers, such as mental health counselors. The expansion of this perspective outside the walls of a community mental health setting encouraged mental health counselors to take employment in outpatient clinics, inpatient health centers, substance treatment facilities, individual and group private practices, and even within business employee assistance programs (EAPs) (Normandy-Doberg, 2010).

Mental health counselors can employ this model to conceptualize the types of services that they wish to offer. If we placed descriptors along the continuum, we might see those at a healthy functional point in their lives at one end. For these individuals who are productive and generally satisfied and happy with their lives, programs and services that facilitate growth and wellness may be the service of choice. But, as we all know, life and normative development can be hit by challenges.

Individuals may at any time be thrown off their physical and mental equilibrium. While continuing to function, these individuals are experiencing stress (distress) and as a result find growth blocked. This may be the case with an individual experiencing the loss of a loved one, a significant career challenge, or perhaps relationship issues. For these individuals, finding support in developing coping skills, possibly by way of short-term individual or group counseling, may be the service needed. Finally, there are individuals for whom the crisis, the distress, is such as to block their normal functioning. Their normal coping and adjustment capabilities have collapsed, and they are experiencing significant changes in their thoughts, behaviors, feelings, and relationships. For these individuals, depending on the severity of their dysfunction, a variety of clinical services and settings may be called into play. The model of the continuum of care allows mental health counselors to not only identify levels of care required but allows for clients to be tracked over time through a comprehensive array of health services spanning all levels of intensity of care (see Table 7.1).

TABLE 7.1 A Sampling of Continuum of Care Services

Health and wellness services: The focus is on what is "well" within the person, not the typical approach that identifies someone as their disease. The goal of these services is to empower individuals with the knowledge, skills, tools, and resources to live healthy, productive, and joyful lives.
Office or outpatient clinic: Services provided on an outpatient basis can include individual, group, or family therapy; individual treatment planning; diagnostic assessments; medication management; and psychological testing.
Intensive case management: Services include psychiatric, legal, medical, and even financial services aimed at assisting a client in living successfully within the community.
Home-based treatment services: Treatment programs brought directly to the client's home.
Day treatment programs: These are typically intensive treatment programs that provide individual and group therapy, with clients often attending 5 days per week.
Partial hospitalization (day hospital): A setting that provides all the treatment services of a psychiatric hospital, but the clients go home each evening.
Emergency/crisis services: 24-hour-per-day services for emergencies (e.g., hospital emergency room, mobile crisis team).
Therapeutic group home or community residence: This therapeutic program usually includes a small group of individuals living together, often with professional supervision, who are typically engaged in a day treatment program.
Crisis residence: This setting provides short-term (usually fewer than 15 days) crisis intervention and treatment. Clients receive 24-hour-a-day supervision.

(*Continued*)

(*Continued*)

Residential treatment facility: Clients receive intensive and comprehensive psychiatric treatment in a campus-like setting on a longer-term basis.

Hospital treatment: Clients receive comprehensive psychiatric treatment in a hospital where the design and length of treatment are a function of numerous variables contributing to the case conceptualization and resulting treatment plan.

Context and Settings for Service Delivery

When considering employment possibilities for mental health counselors, a couple of vectors come together that should be considered. Mental health counselors can provide services not only to a variety of clients and client concerns but deliver those services within a setting or context that may impact the nature of the services they provide. Although several areas and populations served by clinical mental health counselors require or desire special certification or licensing, as might be the case when working in private practice or with addiction counseling (see Chapter 14), for many of the roles performed by clinical mental health counselors, there is no specific certificate. Thus the knowledge and skills required are garnered via experience and on the job supervision.

Clinical mental health counselors find employment in private practice, hospitals, residential care facilities, addiction-related treatment centers, college and university settings, EAPs, and community mental health settings, to name a few. Within each of these settings or contexts, clinical mental health counselors work with individuals, families, groups, and even the community in providing mental health treatment and prevention services.

Because each of these settings and the populations served can influence the very nature of the role and function that is prescribed to the mental health counselor, it is prudent for all mental health counselors to research the characteristics, demands, opportunities, and challenges presented by each of these settings and role definitions.

Community Mental Health Centers

Community mental health centers offer comprehensive mental health services to those within the community and are often utilized by those less fortunate and who are homeless, unemployed, or are experiencing multiple physical, cognitive, and psychological challenges. In response to the Community Mental Health Centers Act (1963), these settings provide a comprehensive range of services near the client's home that are provided regardless of the ability to pay and that focus on strengthening community resources for the prevention of mental illness.

Community mental health centers often offer emergency support, including 24-hour hotlines and stabilization services, inpatient and outpatient treatment, day treatment services, and even partial hospitalization (Cuddeback & Morrissey, 2010). These services will not necessarily be provided within a single building or even by a single agency. Quite often, the term *center* reflects the coordination of several groups, such as a community hospital for inpatient service and an outpatient or even walk-in location.

Those trained as mental health counselors will find the opportunity to employ their knowledge and skills by way of providing short-term individual and group counseling. With community mental health most often operating with governmental funding, the use of evidence-based treatment (see

Chapter 6) and the need to gather accountability data are usually required and will guide the very nature of treatment planning.

Working in a community mental health center often requires the counselors to serve as the front-line contact with those in need and thus requires the mental health counselor to often provide crisis service and screening and triage work. In addition to providing such clinical services, mental health counselors working within a community center may find themselves providing some services unique to this type of setting, such as helping clients carry out essential functions of scheduling appointments, utilizing public transit and other community services, or preparing for applying for a job.

Residential Care

Residential treatment centers are designed to provide a safe and supportive environment for individuals experiencing mental and/or behavioral health disorders; residential treatment centers provide therapeutic services that require patients to leave their homes and reside within the facility for the duration of therapy.

According to the American Residential Treatment Association (ARTA), residential treatment centers can be found in various settings. The facilities can be classified as (1) clinical residential treatment programs, which provide a homelike atmosphere and provide intensive individual and group therapy; (2) group residential communities that provide stable, long-term living arrangements with treatment occurring offsite; (3) farm- or work-based residential programs, which target both clinical treatments as well employment skills development; and (4) apartment-based communities, where residents live in individual or shared apartments while attending therapeutic programs and treatment. Quite often, in apartment-based communities, counselors will come to the apartment for service provision (ARTA, n.d.).

These facilities vary in the services provided. Treatment will be provided to individuals diagnosed with a variety of psychiatric conditions, such as bipolar disorder, schizophrenia, personality disorders, depression, and those with substance abuse and dual diagnoses. Depending on the setting and the specific population served, the counselor may provide individual and group therapy and engage in psychoeducation programming to facilitate client transition and return to their homes and communities.

Note that because residential treatment facilities are responsible for providing care 24/7, counseling professionals in these settings must be prepared to work irregular shifts, including nights, weekends, and even holidays.

Hospitals/Behavioral Health Centers

Clients in a hospitalized setting often have been identified as being of an imminent threat to themselves or others and most often need medication requiring monitoring and regulating. A clinical mental health counselor working in a hospital setting will most often be part of an interdisciplinary team. Treatment would involve the integration of counseling interventions with pharmacotherapy (see Chapter 8). Mental health counselors may also be involved with providing both the patient and the family education about the nature of the disorder, the treatment approach, and the family's role throughout the process.

In this type of setting, clinical mental health counselors may be called upon to assist in client assessment and treatment, facilitate therapeutic groups, provide individual and family counseling, and provide psychoeducation to clients and family. Counselors working with partial-hospitalization programs typically offer group and individual therapy and educational sessions for clients who attend for 6 or more hours a day, most days of the week.

A mental health counselor's role in a hospital setting is not limited to working only with those diagnosed with psychiatric disorders. Mental health counselors can employ their clinical skills to provide support and grief counseling for those experiencing loss. A mental health counselor can help patients and families who may be in long-term acute care to cope with the ongoing stress of the situation and the possible anxiety and depression that can emerge. Finally, mental health counselors can also serve as case managers, providing follow-up and referral for patients needing continued psychological or psychoeducation support upon their discharge.

Substance Abuse Treatment Centers

Since the 1990s, there has been an increasing awareness of the link between substance abuse and mental disorders. In 1994, the Center for Substance Abuse Treatment (CSAT, 1994) provided the Treatment Improvement Protocol (TIP) 9, *Assessment and Treatment of Patients With Coexisting Mental Illness and Alcohol and Other Drug Abuse,* which provided practitioners with an overview of diagnostic criteria, assessment, psychopharmacology, specific mental disorders, and the need for linkage between the mental health services system and the substance abuse treatment system.

Many programs employ an integrated treatment model that stresses a parallel view of recovery, concomitant treatment of mental illness and substance abuse, and the incorporation of strategies from both the mental health and substance abuse treatment fields. The integrated treatment approach is more holistic in its perspective, coordinating substance abuse and mental health interventions (Minkoff, 1989). This approach often involves cross-training practitioners to provide integrated, comprehensive services addressing both disorders concurrently (Biegel et al., 2013).

Mental health counselors engaged in such an integrated treatment are often called upon to assist in client assessment and treatment, facilitate therapeutic groups, provide individual and family counseling, and provide psychoeducation to clients and family. Strategies often employed include contingency management, cognitive-behavioral therapy, and motivational interviewing.

Many substance abuse treatment facilities require their providers to hold a substance abuse specialization certification, something that a clinical mental health counselor may want to consider. However, with their focus on integrated care and the recognition of clients presenting with comorbid or coexisting conditions, such as depression, bipolar disorders, posttraumatic stress disorder (PTSD), and even psychosis (Klott, 2014; Seligman, 1998), many centers employ clinical mental health counselors, tapping their clinical expertise even without a substance abuse specialization certification.

Of particular importance for clinical mental health counselors is that the model involves cross-training of practitioners to provide integrated, comprehensive services addressing both disorders concurrently (Biegel et al., 2013). One of the challenges for those working with this population is the risk or burnout, given the occurrence of client resistance and recidivism.

VA Medical Hospitals and Outpatient Clinics

According to the Watson Institute (n.d.), 2.7 million military veterans have returned from Iraq and Afghanistan since 2001, often with emotional scars needing treatment too. The increasing demand caused the Bureau of Labor Statistics (BLS, 2018) to project job growth of 20% for 26,400 counseling positions by 2024. According to the U.S. Department of Veterans Affairs (2014), there are more than 1,200 VA community-based outpatient clinics, VA hospitals, and VA veteran centers in the United States. Given the traumatic impact of war on those who serve, the VA employs counselors to work with veterans, their spouses, and families to address issues, such as PTSD. Counselors working for the VA provide emergency services, individual and family-based treatment, and even distance/telecounseling.

Given the uniqueness of the population served, counselors working for the VA would do well to understand the very nature of trauma and trauma-informed care, along with evidence-based treatments for PTSD, including cognitive processing therapy (CPT) and prolonged exposure (PE) (APA, 2017).

Correctional Facilities

It should not be surprising that research has identified a high incidence of mental disorders, such as depression, anxiety, substance abuse, and mania, among the incarcerated (Bureau of Justice Statistics, 2006; James & Glaze, 2006). It should also not be a surprise that many of those who are incarcerated can experience significant crises and consider self-harm.

A mental health counselor working in a correctional facility is often called upon to engage in a lethality check. The counselor may also be the first line of screening to identify those inmates who may need to be seen by a psychiatrist for pharmacotherapy. This type of assessment may help identify those individuals who have significant mental illness and, when possible, redirect them to mental health rather than correctional facilities. This might be when an individual, while having broken the law, is assessed as nonviolent and, where an existing psychiatric condition exists, might be assigned to a therapeutic rather than correctional program (Parker et al., 2009).

Other functions served by mental health counselors working in correctional facilities include crisis intervention to stabilize those inmates who are experiencing acute stress and crisis, individual and group counseling, and development of psychoeducational programs geared to facilitating the inmate's re-entrance into society.

Often, as is the case with juvenile settings, the counselor engages families in functional family therapy and multisystemic therapy, an intensive, multimodal family-based approach (Underwood & Washington, 2016).

Beyond the provision of individual therapy, mental health counselors serve to assist inmates in meeting their rehabilitation goals and preventing relapse. Counselors may work in helping inmates in the identification of career goals and the development of the social and behavioral skills necessary for successful employment.

Working within a correctional facility does present some unique challenges. Besides the profile of the clients to be seen, mental health counselors may find that space appropriate for assessment and the delivery of therapy is at a premium. Many of the traditional counseling issues, such as informed consent, confidentiality, and record maintenance, take on some unique characteristics when applied to working within a correction facility. As such, counselors need to have a clear understanding of the rights of inmates (American Bar Association [ABA], 2011).

Employee Assistance Programs

Many businesses recognize that stress, both job related and personal, can interfere with an employee's health, general well-being, and work performance (Society for Human Resource Management [SHRM], 2014). As a result, many have turned to the utilization of employment assistance programs (EAP) designed to provide several support services to their employees. Although many aspiring counselors take for granted opportunities in hospitals, private practices, and mental health or addiction treatment facilities, fewer know about EAPs. These programs offer help for employees and job opportunities for counselors.

EAPs traditionally have assisted workers with issues such as alcohol or substance abuse; however, most now cover a broad range of issues such as child or elder care, relationship challenges, financial or legal problems, wellness matters, and traumatic events like workplace violence. Clients are typically provided with short-term counseling and referral as well as extensive psychoeducational–wellness programming. Given the brief, short-term counseling paradigm employed by EAPs, counselors are often called upon to provide referral and case management for those clients needing more than short-term counseling.

In addition to the more traditional face-to-face modality of service delivery, many counselors employed in EAPs provide service by way of cybercounseling and telehealth modalities (e.g., phone, video-based counseling, email, etc.). Counselors using these methods should review the ethical and legal issues surrounding such a form of service delivery (see the American Counseling Association [ACA], 2014, Section H).

A special consideration when working in EAPs is the constraints of confidentiality. Most companies providing EAPs know that confidentiality is something to be respected and observed. The employees need to know the limits of confidentiality and trust that it will be maintained. In some circumstances, a failure in job performance may result in a supervisory request for the employee to attend counseling. Under these circumstances, the client needs to be provided with the limits (if any) to confidentiality, should the employer seek summary reports. It is not unusual for some company stakeholders to request reports.

Educational Settings

While most states require counselors working as school counselors, pre-K to 12, to hold a school counseling certificate, many schools are turning to clinical mental health counselors as providers of much needed therapeutic assistance within the schools. Data highlight our children's increasing need for mental health support. Cree et al. (2016) reported that 1 in 6 children aged 2 to 9 years has a diagnosed mental, behavioral, or developmental disorder. A study by Ghandour et al. (2018) found that more than 4 million children aged 3 to 17 years have been diagnosed with behavioral problems, 4 million with anxiety, and close to 2 million with depression.

Although the needs are pressing and significant, many of these children and their families fail to receive the therapeutic support they need. Many families have limited access to needed community-based services or are blocked from availing themselves of the services due to socioeconomic factors. As a result, schools have begun to either hire mental health counselors as part of their staff or, as an alternative, enter into collaborative relationships with community providers who, in turn, provide services on site at the school (Baker, 2013; Corthell, 2014). School administrators have found that they can bill Medicaid and/or receive special education funding if the therapy provided by the counselors is identified as a related service on a student's individualized education plan (IEP).

Clinical mental health counselors also find employment on college campuses. In addition to assisting students experiencing normative challenges and crises, mental health counselors working in higher education are often involved with treating students with clinical diagnoses (Gallagher, 2015). Colleges will often seek to employ those counselors who have acquired a license as a licensed professional counselor.

Private Practice

For many mental health counselors working in an individual or group, private practice is their employment goal. To work in private practice, counselors must be licensed to practice in this state in which they wish to provide services. Requirements for licensure vary from state to state (see Chapter 13). However, some qualifications, such as holding a master's degree in a relevant field, having had supervised experience, and achieving a passing score on a written examination such as the National Clinical Mental Health Counseling examination, appear to be somewhat common across states.

Working in private practice is attractive to those who are self-motivated and seek the opportunity to be self-directed in terms of the nature of the services they provide and the clientele they wish to serve. However, this independence in defining one's role and function comes with some challenges.

Running a private practice, which is, in fact, a small business, requires much more than excellent clinical skills. In addition to having the knowledge and skills needed to provide clinical services, the mental health counselor in private practice needs to have business acumen and the ability to manage numerous, nonclinical responsibilities (see Table 7.2).

TABLE 7.2 Considerations for Those Entering Private Practice

Legal Issues
• Are there state and local zoning laws that may limit where you can practice? • Does your location require a business license? • Does your office meet OSHA requirements for accessibility? • Do you have malpractice and professional liability insurance?
Financial Issues
• Have you developed a business budget? • What are the expenses for setting up an office and maintaining it? • How much money do you need to make? How much do you hope to make? • Have you discussed tax implications with an accountant or tax lawyer? • What is your plan for health insurance? Retirement? • How do you cover expenses for short-term disability? • What steps have you taken to be HIPAA compliant?

(Continued)

(Continued)

Practice Management (see Chapter 11)

- What is your marketing plan?
- Is your office secure? Confidential?
- Is your office safe for you (e.g., security management when in session)?
- Will you join insurance panels? If so, which?
- What is your fee schedule, and what forms of payment will you take?
- Do you have a plan and resources if a client is a danger to themselves? Or you?
- Paperwork, paperwork, paperwork. Who will file insurance claims? Who will develop and update forms (e.g., intake, informed consent, policy statements, disclosure forms, etc.)?

Personal Impact/Professional Development

- Working alone can be isolating and lonely. Is that your style, or do you have a plan to find collegial contact and supervision?
- How do you pay for and schedule continuing education (needed for the maintenance of licensure)?

Engaging in private practice often entails long hours, some uncertainty about income flow, and the need to engage in noncounseling business activities ranging from marketing to staffing. As a self-employed professional, the counselor in private practice will also have to attend to those things typically handled by an employer, such as social security taxes, health insurance, sick day and vacation compensations, and retirement contributions.

Integrating Setting, Population, Practice, and YOU

For many, the experience of completing graduate education and the opportunity to begin a career are accompanied by a sense of urgency to "get a job." The pressure to begin work, earn a salary, and start one's professional life is intense and can motivate one to take the jump at the first available employment opportunity.

Although the pressure may be strong, and the needs great, it is helpful to remember that this is not a "job" you are seeking, it is the first step in your vocational journey. As much as it is realistic, it is helpful not only to explore the various settings, populations, and types of practice available for employment but also to engage in self-reflection.

It is often said that working is genuinely not "work" if one enjoys what they are doing. Given the seriousness of what clinical mental health counselors do and the job-related stress that is often encountered, it is essential to reflect upon your values, interests, and goals in light of the various career paths you can pursue. It is important to remember that such a process will be developmental. That is, with added experience, alternative roles, functions, and settings may become more desirable. Take a moment and consider the questions posed in Exercise 7.1. It is crucial to identify your passion as well as your areas of expertise.

Exercise 7.1 A Reflection on Being a Counselor

Directions: As you reflect on each of the following questions, consider how your responses may begin to highlight the type of setting, population, or service you may find most desirable as a mental health counselor.

1. Do you see yourself working for yourself, with all that entails (e.g., marketing, managing, bookkeeping)? Or, at least at this stage, would you prefer working for someone else? Perhaps a little of both?
2. Do you find yourself called to any one particular age group? Preschool age? Early or middle school age? Late adolescent or early adult? Adult? A senior population?
3. Do you see yourself working with individuals? Families? Groups? Organizations?
4. Are you most interested in therapeutic work, or is prevention and wellness more of a calling?
5. Which, if any, of these settings appear most enticing: hospitals, prisons, juvenile detention centers, outpatient mental health clinics, addictions centers, day programs, colleges or university counseling centers, corporate settings. Which ones are least enticing?
6. Which, if any, of the following presenting concerns do you feel most interested and comfortable engaging: developmental transitions; normative life crises; anxiety; depression; alcohol and substance abuse; psychosis; eating disorders; trauma and stressor-related disorders; sexual dysfunctions; personality disorder; impulse-control issues; conduct disorders; neurocognitive disorders?
7. Which of the presenting concerns listed in Question 6 would you not want to treat?
8. Would you prefer to work alone? With similarly trained mental health counselors? Or with a variety of health professionals?

Keystones

- The Community Mental Health Centers Act of 1963 not only mandated the development of a nationwide network of community-based mental health clinics but opened the door for clinical mental health counselor employment.
- Continuum of care is a paradigm for service delivery that views services as ranging from those promoting growth and wellness to those serving the most distressed clients.
- Clinical mental health counselors have the knowledge and skills to be a valuable asset in many settings providing mental health services.
- Mental health counselors find employment in practice, hospitals, residential care facilities, addiction-related treatment centers, schools (pre-K to 12), college and university settings, employment assistance programs (EAPs), and community mental health settings.
- Each setting presents exceptional, unique opportunities and challenges for a mental health counselor and should be considered in light of one's values and career goals.

Additional Resources

Bureau of Labor Statistics. (n.d.). *Substance abuse, behavioral disorder, and mental health counselors.* https://www.bls.gov/ooh/community-and-social-service/substance-abuse-behavioral-disorder-and-mental-health-counselors.htm#tab-5
DeAngelis, T. (n.d.). *Are you really ready for private practice?* https://www.apa.org/gradpsych/2011/11/private-practice
Meyers, L. (2019, March 22). *Establishing a private practice.* https://ct.counseling.org/2019/03/establishing-a-private-practice
SAMHSA-HRSA Center for Integrated Health Solutions (CIHS): https://www.samhsa.gov/integrated-health-solutions
Searight, H. R. (2010). *Practicing psychology in primary care.* Hogrefe.

References

American Bar Association. (2011). ABA standards for criminal justice: Treatment of prisoners (3rd ed.).

American Counseling Association. (2014). *ACA code of ethics.*

American Psychological Association. (2017). *Clinical practice guideline for the treatment of PTSD.* https://www.apa.org/ptsd-guideline/ptsd.pdf

American Residential Treatment Association. (n.d.). Program types. https://artausa.org/residential-mental-health-program-types/

Baker, C. (2013). *School-based mental health services: What can the partnership look like?* https://ct.counseling.org/2013/01/school-based-mental-health-services-what-can-the-partnership-look-like/

Biegel, D. E., Kola, L. A., Ronis, R. J., & Kruszynski, R. (2013). Evidence-based treatment for adults with co-occurring mental and substance use disorders: Current practice and future directions. In J. Rosenberg & S. J. Rosenberg (Eds.), *Community mental health: Challenges for the 21st century* (pp. 215–237). Routledge.

Bureau of Justice Statistics, U.S. Department of Justice. (2006, September). *Mental health problems of prison and jail inmates* (Publication No. NCJ 213600). https://www.bjs.gov/content/pub/pdf/mhppji.pdf

Bureau of Labor Statistics. (2018, November 30). Substance abuse, behavioral disorder, and mental health counselors. *Occupational outlook handbook.* https://www.bls.gov/ooh/community-and-social-service/substance-abuse-behavioral-disorder-and-mental-health-counselors.htm#tab-1

Center for Substance Abuse Treatment. (1994). *Assessment and treatment of patients with coexisting mental illness and alcohol and other drug abuse.* Treatment Improvement Protocol (TIP) Series, no. 9. DHHS Pub. No. (SMA) 95-3061. Substance Abuse and Mental Health Services Administration.

Center for Substance Abuse Treatment. (2005). *Substance abuse treatment for persons with co-occurring disorders.* Treatment Improvement Protocol (TIP) Series, no. 42. Substance Abuse and Mental Health Services Administration. https://www.ncbi.nlm.nih.gov/books/NBK64201/

Colangelo, J. J. (2009). The American Mental Health Counselors Association: Reflection on 30 historic years. *Journal of Counseling and Development, 87*(2), 234–240.

Corthell, K. (2014). *The role of mental health counselors in public schools.* Dissertation, Georgia State University. https://scholarworks.gsu.edu/cps_diss/107

Cree, R. A., Bitsko, R. H., Robinson, L. R., Holbrook, J. R., Danielson, M. L., Smith, D. S., Kaminski, J. W., Kenney, M. K., & Peacock, G. (2018). Health care, family, and community factors associated with mental, behavioral, and developmental disorders and poverty among children aged 2–8 years—the United States, 2016. *MMWR, 67*(5), 1377–1383.

Cuddeback, G. S., & Morrissey, J. P. (2010). Integrating service delivery systems for persons with server mental illness. In T. L. Scheid & T. N. Brown (Eds.), *A handbook of the study of mental health: Social contexts, theories, and systems* (2nd ed., pp. 510–528). Cambridge University Press.

Gallagher, R. P. (2015). *National Survey of College Counseling Centers 2014. Project Report.* The International Association of Counseling Services (IACS). http://d-scholarship.pitt.edu/28178/

Ghandour, R. M., Sherman, L. J., Vladutiu, C. J., Ali, M. M., Lynch, S. E., Bitsko, R. H., & Blumberg, S. J. (2018). Prevalence and treatment of depression, anxiety, and conduct problems in US children. *Journal of Pediatrics, 206,* 256–267.

Hoff, L. A., & Adamowski, K. (1998). *Creating excellence in crisis care: A guide to effective training and program designs.* Jossey-Bass.

James, D. J., & Glaze, L. E. (2006). *Mental health problems of prison and jail inmates* (Publication No. NCJ 213600). https://www.bjs.gov/content/pub/pdf/mhppji.pdf

Klott, J. (2013). *Integrated treatment for co-occurring disorders: Treating people, not behaviors.* Wiley & Sons.

Lourie, I.S. (2003). A history of community child mental health. In A. J. Pumariega & N. C. Winters (Eds.), *The handbook of child and adolescent systems of care: The new community psychiatry.* Jossey-Bass.

Minkoff, K. (1989). An integrated treatment model for dual diagnosis of psychosis and addiction. *Hospital and Community Psychiatry, 40*(10), 1031–1036.

Normandy-Dolberg, J. (2010, September). AMHCA survey results: Concerns cited with managed care, and with funding retirement. *The Advocate,* 6–7.

Parker, T., Foley, G., Moore, K. A., & Broner, N. (2009). Finding common ground in implementing and sustaining jail diversion programs. *American Jails, 23*(4), 25–38.

Seligman, L. (1998). *Selecting effective treatment: A comprehensive, systematic guide to treating mental disorders.* Jossey-Bass.

Society for Human Resource Management (SHRM). (2014). *Employee assistance program (EAP): General: What is an employee assistance program?* https://www.shrm.org/resourcesandtools/tools-and-samples/hr-qa/pages/whatisaneap.aspx

Underwood, L. E., & Washington, A. (2016). Mental illness and juvenile offenders. *International Journal of Environmental Research and Public Health, 13*(2), 228.

U.S. Department of Veterans Affairs. (2014). *Department of Veteran Affairs statistics at a glance.* https://www.bls.gov/ooh/community-and-social-service/substance-abuse-behavioral-disorder-and-mental-health-counselors.htm#tab-1

Watson Institute. (n.d.). *Costs of war.* https://watson.brown.edu/costsofwar/costs/human/veterans

CHAPTER 8

Clinical Mental Health Counselors in an Era of Biologicalization

With the push toward medicalization of mental health treatments, is there any place for a nonprescribing clinical mental health counselor?

—Mimi, doctoral candidate in clinical mental health counseling

The question posed by this doctoral candidate is valid and one that should be of concern to all nonprescribing mental health specialists. It may have been Robert Kaplan, as early as 1990, who observed the *biologicalization* of behavioral and biomedical science (Kaplan, 1990). Whether referred to as *medicalization* or *biologicalization*, it is clear that there has been a steady march toward a more biological or physiological view—not just psychopathology but wellness.

When viewed from this vantage point, all behaviors are rooted in our biology, and problems with our health, including mental health, reflect a disease or pathology. In the case of mental disorders, the focus has increasingly turned to a chemical imbalance hypothesis, that is, having too much or not enough neurotransmitters for the brain to function properly. With this as the proposed etiology of mental disorders, it becomes a tiny step to the view that medication is the first choice of therapy and the course of the action to be taken.

Mental health counselors are not physicians, nor can they prescribe medication, so this issue of biologicalization of emotional problems should be concerning in terms of the implications for the future of clinical mental health counselors, and what, if anything, should they know about the advances of neuroscience and psychopharmacology. This chapter reviews the issue of biologicalization. It describes the unique role that counselors with a more holistic understanding of the human condition can bring to their clients and their collaboration with colleagues from other disciplines.

After completing this chapter, the reader will be able to:

- Describe what is meant by biologicalization of mental health.
- Explain how counselors can employ their understanding of the neuroscience constructs of neurogenesis, epigenetics, default-mode networks, neuroplasticity, and affect asymmetry within their work with clients.
- Describe what is meant by neurocounseling.
- Explain the fundamental physiological/neurochemical bases for antidepressants, antianxiety agents, mood stabilizers, stimulants, and antipsychotics.

The Biologicalization of Mental Health

The contemporary biological model of abnormal behavior assumes that the principal causes of, and the most likely effective treatments for, abnormal behaviors are biological (Carver, 2000). The position taken is that emotional and behavioral disorders are the result of problems in brain structure, brain chemistry, or genetic makeup.

Researchers who focus on brain anatomy have hypothesized that there may be a connection between psychological disorders and chemical exchanges between neurons (Russell-Chapin, 2016; Wakefield, 2016). A tiny space, the synapse, separates one neuron from the next. Hypothetically, when a thought, feeling, or behavior occurs, chemicals called neurotransmitters are released and travel across the synaptic spaces to the receptor sites of other neurons. From a biological causation perspective, emotional and behavioral problems may be the result of too little or too much of one or more neurotransmitters reaching the receptor sites.

Neuroscience and psychiatry have adopted this perspective, with one Nobel prize–winning neuroscientist, Eric Kandel, stating, "All mental processes are brain processes, and therefore all disorders of mental functioning are a biological disease. The brain is the organ of the mind. Where else could [mental illness] be if not in the brain?" (cited by Wakefield, 2016, p. 21).

Increased interest in the role of neurochemistry and brain structure continues and is supported not only by organizations such as the National Alliance for the Mentally Ill (NAMI; see www.nami.org), a broad-based consumer advocacy group that strongly advocates the position that mental illness essentially is a biological brain disorder, but also by the National Institute of Mental Health (NIMH; see https://www.nimh.nih.gov/index.shtml) with its current focus on brain research. The elevation of neurochemistry and biological explanations for mental disorders has resulted in a turning toward medication as a preferred mode of treatment (Cummings et al., 2011).

Psychopharmacology: The Basics

The American Psychiatric Association (APA, 2011) recommends psychopharmacological treatments as the first line of treatment for many mental health disorders. Chemical treatment of mental health disorders has escalated, almost exponentially, since the early 2000s (Bloice, 2005). This move toward psychopharmacology not only reflects but also contributes to the increasingly popular belief within the mental health community that many mental health disorders have a significant biological/chemical basis for existence.

Although clinical mental health counselors cannot prescribe medication, it is very likely they will be called to work with clients taking one or more of these medications. Psychotropic medication, combined with counseling, is considered the standard of care for many mental health disorders. In a 2002 survey, it was found that 89% of counselors reported working with clients on a psychotropic medication (England, 2002). As such, clinical mental health counselors need to have a basic understanding of the medications currently being prescribed.

The medications now available and employed in mental health treatment can be grouped as antidepressants, antianxiety agents, mood stabilizers, stimulants, and antipsychotics. An in-depth discussion of these medications is well beyond the scope of this text. Several excellent resources explaining the "what," "why," and "how" of psychoactive medications are listed at the end of this chapter

Antidepressants

Monoamine oxidase inhibitors (MAOIs) and tricyclic antidepressants were among the first antidepressants to be used. MAOIs, which were introduced in the 1950s, elevate the levels of the neurotransmitters norepinephrine, serotonin, and dopamine by inhibiting the action of monoamine oxidase, an enzyme that usually breaks down these neurotransmitters. Although still prescribed, MAOIs are challenging for clients in that they require strict dietary restrictions.

The second type of antidepressants with a long history are the tricyclic antidepressants. These medications work by inhibiting the reuptake of serotonin, norepinephrine, and to a lesser extent, dopamine, thus allowing them to remain in the synapse and continue their support of neural conductivity. Today, medications such as amitriptyline (Elavil), clomipramine (Anafranil), desipramine (Norpramine), and nortriptyline (Pamelor) are part of this tricyclic class.

Continued work in psychopharmacology has focused on reducing the adverse side effects and increasing the effectiveness of the medications employed. Many of the latest generations of antidepressants are more targeted in their focus, working as specific serotonin reuptake inhibitors, such as fluoxetine (Prozac), fluvoxamine (Luvox), sertraline (Zoloft), paroxetine (Paxil), escitalopram (Lexapro), and citalopram (Celexa), or as norepinephrine reuptake inhibitors, such as venlafaxine (Effexor) and duloxetine (Cymbalta) (see Table 8.1).

TABLE 8.1 Antidepressant Medications

THERAPEUTIC MECHANISM	GENERIC NAME (BRAND NAME)	COMMON SIDE EFFECTS
MAOI derivatives: Inhibit monoamine oxidase and the breakdown of neurotransmitters.	phenelzine (Nardil) tranylcypromine (Parnate) isocarboxazid (Marplan) selegiline (Emsam)	Nausea and vomiting Weight gain Diarrhea Sleepiness Sexual problems
Tricyclics: Increase neurotransmitter presence by inhibiting reuptake.	Serotonin reuptake inhibitors: fluoxetine (Prozac) fluvoxamine (Luvox) sertraline (Zoloft) paroxetine (Paxil) escitalopram (Lexapro) citalopram (Celexa) Norepinephrine reuptake inhibitors: venlafaxine (Effexor) duloxetine (Cymbalta)	Nausea and vomiting Weight gain Diarrhea Sleepiness Sexual problems

According to a research review by Gartlehner et al. (2011), all antidepressant medications work about as well as the others to improve symptoms of depression and to keep depression symptoms from coming back. For reasons not yet well understood, some people respond better to some antidepressant medications than to others. Therefore, it is important to know that some people may not feel better with the first medicine they try and may need to try several medications to find the one that works for them. Others may find that a medicine helped for a while, but their symptoms came back. Clinical mental health counselors need to provide this information to those clients on antidepressant medication and encourage them to work with their prescribing physicians and follow the directions given in terms of dosage and frequency, noting that it may require an extended period (often 4 to 6 weeks) for it to work.

Antianxiety Agents

Antianxiety agents, or anxiolytics, have been employed since the 1960s. Short half-life (or short-acting) benzodiazepines such as lorazepam (Ativan) and beta-blockers are used to treat the short-term symptoms of anxiety.

Benzodiazepines work by enhancing the activity of gamma-aminobutyric acid, or GABA, which is a neurotransmitter that helps an individual feel calm. Beta-blockers reduce anxiety by blocking the effects of norepinephrine, a stress hormone involved in the fight-or-flight response.

Taking these medications for a short period can help the person keep physical symptoms under control and be used "as needed" to reduce acute anxiety. A significant consideration that a client should be made aware of is that benzodiazepine derivates can, with extended use, create physical dependency (see Table 8.2).

TABLE 8.2 Antianxiety Medications

THERAPEUTIC MECHANISM	GENERIC NAME (BRAND NAME)	COMMON SIDE EFFECTS
Benzodiazepines: Enhance the activity of the neurotransmitter GABA, a chemical in the brain that promotes feelings of calmness.	alprazolam (Xanax), diazepam (Valium) lorazepam (Ativan) clonazepam (Klonopin)	Dependency Drowsiness Dizziness
Beta-blockers: Block the effects of norepinephrine, a stress hormone involved in the fight-or-flight response, thus controlling physical symptoms of anxiety.	acebutolol (Sectral) propranolol (Inderal) atenolol (Tenormin)	Fatigue Cold hands Dizziness or light-headedness Weakness
Buspirone: A serotonin receptor agonist that increases actions at serotonin receptors.	buspirone (Buspar, Vanspar)	Dizziness Headaches Nausea Nervousness Light-headedness Excitement Trouble sleeping

Buspirone, a third type of antianxiety agent, is unrelated to the benzodiazepines and is sometimes used for the long-term treatment of chronic anxiety. In contrast to the benzodiazepines, buspirone must be taken every day for a few weeks to reach its full effect. It is not useful on an as-needed basis. Buspirone is from the azapirone class of medications, which includes other anxiolytics and antipsychotics. Buspirone is a serotonin receptor agonist, which means that it increases action at serotonin receptors, which helps alleviate the symptoms of anxiety.

Mood Stabilizers

Mood stabilizers are often employed in the treatment of bipolar disorder (Hauser, 2016). Lithium (lithium carbonate) has been prescribed as a mood stabilizer since the 1970s. The specific biochemical mechanism of lithium action in stabilizing mood is unknown (Chokawala et al., 2020), but it appears to decrease norepinephrine release and increase serotonin synthesis.

Other medications, including anticonvulsants and antipsychotics (see Table 8.3), are also used to reduce extreme highs as might be experienced in manic or hypomanic episodes. Although the actual mechanism through which these work is still unidentified, the most common explanation is that they reduce the "excitability" of the nerve cells (Brunton et al., 2010).

TABLE 8.3 Mood Stabilizers

THERAPEUTIC MECHANISM	GENERIC NAME (BRAND NAME)	COMMON SIDE EFFECTS
Lithium carbonate: Alters sodium transport in nerve and muscle cells and affects a shift toward intraneuronal metabolism of catecholamines, but specific biochemical mechanisms are unknown.	lithium carbonate (Lithobid, Eskalith)	Itching, rash Excessive thirst Frequent urination Tremor (shakiness) of the hands Nausea and vomiting Slurred speech Fast, slow, irregular, or pounding heartbeat Blackouts Changes in vision Seizures Hallucinations (seeing things or hearing voices that do not exist) Loss of coordination Swelling of the eyes, face, lips, tongue, throat, hands, feet, ankles, or lower legs
Anticonvulsants: Hypothesized to reduce the "excitability" of nerve impulses in the brain.	valproic acid (Depakene) divalproex sodium (Depakote) carbamazepine (Tegretol) lamotrigine (Lamictal)	Fatigue Weight gain Nausea Headache Decreased sexual desire Confusion

Stimulants

Much attention has been given to the use of stimulants for conditions such as attention deficit hyperactivity disorder (ADHD). Stimulants used to treat ADHD include dextroamphetamine and amphetamine (e.g., Adderall XR) and methylphenidate (e.g., Concerta, Ritalin LA). These medications are central nervous system stimulants and inhibit the reuptake of dopamine and norepinephrine (Kolar et al., 2008). This increased dopaminergic and noradrenergic activity in the prefrontal cortex is believed to explain the efficacy in increasing executive brain function and treating ADHD (see Table 8.4).

TABLE 8.4 Stimulants

THERAPEUTIC MECHANISM	GENERIC NAME (BRAND NAME)	COMMON SIDE EFFECTS
Stimulants: Increase in dopaminergic and noradrenergic activity in the prefrontal cortex.	dextroamphetamine and amphetamine (Adderall, Adderall XR) methylphenidate (Concerta, Ritalin, Ritalin LA)	Difficulty falling asleep or staying asleep Loss of appetite Stomach pain Headache Weight gain in children Slowed growth in children Can be habit forming

Antipsychotics

Antipsychotic medications such as aripiprazole (Abilify), risperidone (Risperdal), lurasidone (Latuda), haloperidol (Haldol), and chlorpromazine (Thorazine) are thought to rebalance levels of dopamine and/or serotonin. Specific symptoms, such as feeling agitated and having hallucinations, usually go away within days of starting an antipsychotic medication. Symptoms such as delusions often go away within a few weeks, but the medicine's full effects may not be seen for up to 6 weeks (see Table 8.5).

TABLE 8.5 Antipsychotics

THERAPEUTIC MECHANISM	GENERIC NAME (BRAND NAME)	COMMON SIDE EFFECTS
Antipsychotics: Are thought to rebalance levels of dopamine and/or serotonin.	aripiprazole (Abilify) risperidone (Risperdal) lurasidone (Latuda) haloperidol (Haldol) chlorpromazine (Thorazine)	Drowsiness Dizziness Restlessness Weight gain Dry mouth Constipation Nausea Vomiting Blurred vision Low blood pressure Uncontrollable movements, such as tics and tremors Seizures Rigidity

Long-term use of antipsychotic medications may lead to a condition called tardive dyskinesia (TD). TD causes muscle movements, commonly around the mouth, that a person cannot control.

TD can range from mild to severe, and in some people the problem cannot be cured. Sometimes people with TD recover partially or fully after they stop taking antipsychotic medications.

Additional information on antipsychotics and other medications used to manage psychoses and current warnings and advisories is available at the FDA website (https://www.fda.gov).

Neurocounseling

The integration of neuroscience concepts and frameworks into counseling has gained significant momentum in recent years (Beeson & Field, 2017). Neuroscience can both complement and augment mental health counseling when used appropriately. The increased interest in neuroscience is evidenced by the fact that the American Counseling Association (ACA), the Association for Counselor Education and Supervision (ACES), and the American Mental Health Counselors Association (AMHCA) have all established separate Neuroscience and Neurocounseling Interest Networks. Neurocounseling, a new dimension of the counseling process, involves integrating what we know about the brain structure and function as well as related physiological processes into counseling practice to enhance effectiveness (Beeson & Field, 2017).

Knowing the brain and related physiology can give counselors a richer understanding of a client and their presenting concerns and allow counselors to be more intentional about the way they work with clients. For example, understanding that someone who has been traumatized may have a more reactive autonomic nervous system may direct the counselor to employ strategies to arouse the relaxation or parasympathetic response. Teaching mindfulness, grounding skills, basic biofeedback skills of diaphragmatic breathing, and heart rate variability can help.

Linden (2006) suggests that the insights gained from neuroscience research not only can help mental health counselors understand the biological processes involved in the changes they see in their clients as a result of counseling interventions but can also lead to the development and employment of new counseling techniques applied to those with mental disorders and those seeking wellness. However, integration of neuroscience research and counseling practice must be tempered by the recognition that there remain limitations to neuroscience, its research, and its value to counseling (Miller & Dillman-Taylor, 2016). Table 8.6 identifies a number of the fundamental concepts of neuroscience and examples of their inclusion in a neuroscience approach to counseling.

TABLE 8.6 Neuroscience Concepts and Counseling Implications

NEUROSCIENCE CONCEPT	DESCRIPTION	IMPLICATIONS FOR NEUROINFORMED COUNSELING
Epigenetics	The expression of a genetic predisposition is a function person–environment interaction. The behavior of clients can suppress the expression of the gene.	Can be used to provide a client the possibility of growth and change, even in the face of a robust genetic history.

(Continued)

(*Continued*)

NEUROSCIENCE CONCEPT	DESCRIPTION	IMPLICATIONS FOR NEUROINFORMED COUNSELING
Neuroplasticity	The ability of brain areas to increase in organization, level of activation, and amount of connection to other areas based on use and practice (Garrett & Hough, 2018). The brain can change; it is not fixed, and it responds to external environmental events and actions initiated by the individual. Schwartz and Begley (2003) note that "Neuroplasticity can result in the wholesale remodeling of neural networks . . . a brain can rewire itself" (p. 13).	Through learning and engaging in new behaviors, the brain can be rewired. Counselors need to do those things that lead to the establishment and strengthening of specific synaptic connections. For example, negative thinking can develop a self-reinforcing circularity between the amygdala and the frontal cortex, resulting in negative feelings, negative thinking, and negative feelings. Counselors teaching clients to engage in thought-stopping or reframing strategies can begin to break this connection. Cognitive therapy can help clients employ effective executive frontal cortex functioning, focusing on positive and strengths rather than negativity.
Neurogenesis	The brain's capacity to produce new neurons (i.e., nerve cells) (Garrett & Hough, 2018). It is a process than can continue throughout the life span (Fuchs & Flügge, 2014). Neurogenesis can provide clients a sense of hope and serves as a positive metaphor for clients, challenging the conventional wisdom that "an old dog can't learn new tricks."	Neurogenesis can provide clients a sense of hope. Increasing one's activity level (i.e., exercise) has been shown to increase blood flow and release positive neurotransmitters such as serotonin. Thus, a behavioral strategy that shapes increased activity would be a productive element to a treatment protocol of depression. Techniques, including meditation, employment of relaxation training, and bibliotherapy, can stimulate the neurogenic process.
Affect asymmetry	Based on the fact that the left and right frontal cortexes of the brain process emotion differently. The right side tends to focus on the global and has been associated with increased levels of anxiety and depression. Helping clients shift from this global perspective to a more focused left-brain oriented perspective can reduce the feelings of depression and anxiety and result in a more goal-oriented set of behaviors.	Counselors can employ neurofeedback (NFB) as a treatment for assisting clients in recognizing, monitoring, and self-regulating brain wave activity to alleviate clinical symptoms as well as enhance wellness. NFB employs electroencephalographs (EEG) to provide feedback to clients on brain activity during a period of distress and emotional upheaval. This technique has been used to assist in anxiety, depression, and sexual behavior problems (Myers & Young, 2012).
Default-mode networks	The brain's neural networks are not easy to change, and as a result, brain activity can fall back to old, less desirable patterns. Therapy doesn't erase previous existing patterns; it attempts to develop more facilitative patterns that will override these previous patterns. As a result, regression or recidivism is possible.	Clients who find themselves ruminating about past negative experiences or engaging in negative self-reflection need to be helped to understand the difficulty involved with changing old patterns. Counselors can employ analogies to teach clients about the retention of old patterns while highlighting that they need not be used once a new pattern is available. For example, many clients can relate to having employed some euphemistic term for a private body part of biological function. While these are still present and available to be called upon, it is unlikely that the client employs them, having developed a new, now more robust alternative reflecting more accurate medical terminology.

Role and Challenges for Clinical Mental Health Counselors

Although the medicalization of mental health—that is, the increasing focus on psychopharmacology as a treatment of choice—may upon initial review appear to be a threat to the value of mental health counseling, such need not be the case. For those clients for whom medication may be of value, counselors can continue in supportive and therapeutic roles.

Counselors are not being asked to implicitly or explicitly endorse a pharmacological approach to treatment. Still, given the reality of our current situation, an informed counselor can help clients understand the role and impact of medications, make informed decisions regarding the employment of medication, and, once engaged, be supportive of clients as they adhere to the protocol.

Working in coordination and collaboration with medical providers, mental health counselors can support clients by addressing their misgivings or misunderstanding regarding the medication and assisting them in maintaining proper compliance with the treatment protocol. We live in a culture of immediate results, and sadly much of the marketing efforts suggest that taking medication will solve all problems immediately. Therefore, it is not unusual for a client to complain that the medication "isn't working" and thus abandon the protocol. Clients might assume that their psychotropic drug will work as quickly as aspirin, an antacid tablet, or even an injection of insulin. Clients must understand that psychotropic medications require time to reach critical blood levels and become effective. Clients should understand that these medications can take up 12 weeks to show full benefits, and even in those cases where they provide faster relief, it still may be 3 to 4 weeks to develop essential levels. Counselors can provide support during this "waiting period."

Although supporting the medical protocol, counselors can and need to continue in their role as therapeutic agents. The integration of neuroscience research into a counselor's treatment planning is an added tool in the counselor's toolbox. Biological interventions can help deal with mental health problems, even those associated with environmental conditions, such as the use of anxiolytics as effective biological treatments of symptoms associated with PTSD. It is also clear that counseling strategies, such as cognitive-behavioral interventions, can be effective, even with symptoms of disorders that are biological in origin. For example, cognitive-behavioral therapy techniques have been demonstrated to help manage delusional and reclusive behaviors in schizophrenic patients (Butler et al., 2006).

Having the knowledge and skill necessary to integrate, when possible, findings from neuroscience into the mental health counseling treatment plan is not only a good idea; it is an ethical mandate. When applied to the inclusion of medicine in a treatment plan, counselors must legally and ethically defer to prescribers. However, this deference does not remove the counselor's ethical responsibility to protect their clients by assisting them in gaining the information they need to provide informed consent. Counselors need to understand how psychotropic medication can impact a client both positively and negatively and how to act on that knowledge. The professional organizations are clear on this matter.

The ACA, for example, directs its member to remain informed and up to date on "current scientific and professional information in their fields of activity" (2014, Section C.2) The AMHCA in its standards for practice (2020) similarly notes for its members that an understanding "of the biological bases of behavior helps clinical mental health counselors not only be more precise in our diagnosis and treatment of mental disorders, but also in the promotion of wellness, peak performance, and quality of life" (p. 9). The AMHCA directs its members to have the knowledge and skills necessary to "articulate the basic principles of pharmacology (e.g., dose-response, side-effects, interactions pharmacokinetics, pharmacodynamics, routes of administration, distribution) and adaptation (e.g., tolerance, sensitization, withdrawal, placebo, nocebo) associated with commonly used drugs" (2020, p. 11).

It is fair to assume that the movement toward the biologicalization of mental health treatment will continue. It is also clear that clinical mental health counselors have a unique role and responsibility to play in this movement.

Keystones

- The contemporary biological model of abnormal behavior assumes that the principal causes of, and the most likely effective treatments for, abnormal behaviors are biological.
- The American Psychiatric Association (APA) recommends psychopharmacological treatments as a first line of treatment for many mental health disorders.
- The medications currently available and employed in mental health treatment can be grouped as antidepressants, antianxiety agents, mood stabilizers, stimulants, and antipsychotics.
- Monoamine oxidase inhibitors (MAOIs) and tricyclic antidepressants were among the first antidepressants to be used.
- Antianxiety agents such as benzodiazepines and beta-blockers are used to treat short-term symptoms of anxiety.
- Lithium has been prescribed as a mood stabilizer since the 1970s. The specific biochemical mechanism of lithium action in stabilizing mood is unknown.
- Stimulants used to treat ADHD include dextroamphetamine and amphetamine. They inhibit the reuptake of dopamine and norepinephrine.
- Antipsychotic medications are thought to rebalance levels of dopamine and/or serotonin.
- Neurocounseling, a new dimension of the counseling process, involves the integration of our knowledge of brain structure and function, as well as related physiological processes, into counseling practice to enhance effectiveness.
- While being supportive of the medical protocol, counselors can and need to continue in their role as therapeutic agents. The integration of neuroscience research into a counselor's treatment planning is an added tool in the counselor's toolbox.

Additional Resources

Field, T. A., Jones, L. K., & Russell-Chapin, L. A. (Eds.). (2017). *Neurocounseling: Brain-based clinical approaches*. American Counseling Association.

Luke, C. (2020). *Neuroscience for counselors and therapists* (2nd ed.). Cognella Academic Publishers.

Neuroscience-Informed Cognitive-Behavior Therapy (nCBT). A site devoted to current empirical studies in nCBT: https://www.n-cbt.com

References

American Counseling Association. (2014). *ACA code of ethics.*

American Mental Health Counselors Association. (2020). *AMHCA standards for the practice of clinical mental health counseling.* https://www.amhca.org/HigherLogic/System/DownloadDocumentFile.ashx?DocumentFileKey=15a3f054-c284-c0f8-7ac6-d1ac96ca20d4&forceDialog=0

American Psychiatric Association. (2011). *American Psychiatric Association practice guidelines.* https://psychiatryonline.org/guidelines

Beeson, E. T., & Field, T. A. (2017). Neurocounseling: A new section of the *Journal of Mental Health Counseling. Journal of Mental Health Counseling, 39,* 71–83. https://doi.org/10.17744/mehc.39.1.06

Bloice, C. (2005). Why is this woman smiling? The hard sell of bad medicine. *Revolution: The Journal for RNs & Patient Advocacy, 6*(1).

Brunton, L., Chabner, B., & Knollman, B. (2010). *Goodman and Gilman's the pharmacological basis of therapeutics* (12th ed.). McGraw-Hill Professional.

Butler, A. C., Chapman, J. E., Forman, E. M., & Beck, A. T. (2006). The empirical status of cognitive-behavioral therapy: A review of meta-analysis. *Clinical Psychology Review, 26*(1), 17–31.

Carver, J. (2000). *Dopamine: Parkinson's disease and ADHD to smoking and paranoia.* http://www.enotalone.com/article/4115.html

Chokhawala, K., Lee, S., & Saadabadi, A. (2020). *Lithium.* StatPearls [Internet]. StatPearls Publishing. https://www.ncbi.nlm.nih.gov/books/NBK519062/

Council for Accreditation of Counseling and Related Educational Programs. (2015). *2016 CACREP standards.*

Cummings, N. A., O'Donohue, W. T., & Cummings, J. L. (2011). The financial dimension of integrated behavioral/primary care. In N. A. Cummings & W. T. O'Donohue (Eds.), *Understanding the behavioral healthcare crisis: The promise of integrated care and diagnostic reform* (pp. 33–58). Routledge.

England, J. T. (2002). Mental health counselors' perceptions regarding psychopharmacological prescriptive privileges. *Journal of Mental Health Counseling, 24,* 36–50.

Fuchs, E., & Flügge, G. (2014). Adult neuroplasticity: More than 40 years of research. *Neural Plasticity,* Article ID 541870. https://doi.org/10.1155/2014/541870

Garrett, B., & Hough, G. (2018). *Brain and behavior: An introduction to biological psychology* (5th ed.). Sage.

Gartlehner, G., Hansen, R. A., Morgan, L. C., Thaler, K., Lux, L. J., Van Noord, M., Mager, U., Gaynes, B. N., Thieda, P., Strobelberger, M., Lloys, S., Reichenpfader, U., & Lohr, K. N. (2011). Second-generation antidepressants in the pharmacologic treatment of adult depression: An update of the 2007 Comparative Effectiveness Review [Internet]. Agency for Healthcare Research and Quality (Comparative Effectiveness Reviews, No. 46). https://www.ncbi.nlm.nih.gov/books/NBK83442/

Hauser, J. (2016). Mood Stabilizers for bipolar disorder. *Psych Central.* Retrieved from https://psychcentral.com/lib/mood-stabilizers-for-bipolar-disorder/

Kaplan, R. M. (1990). Behavior as the central outcome in health care. *American Psychologist, 45*(11), 1211–1220. https://doi.org/10.1037/0003-066X.45.11.1211

Kolar, D., Keller, A., Golfinopoulos, M., Cumyn, L., Syer, C., & Hechtman, L. (2008). Treatment of adults with attention-deficit/hyperactivity disorder. *Neuropsychiatry Disease Treatment, 2,* 389–403. https://doi.org/10.2147/ndt.s6985

Linden, D. E .J. (2006). How psychotherapy changes the brain-the contribution of functional neuroimaging. *Molecular Psychiatry, 11,* 528–538.

Miller, R., & Dillman-Taylor, D. (2016). Does Adlerian theory stand the test of time? Examining individual psychology from a neuroscience perspective. *Journal of Humanistic Counseling, 55,* 111–128. https://doi.org/10.1002/johc.12028

Myers, J. E., & Young, J. S. (2012). Brain wave biofeedback: Benefits of integrating neurofeedback in counselling. *Journal of Counseling and Development, 90,* 20–28.

Russell-Chapin, L. A. (2016). Integrating neurocounseling into the counseling profession: An introduction. *Journal of Mental Health Counseling, 38*(2), 93–102. https://doi.org/10.17744/mehc.38.2.01

Schwartz, J., & Begley, S. (2003). *The mind and the brain: Neuroplasticity and the power of mental force.* Regan.

Wakefield, J. C. (2016, September). *The medicalization of society.* Grand Valley State University, DeVos Medical Ethics Colloquy. https://www.gvsu.edu/cms4/asset/22BEB039-C05E-34A5-13EB6F73BBBC1CBE/24_-_onlineonly_-_medicalization_of_society_9.26.2016_-_tagged_ada.pdf

CHAPTER 9

Clinical Mental Health Practice Within a Multicultural Society

Can you imagine? She is turning down a full scholarship to a Tier I school to work in the family restaurant.

—G. O'Malley, high school counselor

Mr. O'Malley, the high school counselor quoted above, is reacting to one of his "star" students, who although being valedictorian of her graduating class and having multiple scholarships offers, has just informed him that she is not going to go to college, but rather that she will work, like her siblings, in the family restaurant. Can you imagine? The answer is yes. It is yes for any counselor who understands the Latino cultural concept of familism.

Familism reflects a Latino value that promotes loyalty, cohesiveness, and obedience with the family. Familism reflects strong family identification and subjugation of one's individual needs to those of the family (Lugo Steidel & Contreras, 2003). So, yes. His student is making a difficult yet personally meaningful decision. Her decision viewed within this cultural light can be seen as one of family love, devotion, and service.

Clinical mental health counselors now serve in a world that is enriched by diversity. Our clients bring with them values, beliefs, experiences, and worldviews that may differ from our own. The implications for mental health counselors are profound.

We have become painfully aware that many of our assumptions, theories, and techniques reflecting the influence of White, Western, male values need to be revisited and reassessed for validity and utility, especially when used with clients whose cultural experiences differ from those of the White, Western, dominant culture. For too long, counselors have ignored the relevance of cultural factors and the role of social context in human development and human behavior.

The need is clear. Counselors in the 21st century need to be sensitive to client diversity and have the competency to work with multiculturalism and diversity issues. The recognition of the inadequacy of our models, our approaches when employed with culturally diverse populations, has stimulated a call to all counselors to gain the knowledge, skills, attitudes, and perspective required to operate from a multicultural framework.

After reading this chapter, readers will be able to:

- Describe the components of the multicultural counseling competencies.
- Explain the need for counselors to be advocates for social justice.
- Describe what is meant by micro, meso, exo, and macro systems and how counselors can work with each as an advocate for their clients.

Multicultural Counseling Perspective

It has been suggested that there are universal aspects of counseling that apply to all individuals, regardless of culture. Perhaps, if one considers the relational elements, such as a counselor's genuineness and unconditional valuing of a client, this position of universality may be true. But for counselors to truly accept and respect their clients, they must be able to "bracket" their worldviews and be open to the richness of another's perspective.

Mental health counselors have been directed to "not condone or engage in any discrimination based on ability, age, color, culture, disability, ethnic group, gender, gender identity, race, religion, national origin, political beliefs, sexual orientation, relationship status, or socioeconomic status (American Mental Health Counselors Association [AMHCA], 2020, C.2.a). Counselors are called to understand their worldviews and biases and take steps to prevent these biases from interfering with their counseling process (AMHCA, 2020, C.2.c).

These directives and prohibitions are necessary, but they are not sufficient for the clinical mental health counselor's engagement in ethical practice. The ethical mental health counselor does more than constrain or bracket personal bias when engaged with clients. Mental health counselors need to be culturally competent and use their awareness of their worldview and those of their clients to monitor assessment and diagnostic procedures and develop intervention strategies that are culturally informed.

The 1973 Vail Conference Follow-up Commission of the American Psychological Association highlighted the inadequacy of mental health counselor training and service delivery to those with culturally diverse backgrounds. It declared that practice in the absence of multicultural competency was unethical (Korman, 1976). Emphasis on multicultural competency for mental health providers has grown significantly from these early days. In the 1990s, it moved from being viewed as an add on to fundamental counseling skills to becoming an integral part of the counseling relationship and dynamic.

As noted by Pederson (1994), a multicultural counseling perspective is a "generic rather than an exotic perspective" (p. 6). Culture is an invisible but imperative participant in all counseling (Draguns, 2008). Therefore, at its core, counseling competence is multicultural counseling competence (Ridley et al., 2011).

There has been a paradigm shift, one that has seen mental health counselors understanding the force of culture on the human condition and valuing the need to employ a multicultural perspective (Pederson, 2001). Mental health counselors understand the complexity of diversity. Mental health counselors view the client's experience as a result of the intersection of factors such as race, ethnicity, gender, age, sexual orientation, religious identity, and economic status. Case Illustration 9.1 highlights the impact of ethnicity, gender, age, and economic status on one client's decision not to pursue higher education.

CASE ILLUSTRATION 9.1 Luciana

Luciana is a 17-year-old senior at Delray High School. Luciana lives with her parents and six siblings. As the youngest female in the family, Luciana has had to share her time and energy between school and working in the family restaurant. Her parents came to the United States from Mexico to work as cooks. Luciana's mother passed when she was 11 years old, and since that time she has taken on many of the household duties that had been performed by her mom, such as cooking, cleaning, and laundry for her dad and six male siblings. In addition to these household duties, Luciana has been required to work 3 nights a week, as cashier, at the family-owned restaurant. The restaurant is truly a family-run business with all of her brothers and her dad working there.

Luciana is a talented student and has expressed interest in becoming an engineer. As a result of her hard work, Luciana has been recognized as the valedictorian for her graduating class. Her counselor, Mr. O'Malley, has worked with Luciana since her freshman year. He was thrilled at her selection as valedictorian but now is even more excited to tell her the news. Luciana has been awarded three full scholarship offers from Tier I engineering programs.

Mr. O'Malley: I bet you can tell from my smile that I have something super to tell you.
Luciana: (smiling) You do look pretty excited, what's up?
Mr. O'Malley ceremoniously removes three letters from his desk and begins to read. He reads each letter announcing that Luciana has not only gained admission to the top three colleges of her choice but also offered a full 4-year scholarship. He cannot contain his excitement. As he finishes, he notices that Luciana is looking down and appearing sad, not happy as he expected.
Mr. O'Malley: Luciana, what's wrong?
Luciana: (with a quiver in her voice) Mr. O'Malley, this is wonderful. I am shocked. I know we worked hard—I can't thank you enough for all of your help, and I don't want you to be upset with me, but I have decided not to go to college, at least not go, right after I graduate. I ...
Mr. O'Malley: (interrupting) What? You're joking, right? These are the three schools you hope to get into AND they are going to pay everything to have you on their campus. Luciana, this is your dream come true?
Luciana: It is really wonderful. My dad said, not now. He wants me to work in the restaurant like everyone else. Honestly, my family needs me. I need to help my father. I also need to support the family since mom is no longer here. Maybe later. Perhaps, then I will go to college and become an engineer.

Yes, Luciana, the client in Case Illustration 9.1, had a bright future, and she still does. Although confusing to her Irish Catholic, middle-class counselor, Luciana's vocational choice is understandable once Mr. O'Malley understands familism, a multifaceted traditional Latino cultural value that lies at the heart of her decision.

Luciana was raised and lives within a culture that places family needs over individual desires. It is a culture that emphasizes obedience and respect for those in positions of authority within the family (e.g., parents, elders; Lugo Steidel & Contreras, 2003).

A counselor working with Luciana, who understood these cultural values, would appreciate that this bright young female has values and priorities different from those of the dominant culture. For this counselor, energies would not be solely focused on getting her to select a college and a scholarship, a decision and a path that would move her away from familism. Instead, a counselor with multicultural sensitivity would work collaboratively with Luciana and her parents to see if there would be a creative way in which to foster her academic development while at the same time allowing her to be of higher service to the family.

Counselors working with clients similar to Luciana cannot ignore the cultural forces that are at play. More than merely recognizing these forces, the multiculturally competent mental health counselor values them and their influence on their clients and attempts to work with these forces in the service of their clients.

Standards for Training and Practice

Numerous professional associations and accreditation bodies have emphasized multicultural competence (e.g., American Counseling Association [ACA], 2014; AMHCA, 2020; American School Counseling Association [ASCA], 2015; American Psychological Association [APA], 2017; Council on Accreditation of Counseling and Related Education Programs [CACREP], 2016). The importance of the development of multicultural competencies can be seen in the fact that CACREP includes social and cultural diversity as one of the eight common core curricular areas (2016, F1.2). It directs clinical mental health trainees to understand the nature of context in their provision of service by recognizing the "cultural factors relevant to clinical mental health counseling" (CACREP, 2016, C.2.j).

In 1996, the Association for Multicultural Counseling and Development (AMCD), a division of the ACA, adopted the multicultural counseling competencies (MCC) model (Arredondo et al., 1996). The tripartite model of MCC is widely recognized for guiding training and research. The three dimensions of the model include (1) *awareness* of the counselors' own cultural beliefs, (2) *knowledge* of the culture as well as historical and sociopolitical backgrounds of their clients, and (3) *skills* necessary to apply the techniques and treatments they employ. Table 9.1 highlights the specific beliefs, attitudes, knowledge, and skills deemed essential for multicultural competency. It may prove useful to review each of these domains of competencies and identify the degree to which they are present in your current professional formation and formulate a plan for their ongoing development throughout your path toward multicultural competency.

TABLE 9.1 AMCD Multicultural Counseling Competencies

I. Counselor Awareness of Own Cultural Values and Biases

A. Attitudes and Beliefs

1. Culturally skilled counselors believe that cultural self-awareness and sensitivity to one's own cultural heritage is essential.
2. Culturally skilled counselors are aware of how their own cultural background and experiences have influenced attitudes, values, and biases about psychological processes.
3. Culturally skilled counselors are able to recognize the limits of their multicultural competency and expertise.
4. Culturally skilled counselors recognize their sources of discomfort with differences that exist between themselves and clients in terms of race, ethnicity, and culture.

B. Knowledge

1. Culturally skilled counselors have specific knowledge about their own racial and cultural heritage and how it personally and professionally affects their definitions and biases of normality/abnormality and the process of counseling.
2. Culturally skilled counselors possess knowledge and understanding about how oppression, racism, discrimination, and stereotyping affect them personally and in their work. This allows individuals to acknowledge their

(Continued)

(*Continued*)

own racist attitudes, beliefs, and feelings. Although this standard applies to all groups, for White counselors it may mean that they understand how they may have directly or indirectly benefited from individual, institutional, and cultural racism as outlined in White identity development models.

3. Culturally skilled counselors possess knowledge about their social impact upon others. They are knowledgeable about communication style differences, how their style may clash with or foster the counseling process with persons of color or others different from themselves based on the A, B, and C dimensions, and how to anticipate the impact it may have on others.

C. Skills

1. Culturally skilled counselors seek out educational, consultative, and training experiences to improve their understanding and effectiveness in working with culturally different populations. Being able to recognize the limits of their competencies, they (a) seek consultation, (b) seek further training or education, (c) refer out to more qualified individuals or resources, or (d) engage in a combination of these.
2. Culturally skilled counselors are constantly seeking to understand themselves as racial and cultural beings and are actively seeking a non-racist identity.

II. Counselor Awareness of Client's Worldview

A. Attitudes and Beliefs

1. Culturally skilled counselors are aware of their negative and positive emotional reactions toward other racial and ethnic groups that may prove detrimental to the counseling relationship.
2. They are willing to contrast their own beliefs and attitudes with those of their culturally different clients in a nonjudgmental fashion.
3. Culturally skilled counselors are aware of their stereotypes and preconceived notions that they may hold toward other racial and ethnic minority groups.

B. Knowledge

1. Culturally skilled counselors possess specific knowledge and information about the particular group with which they are working. They are aware of the life experiences, cultural heritage, and historical background of their culturally different clients. This particular competency is strongly linked to the "minority identity development models" available in the literature.
2. Culturally skilled counselors understand how race, culture, ethnicity, and so forth may affect personality formation, vocational choices, manifestation of psychological disorders, help seeking behavior, and the appropriateness or inappropriateness of counseling approaches.
3. Culturally skilled counselors understand and have knowledge about sociopolitical influences that impinge upon the life of racial and ethnic minorities. Immigration issues, poverty, racism, stereotyping, and powerlessness may impact self-esteem and self-concept in the counseling process.

C. Skills

1. Culturally skilled counselors should familiarize themselves with relevant research and the latest findings regarding mental health and mental disorders that affect various ethnic and racial groups. They should actively seek out educational experiences that enrich their knowledge, understanding, and cross-cultural skills for more effective counseling behavior.
2. Culturally skilled counselors become actively involved with minority individuals outside the counseling setting (e.g., community events, social and political functions, celebrations, friendships, neighborhood groups, and so forth) so that their perspective of minorities is more than an academic or helping exercise.

III. Culturally Appropriate Intervention Strategies

A. Beliefs and Attitudes

1. Culturally skilled counselors respect clients' religious and/or spiritual beliefs and values, including attributions and taboos, because they affect worldview, psychosocial functioning, and expressions of distress.
2. Culturally skilled counselors respect indigenous helping practices and respect [helping] networks among communities of color.

3. Culturally skilled counselors value bilingualism and do not view another language as an impediment to counseling (monolingualism may be the culprit).

B. Knowledge

1. Culturally skilled counselors have a clear and explicit knowledge and understanding of the generic characteristics of counseling and therapy (culture bound, class bound, and monolingual) and how they may clash with the cultural values of various cultural groups.
2. Culturally skilled counselors are aware of institutional barriers that prevent minorities from using mental health services.
3. Culturally skilled counselors have knowledge of the potential bias in assessment instruments and use procedures and interpret findings keeping in mind the cultural and linguistic characteristics of the clients.
4. Culturally skilled counselors have knowledge of family structures, hierarchies, values, and beliefs from various cultural perspectives. They are knowledgeable about the community where a particular cultural group may reside and the resources in the community.
5. Culturally skilled counselors should be aware of relevant discriminatory practices at the social and community level that may be affecting the psychological welfare of the population being served.

C. Skills

1. Culturally skilled counselors are able to engage in a variety of verbal and nonverbal helping responses. They are able to send and receive both verbal and nonverbal messages accurately and appropriately. They are not tied down to only one method or approach to helping, but recognize that helping styles and approaches may be culture bound. When they sense that their helping style is limited and potentially inappropriate, they can anticipate and modify it.
2. Culturally skilled counselors are able to exercise institutional intervention skills on behalf of their clients. They can help clients determine whether a "problem" stems from racism or bias in others (the concept of healthy paranoia) so that clients do not inappropriately personalize problems.
3. Culturally skilled counselors are not averse to seeking consultation with traditional healers or religious and spiritual leaders and practitioners in the treatment of culturally different clients when appropriate.
4. Culturally skilled counselors take responsibility for interacting in the language requested by the client and, if not feasible, make appropriate referrals. A serious problem arises when the linguistic skills of the counselor do not match the language of the client. This being the case, counselors should (a) seek a translator with cultural knowledge and appropriate professional background or (b) refer to a knowledgeable and competent bilingual counselor.
5. Culturally skilled counselors have training and expertise in the use of traditional assessment and testing instruments. They not only understand the technical aspects of the instruments but are also aware of the cultural limitations. This allows them to use test instruments for the welfare of culturally different clients.
6. Culturally skilled counselors should attend to as well as work to eliminate biases, prejudices, and discriminatory contexts in conducting evaluations and providing interventions, and should develop sensitivity to issues of oppression, sexism, heterosexism, elitism and racism.
7. Culturally skilled counselors take responsibility for educating their clients to the processes of psychological intervention, such as goals, expectations, legal rights, and the counselor's orientation.

Source: Patricia Arredondo, et. al., "AMCD Multicultural Counseling Competencies," *Journal of Multicultural Counseling and Development*, vol. 24, no. 1, pp. 1–3. Copyright © 1996 by American Counseling Association. Reprinted with permission.

Self-Awareness

A mental health counselor's foundation of multicultural competence is cultural self-awareness of their biases, stereotypes, and beliefs. Counselors must engage in self-reflection and self-examination to identify values, beliefs, feelings, and worldviews. Such a self-examination may be uncomfortable, but it is necessary (Sue & Sue, 2013).

This self-examination is not meant to focus on one particular issue (e.g., abortion) or one specific group (e.g., indigenous peoples). Mental health counselors need to review their beliefs and values regarding race, ethnicity, gender, sex roles, spirituality/religion, socioeconomic status, even issues such as personal responsibility, nature versus nurture, and mental disorders. This self-reflection process is not a one-time examination to be done and then checked off the list of things to do. A culturally competent mental health counselor recognizes that experience can impact one's beliefs, values, feelings, and worldview, and thus commits to the ongoing process of self-reflection.

Client's Worldview

Each of us has a perception of the world that has developed as a result of our experiences, socialization processes, and interactions with others, and this worldview affects how we perceive and evaluate situations and the action needed (Sue & Sue, 2013). Counselors need to understand the client's worldview if they are to understand the client.

Counselors also need to be able to "bracket" their worldview with their values, beliefs, and expectations in order to prevent them from being imposed on the client's narrative and resulting in actions that are anything but supportive of the client. Zhang and Parsons (2016) illustrate just how a counselor, absent of an understanding of a client's culture and uncritically applying their own set of expectations, can result in actions that are ill-guided (see Case Illustration 9.2).

CASE ILLUSTRATION 9.2 Robert: A Case of Child Abuse?

Kelly graduated from a CACREP-accredited counseling program 5 years ago and was hired by one of the schools in a state on the East Coast as a school counselor. As a graduate student, Kelly did very well in all her coursework and completed her practicum and internship with all As. As a certified school counselor, Kelly's expertise lies in working with kids whose ages range from 6 to 12. Being an employee, Kelly has been very conscientious and goes above and beyond what is required. For this reason, she is liked by teachers and students alike. However, because of a busy schedule and her kids and family, Kelly never had time to attend workshops to advance her knowledge and skills.

One day the English teacher, Mrs. Christopher, referred one of her students, Robert, a 9-year-old boy, to Kelly, saying that Robert was struggling with his English homework and was not able to concentrate in the class. Robert was born in Vietnam. After his father died, his mother married a Chinese-Vietnamese American man and brought Robert to the United States at about 5 years of age. Robert was always quiet and was doing ok in all other classes but English.

When Robert was brought to Kelly's office, he showed some nervousness. As an experienced counselor, Kelly was able to place Robert in a chair and calm him down quickly. However, while Robert lifted his right hand over his shoulder, scratching his back, Kelly noticed some bruises on his side. "What is that on your body?" asked Kelly. Instead of responding verbally, Robert "asked" what she meant by opening his eyes. "The bruises I see on your body? Can I take a look?" asked Kelly. Robert was a little bit reluctant but said, "Ok." Kelly stood up and lifted Robert's t-shirt. Kelly opened her eyes widely when she saw bruises all over Robert's back. "What happened, Robert? Who did it?" asked Kelly. "Hmm ... Mom," said Robert.

Source: Zhang, N., & Parsons, R. D. (2016). *Field experience: Transitioning from student to professional*, 182–183. Sage.

As you read the case of Robert, you, like Kelly, the school counselor, may have seen the physical markings as evidence of child abuse and, as a mandated reporter, immediately contacted legal authorities such as children and youth services. Perhaps with additional information and a deeper understanding of Robert's Vietnamese culture, you may have proceeded somewhat differently.

Zhang and Parsons (2016) explain that Robert's family employs Chinese medical treatments. In this case, the procedure called for was *gua sha*, a therapy that involves the scraping of the skin to produce a light bruising. The treatment is based on the belief that such scraping releases unhealthy elements from injured areas and stimulates blood flow and healing. The technique, although nontraditional in Western culture, has been found to provide medical benefits (e.g., Lee et al., 2010).

Mental health counselors, seeking to develop multicultural competency, would do well to step outside of their own "worlds" and cultural experiences to engage in community activities, meetings, and services of those from other cultures. Sharing the experience versus merely reading about it may be an effective way to increase awareness and sensitivity to the value of diversity.

Reflection and Review of Strategies Employed

For too long, we in mental health counseling have approached our profession and practices with the belief that our theories and strategies had universal value. We failed to appreciate that often what we did, and how we did it, had little value for large groups of individuals. Our failure to consider the culture and client diversity in our assessments has resulted in the misdiagnosis and overpathologizing of African American, Hispanic, and Latino clients (Johnson, 2013; Sue & Sue, 2013).

Counselors are called to recognize this history of our profession and address such biases within their practice (ACA, 2014, E.5.c). The ACA (2014) code of ethics is clear in directing its members to be mindful of client diversity when assessing and diagnosing and further directs its members to "recognize that culture affects the manner in which clients' problems are defined and experienced. Clients' socioeconomic and cultural experiences are considered when diagnosing mental disorders" (E.5.b).

Many of the fundamental "truths" upon which we, as counselors, have based our decisions, "truths" such as the definition of what is "normal," the universality of linear thinking, the focus on the individual and psychological primacy of independence, are now being reconsidered in light of our understanding of cultural diversity (Sue & Sue, 1999). Further, we now understand the limitations to theories that reflect primarily White, male, Western views of the human condition.

With multicultural competency, mental health counselors employ interventions that not only assist the client directly but also extend into the systems and context that contribute to the client's challenges and difficulties (Ratts et al., 2016). With an understanding of culture's role in the effective delivery of service, the multiculturally competent counselor is open to consulting with healers or spiritual leaders that can provide insight into the client's struggle and culturally valued approaches to intervention (Robinson & Howard-Hamilton, 2000). The multiculturally competent mental health counselor is not only aware of indigenous models of helping but, as appropriate, engage with clients with these culturally responsive and supportive resources (Lee & Armstrong, 1995). Again, this approach is not only a good idea but is an ethical mandate:

> Counselors recognize that support networks hold various meanings in the lives of clients and consider enlisting the support, understanding, and involvement of others (e.g., religious/spiritual/community leaders, family members, friends) as positive resources, when appropriate, with client consent. (ACA, 2014, A.1.d)

Knowing One's Limitations

It is aspirational for all mental health counselors to be free of bias and prejudice, fully understand and value their clients' worldviews, and be knowledgeable and skilled in adapting assessment and intervention strategies in culturally sensitive ways. Aspirational, yes. Realistic, probably not.

As with all aspects of professional practice, mental health counselors must know the limitations of their abilities and practice within the boundaries of their competency. The ACA code of ethics (2014) directs its members to refer clients when they practice outside the scope of their competence. While this directive may be applied to working with clients who would benefit from a specific form of treatment, one for which the mental health counselor has not been adequately trained, it is also applicable to those situations where a culturally diverse client would benefit from working with another professional who is more in tune with their unique cultural story and context. Mental health counselors who make such a referral demonstrate respect and concern for the client. There is a caveat, however.

If a referral of specific client populations becomes a pattern for any one counselor, such referral, while perhaps needed, is not the only thing this counselor needs to do. It is the ethical responsibility of all mental health counselors to seek ongoing professional education and supervision to gain the knowledge and skill required of working with clients—of all backgrounds. In some cases, a counselor may find that in addition to such education, personal counseling may be beneficial to gain greater insight into their worldview and the factors that may be making it difficult to be genuine, empathic, and valuing of all those whom they treat.

Clinical Mental Health Counselors as Advocates Employing an Ecological Systems Approach

With increased multicultural competence comes an increased awareness of the oppressive forces that permeate our society. Mental health counselors are called to act in the best interest of their clients. Clinical mental health counselors will be tasked not only with facilitating a client's growth within the counseling relationship but also act as advocates for social justice and equity, for this client and all who are similarly experiencing such injustice and oppression.

Historically, the counseling approach to clients struggling to function within society was to seek to facilitate the adjustment of the individual to the system. While this still may be of value in many circumstances, the truth is also that often it is the system that unjust and interfering with the individual's growth and well-being. Under these conditions, mental health counselors must engage in intentional action(s) to assist in removing the external obstacles and oppressive forces impeding clients' well-being (Toporek, 2000). The ACA is explicit in calling members when appropriate to "advocate at individual, group, institutional and social levels to examine potential barriers and obstacles that inhibit access and/or the growth and development of clients" (2014, A.7.a).

In 2003, the ACA commissioned a task force to look at advocacy and advocacy competencies. These competencies were updated in 2018 (Toporek & Daniels, 2018). The advocacy competencies described outline "counselor skills, knowledge and behavior that can be implemented to address systemic barriers and issues facing students, clients, client groups or whole populations" (Toporek & Daniels, 2018, p. 2).

Counselors were and are encouraged to view client issues from a multilevel, systemic perspective. The ecological systems approach, with its review of client–context interaction, directs counselors and clients to the identification of the roots of the issue for the client and to help identify factors that potentially could impact the maintenance of the problem for the client and the creation of similar problems for others within that ecology. One model of such an ecological perspective defines counseling as "contextualized help-giving that is dependent on the meaning clients derive from their environmental interactions" (Conyne & Cook, 2004, p. 6). Any efforts at intervening with a client who experiences systemic disenfranchisement and oppression will most likely prove ineffective or, at best, short-lived without such an ecological approach. Mental health counselors must view clients' issues from an ecological perspective, highlighting the role and influence of a client's physical, social, and institutional realities.

Urie Bronfenbrenner (1979, 2005) presented an ecological framework that can aid in understanding the various systems (i.e., micro, meso, exo, and macro) in which a client functions and how these interact to impact a client's well-being. Mental health counselors operating with advocacy competencies will advocate for their clients by engaging at the level of each of these systems (Ratts et al., 2010).

Microsystems

For Bronfenbrenner (1979, 2005), the microsystems were the most immediate of the systems in which one operates. The microsystem is the level of daily interactions that occur at home, work, school. These are social interactions with family members, coworkers, peers, and community members. These interactions are reciprocal. As such, a client's style and behavior with friends after work might prove quite different than that client's interactional patterns when engaged with family members.

Microsystem work for the mental health counselor entails their style of interaction and relationship as they provide counseling to individuals, families, and small groups. Microsystem advocacy strategies focus on empowering clients at the individual level. These may include working with clients by helping them understand their situation in context and then helping them develop self-advocacy skills.

Mesosystems

The next level is termed the mesosystem (or mezzo level). The mesosystem is the composite of interactions among the various microsystems. Thus, a client's engagement at work or in school may be the outcome of the interaction not only of the microsystem of the setting, for example, the supervisor–worker interactions or teacher–student exchanges but also how these interact with the microsystems of peer involvement or home life.

Consider the potential impact of a teacher praising a client (microsystem) for volunteering to come to the board. Such interaction of teacher–student is then met with mocking commentary coming from that student's peers. In this case, the mesosystem is one of conflicting values between the microsystems of teacher–student and student–student.

Mental health counselors working at the mesosystem level continue to provide direct support to their clients. However, when working at this level, mental health workers may move outside of the office and engage in one-on-one contact with the client at the client's workplace, school, or even community. Mental health counselors engaging at this level will employ collaboration skills to create programs that can be implemented at these various arenas to remove those factors negatively impacting the client and increasing elements that would be supportive of the client's growth.

Exosystem

The exosystem refers to the broader social system. The client is not a direct participant in their exosystem but is impacted by the structures in this system as they interact with some structure in the client's microsystem (Berk, 2000). For example, a community mental health counselor, recognizing the growth in the number of ESL (English as Second Language) families moving into their school district, may go to a community school to advocate for additional ESL support programming. Perhaps a counselor observing the economic decline of her community and the increased stress created by job loss may approach a business and invite their consideration of providing their employees access to mental health services through an employee assistance program (Chapter 7). In both cases, the client or clients were not directly involved in these interventions, but they and others will benefit.

Macrosystem

The macrosystem comprises the clients' culture (values, beliefs, patterns, customs) and the political, legal, and economic systems in which they live. Thus, the focus is on the broad view of systemic causes for attacks on mental health and well-being, whether at the community, state, or national levels.

Services provided by the mental health counselor working at the macrosystem level indirectly, and yet effectively, impact the constituencies of concern. For example, a mental health counselor working in the school may implement a schoolwide positive behavior program or an antibullying program. The mental health counselor working in a community setting may develop and distribute antismoking, antidrug informational materials through schools, churches, and other community agencies. When working at the macrosystem level, the mental health counselors will attempt to highlight all of the issues involved and, through collaboration and education, invite change in the social norms and even social policies that may be undermining the well-being of specific peoples.

Table 9.2 provides a sampling of targets that mental health counselors, using an ecological approach to practice, can address.

TABLE 9.2 Sampling of Targets for Advocacy in the Ecological Systems Framework

Microsystem
- Use culturally sensitive, respectful, and inclusive language.
- Understand the cultural implications of nonverbals.
- Discuss privacy concerns, especially in situations where culture is collectivistic.
- Assist the client in developing the skills needed to self-advocate.
- Invite the client to help you understand their worldview and lived experiences.
- Integrate the client's worldview and cultural resources into the helping process.

Mesosystem
- Assist the client in developing a range of behaviors applicable to each of their microsystem encounters (e.g., with neighborhood peers, within a school, church, etc.).
- Help the client understand the resources available through other systems.
- Help the client understand the impact of various microsystems on their situation, including identifying forces of oppression, both those internalized and those systemically imposed.
- Develop school–agency–family–community partnerships (Luke, 2008).

Exosystem
- Increase knowledge of and access to structures and systems that, if engaged, can be supportive of this and similar clients.
- Coordinate and advocate for services needed by the clients and others in similar circumstances.
- Negotiate relevant services and education systems on behalf of the client.
- Facilitate client access to community services and resources.

Macrosystem
- Participate in social action targeting group, institutional, state, federal and social policies, programs, actions (or inactions) that inhibit growth, development, and wellness.
- Engage in collaboration with political and professional advocacy groups to develop social policies that can reduce systemic "isms."
- Call legislators to accountability when failing to promote policies necessary to remove oppression and disenfranchisement.
- With allies, use data supporting desired change, lobby policymakers.

Not an Either-Or Approach

When working from an ecological systems framework, counselors should not view each of these systems (i.e., micro, meso, exo, macro) as unique and as singular targets for service. A better perspective is that entering at any one of these system levels invites the counselor to think of possible services addressing the issues at hand by targeting the other system levels. For example, when working with a veteran diagnosed with PTSD, the mental health counselor may engage at the microsystem level and employ best practice strategies such as eye movement desensitization and reprocessing (EMDR). Attempts at providing support and addressing the issue of PTSD need not stop at this microsystem level.

The mental health counselor engaged with this client may offer services to family members to help them understand the client's challenges and find ways to support (mesosystem). The counselor working at the mesosystem level may review programs available for assisting others with trauma-induced disorders. At the macrosystem level, the counselor may investigate the accessibility of healthcare services for veterans and economic support to reduce additional stressors in veterans' lives. Additionally, the mental health counselor working at the macrosystem level might investigate policies or laws that prevent or inhibit access to trauma-informed mental health services and those that promote recovery.

Keystones

- Given the fact that their worldviews will shape all interactions between counselor and client, it is incumbent on all ethical counselors to gain knowledge, personal awareness, sensitivity, dispositions, and skills necessary to be a culturally competent counselor (ACA, 2014, C.2.a).
- There has been a paradigm shift, one that has seen mental health counselors understanding the force of culture on the human condition and thus valuing the need to employ a multicultural perspective.
- Mental health counselors need to be culturally competent and use their awareness of their worldview, and the worldview of their clients, to monitor assessment and diagnostic procedures and develop intervention strategies that are culturally informed.
- Numerous professional associations and accreditation bodies have emphasized the development of multicultural competence (e.g., ACA, 2014; AMHCA, 2020; APA, 2017; ASCA, 2015; CACREP, 2016).
- The cultural counseling competencies model is a tripartite model of guiding multicultural training and research. The three dimensions of the model include: (1) *awareness* of counselor's own cultural beliefs, (2) *knowledge* of the culture as well as historical and sociopolitical backgrounds of their clients, and (3) *skills* necessary to apply the techniques and treatments they employ.
- Clinical mental health counselors will be tasked not only with facilitating their client's growth within the counseling relationship but also act as advocates for social justice and equity, for their client and all who are similarly experiencing such injustice and oppression.
- When appropriate, counselors are called to "advocate at individual, group, institutional and social levels to examine potential barriers and obstacles that inhibit access and/or the growth and development of clients" (ACA, 2014, A.7.a).
- Urie Bronfenbrenner (1979, 2005) presented an ecological framework that helps understand the various systems (i.e., micro, meso, exo, and macro) in which a client functions and how these interact to impact the client's well-being. Mental health counselors, operating with advocacy competencies, will advocate for their clients by engaging at the level of each of these systems.

Additional Resources

American Counseling Association. (n.d.). *Competencies*. https://www.counseling.org/knowledge-center/competencies

Cook, E. P. (Ed.). (2012). *Understanding people in context: The ecological perspective in counseling*. American Counseling Association.

Durodoye, B. A. (2013). Ethical issues in multicultural counseling. In C. Lee (Ed.), *Multicultural issues in counseling: New approaches to diversity* (4th ed., pp. 295–308). American Counseling Association.

Lebeauf, I., Smaby, M., & Maddux, C. (2009). *Adapting counseling skills of multicultural and diverse clients*. American Counseling Association. http://www.counseling.org/resources/library/vistas/2009-v-print/Article%204%20LeBeaufSmabyMaddux.pdf

McAuliffe, G., & Associates. (2012). *Culturally alert counseling: A comprehensive introduction*. Sage.

References

American Counseling Association. (2003). Governing Council, March 20–22.

American Counseling Association. (2014). *Code of ethics and standards of practice*. http://www.counseling.org/Resources/aca-code-of-ethics.pdf

American Mental Health Counselors Association. (2020). *Code of ethics*. https://www.amhca.org/HigherLogic/System/DownloadDocumentFile.ashx?DocumentFileKey=24a27502-196e-b763-ff57-490a12f7edb1&forceDialog=0

American Psychological Association. (2017). *Multicultural guidelines: An ecological approach to context, identity, and intersectionality.* http://www.apa.org/about/policy/multicultural-guidelines.pdf

American School Counseling Association. (2015). *The school counselor and cultural diversity.* https://www.schoolcounselor.org/asca/media/asca/PositionStatements/PS_CulturalDiversity.pdf

Arredondo, P., Toporek, M. S., Brown, S., Jones, J., Locke, D. C., Sanchez, J., & Stadler, H. (1996). *Operationalization of the multicultural counseling competencies.* Association for Multicultural Counseling and Development.

Berk, L. E. (2000). *Child development* (5th ed.). Allyn and Bacon.

Bronfenbrenner, U. (1979). *The ecology of human development: Experiments by nature and design.* Harvard University Press.

Bronfenbrenner, U. (2005). *Making human beings human: Bioecological perspectives on human development.* Sage.

Council on Accreditation of Counseling and Related Educational Program. (2016). *Section 2: Professional counseling identity.* https://www.cacrep.org/section-2-professional-counseling-identity/

Coyne, R. K., & Cook, E. P. (2004). Understanding persons within environments: An introduction to ecological counseling. In R. K. Coyne & E. P. Cook (Eds.), *Ecological counseling: An innovative approach to conceptualizing person-environment interaction.* American Counseling Association.

Draguns, J. G. (2008). Universal and cultural threads in counseling individuals. In P. B. Pedersen, J. G. Draguns, W. J. Lonner, & J. E. Trimble (Eds.), *Counseling across cultures* (6th ed., pp. 21–36). Sage.

Johnson, R. (2013). Forensic and culturally responsive approach for the DSM-5: Just the FACTS. *The Journal of Theory Construction & Testing, 17,* 18–22.

Korman, M. (1976). Conference follow-up. In M. Korman (Ed.), *Levels and patterns of professional training in psychology* (pp. 129–140). American Psychological Association. https://doi.org/10.1037/10047-010

Lee, C. C., & Armstrong, K. L. (1995). Indigenous models of mental health interventions. In J. C. Ponterroto, J. M. Casas, L. A. Suzuki, & C. M. Alexander (Eds.), *Handbook of multicultural counseling* (pp. 441–456). Sage.

Lee, M. S., Choi, T. Y., Kim, J. I., & Choi, S. M. (2010). Using Guasha to treat musculoskeletal pain: A systematic review of controlled clinical trials. *Chinese Medicine, 5,* 5. https://doi.org/10.1186/1749-8546-5-5

Lugo Steidel, A. G., & Contreras J. M. (2003). A new familism scale for use with Latino populations. *Hispanic Journal of Behavioral Sciences, 25,* 312–330.

Luke, M. (2008). School–family–community partnerships: Implications for school counselors to bridge the gap in urban schools. *New York State School Counseling Journal, 5*(2), 13–22.

Pedersen, P. (1994). *A handbook for developing multicultural awareness* (2nd ed.). American Counseling Association.

Pederson, P. (2001). Multiculturalism and the paradigm shift in counselling: Controversies and alternative futures. *Canadian Journal of Counseling, 35*(1), 15–25.

Ratts, M. J., Sing, A. A., Nassar-McMillan, S., Butler, S. K., & McCullough, J. R. (2016). Multicultural and social justice counseling competencies: Guidelines for the counseling profession. *Journal of Multicultural Counseling and Development, 44,* 28–48. doi: 10.1002/jmcd.12035.

Ridley, C. R., Mollen, D., & Kelly, S. M. (2011). Beyond microskills: Toward a model of counseling competence. *The Counseling Psychologist, 40*(3), 1070–1077.

Robinson, T. L., & Howard-Hamilton, M. F. (2000). *The convergence of race, ethnicity, and gender: Multiple identities in counseling.* Merrill.

Sue, D. W., & Sue, D. (1999). *Counseling the culturally different: Theory and practice.* Wiley.

Sue, D. W., & Sue, D. (2013). *Counseling the culturally diverse: Theory and practice* (6th ed.). John Wiley & Sons.

Toporek, R. L. (2000). Developing a common language and framework for understanding advocacy in counseling. In J. A. Lewis & L. Bradley (Eds.), *Advocacy in counseling: Counselors, clients, and community* (pp. 5–14). ERIC/CASS.

Toporek, R. L., & Daniels, J. (2018). *American Counseling Association advocacy competencies.* https://www.counseling.org/docs/default-source/competencies/aca-advocacy-competencies-updated-may-2020.pdf?sfvrsn=f410212c_4

Zhang, N., & Parsons, R. D. (2016). *Field experience: Transitioning from student to professional.* Sage.

CHAPTER 10 Accountability

Thank God I kept good notes.

—Philip, licensed professional counselor

Philip, the counselor quoted above, was sued by a client claiming malpractice. The details of the suit are not necessary; what is of importance is that Philip kept meticulous records, including those demonstrating acquisition of client informed consent on multiple occasions. Those records resulted in immediate dismissal of the suit.

While records providing evidence of practice decisions are valuable in terms of litigation, their value extends beyond buffering one from legal trouble. Documents and clinical notes are practical in that they facilitate adherence to treatment plans, modification of plans as needed, communication with other professionals, and even obtaining third-party payments.

The maintenance of professional records is an essential component of professional practice and a primary vehicle to demonstrate clinical accountability. The current chapter reviews the issues of professional accountability and documentation.

After reading this chapter, readers will be able to:

- Describe the purpose, process, and importance of accurate and thorough record keeping.
- Identify the common elements most often included in a client's record.
- Describe three approaches to developing progress notes.
- Describe the ethical and legal concerns regarding the maintenance of client records.

Documentation and Record Keeping

For professional counselors, record keeping and documentation is not only a practical, useful guide to practice, but it is also an ethical mandate and legal requirement. The documentation of our practice decisions provides evidence of our maintenance of a standard of care that reflects the ethical performance of our duties. Maintaining documentation and records is valued at those times of referral and the sharing of professional communications. Our records provide the structure for the continuation of care. They may be necessary not only for obtaining third-party payment but also as justification for our practice decisions when called forth in legal proceedings (Mitchell, 2007).

As noted in the American Counseling Association's (2014) code of ethics:

> Counselors create, safeguard, and maintain documentation necessary for rendering professional services. Regardless of the medium, counselors include sufficient and timely

> documentation to facilitate the delivery and continuity of services. Counselors take reasonable steps to ensure that documentation accurately reflects client progress and services provided. If amendments are made to records and documentation, counselors take steps to properly note the amendments according to agency or institutional policies. (A.1.b)

Although the maintenance of clinical records can undoubtedly aid the counselor's memory, especially when working with extensive caseloads, record keeping is about more than merely remembering details of client sessions and the direction to be taken. Luepker (2012) outlines six reasons that keeping clinical records is essential:

1. Clinical records help facilitate the communication process between the client and the counselor. Good record keeping demonstrates a commitment to the client's welfare, and discussing records with clients can open dialogue and create an atmosphere of "safety and mutual respect" (p. 2).
2. Records are an essential part of the diagnosis and treatment planning process. A systematic review of records allows the counselor to evaluate and revise treatment plans as necessary.
3. Good documentation facilitates continuity of care. The better the record keeping, the more likely it is that another practitioner can understand what has happened during the therapeutic process and provide appropriate treatment based on previous sessions. In cases where the clinician can no longer provide treatment, client records may be the only tool a new counselor has to pick up where treatment is left off.
4. Case files can be used in the clinical supervision process. Counselors and supervisors can review client records to provide feedback to the counselor and develop future treatment strategies.
5. Documentation is often required for third-party billing. Insurance companies will likely require a diagnosis and/or treatment plan to reimburse the clinician for services.
6. Documentation is the best defense counselors have against accusations of illegal and unethical behavior. Should a client file a lawsuit or ethics complaint against the counselor, the documentation kept during the therapeutic process may be the difference between losing or winning in court or an ethics hearing.

Nature of Clinical Records

It might be said that a counselor's records include anything involving contact between the counselor and the client that is written down or electronically recorded. Clinical documentation would consist of a counselor's notations about the client, progress achieved, goals established, recommendations, and treatment decisions made, and the rationale for each (Barnett & Johnson, 2014). While taking many forms and ranging in degree of detail and extensiveness, clinical documents are not random thoughts.

Counseling records should provide an overview of the client—their issues and the counseling relationship's nature and direction. Counseling records should, according to Luepker (2012), "convey, in humane, legible, and plain language, accurate and contemporaneous answers to 'who, why, what, when, and how?' of the counseling relationship" (p. 22).

For these records to have professional utility, they must be pertinent to the counseling and not be superfluous. Professional documents should be as objective and as empirical as possible, separating that which is directly observed from clinical judgment. Additionally, clinical records should follow a rational progression, such as moving from data reflecting demographics to those supporting clinical assessment, diagnosis, and treatment planning. As part of this progression, clinical notes should be maintained in chronological order from intake to termination, thus providing a complete picture of the evolving nature of the counseling relationship and the counseling process.

Data Collected and Retained

The specific types of data collected and the documentation format employed will vary as a function of the individual counselor, the setting in which they work, and even the nature of the population served (e.g., minors, emergency, hospitalized, etc.). However, some data are essential and fundamental to any ongoing case service. These data reflect the client's general condition and situation and the client's presenting concerns, as well as data that reflect the dynamic and progress of the counseling relationship from intake to termination (see Table 10.1).

TABLE 10.1 Overview of Client Data and Documentation

General Information • Identifying data (e.g., name, client I.D. number) • Contact information (e.g., phone number, address, next of kin) • Fees and billing information • Where appropriate, guardianship or conservatorship status • Documentation of informed consent or assent for treatment • Documentation of waivers of confidentiality and authorization or consent for release of information • Documentation of any mandated disclosure of confidential information (e.g., report of child abuse, release secondary to a court order) • Presenting complaint, diagnosis, or basis for the request for services • Plan for services, updated as appropriate (e.g., treatment plan, supervision plan, intervention schedule, community interventions, consultation contracts) • Health and developmental history
Contact and Session Notes • Date of service and duration of a session • Types of services (e.g., consultation, assessment, treatment, training) • Nature of professional intervention or contact (e.g., treatment modalities, referral, letters, emails, phone contacts) • Formal or informal assessment of client status • Functional status • Danger to self/others • Progress notes (e.g., SOAP, DAP, DART) • Treatment compliance/lack of compliance
Termination/Summary • The what, when, and why of termination • Issues related to the termination • Referral or follow-up made

Intake Information

The information collected either as a prescreening before meeting with a client or at the first session typically falls under the category of intake information. The types of data collected for intake will vary from setting to setting, clinician to clinician. At a minimum, intake data will include basic demographics, such as name, date of birth, gender orientation, address, contact information, emergency information, data on living circumstances, and so on, as well as a preliminary description of the client's presenting concerns or stated goals for coming to counseling.

As a reflection of the counselor's valuing of the client's autonomy, counselors will provide the client with information about the approach to be taken, what the client may be expected experience in the counseling process, the parameters of service (when, where, how long, and cost), and the recourse for the client who feels that the service was inappropriate or ineffective. This information should be summarized in a written document and clients invited to sign as evidence of their understanding and acceptance. This signed informed consent document would be included as part of the intake data.

Mental health counselors will typically employ this intake session to gather the preliminary information for case conceptualization, including predisposing conditions, precipitative events, perpetuating factors, and protective factors (see Chapter 5). Of particular importance during an initial intake is for the mental health counselor to gather data about significant medical history or comorbid conditions and client's use of drugs and alcohol. Some counselors use this initial meeting to also engage in a mental status exam (MSE), recording their observations of the client's mood, cognition, perception, thoughts, behaviors, insight, and judgment. Finally, depending on the presenting concern and the client's manner of presentation, the counselor may engage in an assessment of the degree to which the client is at risk for self-harm or for harming others.

Assessment Information

In support of the counselor's case conceptualization, data reflecting the client's biopsychosocial levels of functioning will be gathered. The data described in this section may be included in the intake section of the documentation, as may be the case when collecting mental status data, or they may be included in a separate section, as the relationship develops.

Assessments may include data such as the clinical diagnosis assigned to the client, symptoms (including severity and duration), and any diagnostic assessment or inventory data collected. Although much of the data may be acquired through clinical interviews, some counselors will employ structured assessments and inventories, such as the Beck Depression Inventory (BDI) or the Myers-Briggs Type Indicator (MBTI).

Case Conceptualization and Treatment Planning

In Chapter 5, case conceptualization and treatment planning were reviewed. Counselors gather data to help in the development of their case conceptualization, which directs them to a treatment plan. Counselors need to document the bases for their ethical decision making in terms of the inclusion of specific intervention strategies, which not only highlights their consideration of best practice (see Chapter 6) but, once documented, facilitates continuity of care should the client need to be seen by another healthcare provider.

The creation and documentation of a treatment plan are essential to successful outcomes in the counseling process; the treatment plan is the "roadmap" of the process. The plan is developed based on the client's diagnosis and symptoms and provides both the client and the counselor with a direction in the forms of goals and intervention strategies. Both diagnoses and treatment plans are fluid documents; they should be revisited regularly and revised as necessary (Luepker, 2012). As treatment progresses, client responses to treatment (both positive and negative) should be noted, and the plan should be updated accordingly.

The information included in a treatment plan will vary, again, as a function of the counselor's orientation, the client, and the setting or context within which the services are provided. However, most treatment plans will include a description of the client's presenting concerns along with duration and severity. The plan will most often identify goals and objectives for counseling and connect them to specific intervention strategies. Treatment plans will often reflect the theoretical model employed. As such, a counselor engaged with a cognitive-behavioral approach will develop a treatment plan that may appear quite different than that created by a counselor with a psychodynamic orientation. In either case, the counselor should document the client's engagement in the formulation of the goals, objectives, and treatment modality and include that evidence as part of the informed consent.

Case Notes

Case notes, or progress notes, reflect the session-to-session process. These notes should be recorded immediately after a session, document what occurred in each counseling session, and identify progress toward client goals (Cameron & turtle-song, 2002; Luepker, 2012). There are various ways to approach recording progress notes. Three of the most commonly employed note-taking methods are SOAP (Subjective, Objective, Assessment, Plan), DAP (Description, Assessment, and Plan), and DART (Description, Assessment, Response, and Treatment Plan).

SOAP Notes

Used extensively in medical practice, mental health counselors also find SOAP notes useful to their practice. A counselor will document data gathered from the client regarding their shared thoughts, feelings, perspective, and experience with relationships. These data are considered *subjective.*

Data will also be gathered, reflecting factual information, perhaps collected by the counselor or another significant observer (e.g., family member, partner, manager, colleague). These data might include observations of the client's appearance, evidence of compliance with medication or treatment regimen, and behavior in and out of session. These data are identified as being *objective* because they are gathered by observation and not inference. As with any data included in the client's file, that which is recorded should have direct relevance to the case conceptualization and treatment plan and be included with the realization that others (e.g., client, other professionals, the courts) may have access.

The third group of data collected with the SOAP format reflects the counselor's syntheses of the subjective and objective data gathered and their formulation into an assessment or clinical impression. The *assessment* data might be stated or presented as a diagnosis based on the DSM-5 (American Psychiatric Association, 2013) (see Chapter 4).

The SOAP format's final element is a reflection of the action or treatment plan (*plan*). These data highlight the dates of contact, nature of the contact, interventions employed, and direction to be taken. Table 10.2 provides a summary of the elements of a SOAP method of documentation.

TABLE 10.2 SOAP Notes

SECTION	TYPES OF CONTENT	EXAMPLES
Subjective (S)	What the client tells you What pertinent others tell you about the client Basically, how the client experiences the world	Client's feelings, concerns, plans, goals, and thoughts. Intensity of problems and impact on relationships. Pertinent comments by family, case managers, behavioral therapists, etc. Client's orientation to time, place, and person. Client's verbalized changes toward helping.
Objective (O)	Factual What the counselor personally observes/ witnesses Quantifiable: what was seen, counted, smelled, heard, or measured Outside written materials received	The client's general appearance, affect, behavior. Nature of the helping relationship. Client's demonstrated strengths and weaknesses. Test results, materials from other agencies, etc.
Assessment (A)	Summarizes the counselor's clinical thinking A synthesis and analysis of the subjective and objective portion of the notes	For counselor: Include clinical diagnosis and clinical impressions (if any). For care providers: How would you label the client's behavior and the reasons (if any) for this behavior?
Plan (P)	Describes the parameters of treatment Consists of an action plan and prognosis	Action plan: Include interventions used, treatment progress, and direction. Counselors should include the date of next appointment. Prognosis: Include the anticipated gains from the interventions.

Source: Cameron, S., & turtle-song, i. (2002). Learning to write case notes using the SOAP format. *Journal of Counseling & Development, 80*, 290.

DAP Notes

DAP is another format for gathering session or progress notes that is useful for mental health providers. DAP is an acronym for Data, Assessment, and Plan (sometimes referred to as Description, Analysis, and Plan).

As might be anticipated, *data* (*description*) includes factual information gathered during the session. The description would include observations of client behaviors, recording significant client statements, and data reflecting the client's emotions, thoughts, and reactions to treatment. Thus, a counselor may record that the client entered the session crying and physically shaking and quote the client as stating that she "just received a legal document saying her spouse filed for divorce."

While including objective data, this section also includes the counselor's subjective impressions and hypotheses about the client's disclosures. The counselor, for example, may note that although it appears that the client is saddened, on further reflection "it appears to me that the client is more anxious than sad, anxious about her financial situation."

The second category of data is that reflecting *assessment* (*analysis*). Data would include screening and test results as well as any other assessment data. Suppose we continue the brief illustration regarding the upset client. In that case, the counselor may test her hypothesis regarding the anxiety by merely reflecting what she observes and pose a question, as assessment, to the client: "It is clear this is very upsetting. I know we talked about it in our past sessions, and you shared how you were concerned about the possible impact of a divorce on your financial security. I wonder, is that uncertainty about your financial future what you are feeling at the moment and serving as the foundation for you upset?"

As more data are acquired, new interpretations that may be rendered, and assessment of those interpretations need to be included as a reflection of the counselor's understanding of the client's problem(s) and their evolving case conceptualization (see Chapter 5) and the client's response to treatment.

The final section of progress notes when employing the DAP format is a statement of the *plan*. With each session, counselors will highlight the treatment plan's current direction, with adjustments to goals and strategies as appropriate. Thus, in the present illustration, the counselor may support the client in her moment of emotional turmoil, and the crisis of the moment, while inviting her to identify the issues that are immediately most concerning more concretely. Once these issues are identified, they would work together to develop a plan to reduce the crisis and attack these issues of concern. This plan section would also include identification of the next step, including homework, referral, and the next scheduled session.

DART Notes

DART is a progress notes system created for mental health professionals by Brian N. Baird (2002). It is an acronym for Description, Assessment, Response, and Treatment Plan. The author created the DART system because he felt that other systems, specifically SOAP, with its use of medical terminologies, was problematic for those working in psychological settings. Like the other note-taking models, counselors record observations and data that reflect the client's current situation and status and an assessment of the dynamics that have led to this current situation (i.e., case conceptualization).

In the *description* section, counselors are encouraged to gather data that answers questions of the when, where, who, and what. Notes included in this section would consist of a description of the event and time, location, and people engaged. The *assessment* section presents the counselor's hypotheses about why this is happening (case conceptualization) and the assumption of the best way to assist the client in addressing the concerns and issues (treatment planning). Somewhat unique to this documentation method is the counselor's recording of their response to the dynamics being encountered. In the *response* section, the counselor records not only the actions taken, or not taken, but the reason guiding their clinical decision. In this section, the counselor provides a rationale for the treatment approach and practice decision (Baird, 2002). Some suggest that this section may be of use in the event of future legal action where clinical judgment may be under question (Zhang & Parsons, 2016).

The final section of the DART notes is the description of the *treatment plan*. Goals and objectives for the plan and the specifics, such as homework assigned, would be included in this section. It is helpful for counselors to not only describe the treatment plan but the rationale for this approach. Case Illustration 10.1 explores the use of DART notes for a session.

CASE ILLUSTRATION 10.1 Rachael

DART Notes Session: August 25, 2020

D (description): Session timing—6 p.m. to 6:50 p.m., Tuesday, 8/25/20. Session focus—individual intake session with Rachael, a self-referred 31-year-old female. Rachael entered the session on time. In extending her hand as a greeting, she apologized for it being moist, noting that she was very nervous. The client freely disclosed her anxiety and how it impacted her ability to engage in social encounters. Rachael pointed out that her romantic relationship of 3 years was abruptly ended by her significant other. Rachael expressed that "not only does it make me sad, but I am ashamed to go out in public ... what will people think of me?" The client stated that she is continuing to function at her law firm, where she is a patent attorney, but has begun to withdraw from social contact outside of work. She noted since the breakup that she has been experiencing "mini-panic attacks" when introduced to new people.

A (assessment): The client presented as professionally dressed (having just come from her work), was fluid in her speech, and presented as self-reflective. She reported being anxious when meeting new people, describing heart palpitations, sweating, shortness of breath, and a couple of times feeling dizzy, "as if I was going to pass out." She noted that while she had similar experiences in college—that this was recent and appeared to have followed her recent breakup. When discussing her current relationship, she started to cry. She shared it was getting her down and "that she is afraid of opening herself up to others in anticipation of their rejection." The client's self-reporting of withdrawal from social encounters and the anxiety provoked by social situations would indicate a social anxiety disorder. The freedom with which she disclosed and my reflections' apparent accuracy supports my feeling that the beginning of a meaningful working alliance has been established.

R (response): During the session, Rachael identified that she feels as if her self-esteem is plummeting and that she is developing social anxiety. As she spoke, she noted that she has always been self-confident and assertive and remains so in formal situations or business-related encounters. She feels that this recent breakup has undermined her self-confidence and believes that others will reject her as well.

T (treatment): Albeit early in the relationship, it appears that a cognitive-behavioral approach might be of value. I provided a brief explanation of the connection of thoughts to feelings and invited Rachael to begin a thought diary. Her homework was to identify times of anxiety and record her thoughts, feelings, actions, and the context and events in which they occurred. The hope is to use the thought diary as the data for our next session, in which I would like to help her understand CBT and set goals in line with that approach. The next session is scheduled, September 7, at 6 p.m.

Signed, J. L. Plimton, MS, LPC. August 25, 2020

Termination Documentation

A counseling relationship is expected to terminate and may end for various reasons. The desired rationale for termination is that the treatment successfully helped the client achieve their goals, and thus continued counseling is not needed. It is also possible that a specific counseling relationship is terminated due to restrictions presented by the agency or third-party payers. This would be the case where the number of sessions has been limited by an employee assistance program (see Chapter 7). Regardless of the reason for termination, documenting the what and what next is essential.

Counselors should develop a summary that includes brief descriptions of (1) why the client initially came to counseling, (2) how the issues or goals may have changed throughout counseling, (3) the approach taken in treatment, (4) an assessment of the impact of treatment at the point of termination, (5) the reason for termination, and (6) the direction (if any) provided by the counselor to the client at termination.

Documentation: Ethical-Legal Considerations

Counselors must understand the importance of record keeping. Keeping and maintaining records is not merely a secretarial obligation. Clinical records can genuinely impact a client in life-altering ways. The data counselors include in their records, data reflecting facts, inferences, conclusions, or even the absence of these data, can come to play in a client's custody battle or desire to gain security clearance for a job. These data contain sensitive information. These data need to be respected and protected against access—either accidental or deliberate—by those for whom the information was not intended for release.

Protecting Client Data

Clients assume confidentiality when engaging with a professional counselor. This assumption is confirmed and defined by counselors during their initial contact with clients. While mental health counselors help the client understand the limits of confidentiality and acquire their informed consent to engage in counseling, this is insufficient as a step toward fulfilling the counselor's fiduciary responsibilities to the client.

The American Counseling Association is clear in its directive to its members that counselors "ensure that records and documentation kept in any medium are secure and that only authorized persons have access to them" (2014, B.6.b). This responsibility continues even when the counselor is no longer in practice: "Counselors take reasonable precautions to protect client confidentiality in the event of the counselor's termination of practice, incapacity, or death and appoint a records custodian when identified as appropriate" (ACA, 2014, B.6.i).

Counselors must develop processes and procedures to protect the physical and electronic records from inadvertent or unauthorized disclosure. It is essential that mental health counselors understand not just the ethical mandates regarding confidentiality but also state and federal regulations and statutes regarding such things as HIPAA restrictions (2013), mandated reporting, and the handling of data on sexually transmitted infections or chemical dependency treatment records.

An added responsibility for those counselors who employ clerical or paraprofessionals within their practice is to take reasonable steps to ensure that these individuals are educated about the nature of the records and the processes needed to maintain confidentiality and protect the documents from inappropriate disclosure.

HIPAA

The federal Health Insurance Portability and Accountability Act (HIPAA) of 1996 was passed to establish a national framework for security standards and protection of confidentiality concerning healthcare data and information. HIPAA also has specific regulations stipulating health professionals' behaviors in terms of documentation (U.S. Department of Health and Human Resources, 2013).

Although not all counselors are considered "covered entities" that must comply with HIPAA requirements, anyone intending to engage in private practice would do well to understand HIPAA requirements and develop procedures to position themselves to be HIPAA compliant.

There are numerous aspects to HIPAA compliance, but two are of particular note for mental health counselors. First, HIPAA-compliant counselors provide a document to all clients that explains how the practice handles the release of confidential information. The second document is a notice of client rights under state and federal law. An excellent review of these HIPAA elements was developed by Walsh and Dasenbrook (2005) for the American Counseling Association and is available at https://www.counseling.org/Kaplan/hipaa.pdf.

Maintain Records

The length of time one should maintain a client's records has not been standardized, and as such, counselors need to review the policies of the agencies in which they work, and if in private practice check with state laws. As a practical rule of thumb most individuals in mental health practice abide by the 7-year rule.

In the absence of a mandate, it is useful to maintain records for a minimum of 7 years for adult clients. For counselors working with Medicaid clients or those receiving other federal government assistance, the period should be extended to 10 years because federal "false claims" actions can be brought against healthcare providers for up to 10 years. Finally, for those treating children (minors), a good rule to follow is maintaining the records at least up to that client's age of majority.

The Release of Client Records

Counselor notes are client notes, and clients have a right to access them. That does not mean that they can take the file, but they have the right to review the file (especially with the interpretive help of the counselor) and even ask for duplications or summarizations. Others may also seek access to the records.

As a general rule, client records must be maintained as confidential documents. The release of these records in full or in part must occur with the client's permission and formal signing of a Consent for Release of Information document. There are exceptions to this rule.

If a counselor's records are subpoenaed by the courts (i.e., a judge), the counselor is legally obligated to comply by releasing the specific clinical documentation requested (Stolsmark, 2015). The ACA's code of ethics, however, directs members to disclose only essential information (2014, B.1.c, B.2.d, & B.2.e).

Anytime records are requested, a counselor would do well to not only inform the client and acquire a signed client release of information form but also seek legal advice.

Keystones

- Record keeping and documentation is not only a practical, useful guide to practice, but it is an ethical mandate and legal requirement.
- Documentation of practice decisions provides evidence of ethical performance of duties, facilitates consultation and referral, assists in continuation of care, and provides data for third-party payment, and, if needed, for legal proceedings.
- At minimum, clinical documentation includes notations about the client, progress achieved, goals established, recommendations, and treatment decision made, and the rationale for each.
- Clinical documentation typically includes intake information, assessment data, case conceptualization and treatment plans, progress notes, and termination summaries.
- Case notes, or progress notes, are reflections of the session-to-session process and document what occurred in each counseling session and identify progress toward client goals.
- There are various ways to approach recording progress notes. Three of the commonly employed methods are SOAP, DAP, and DART.
- The ACA is clear in its directive to its members that counselors "ensure that records and documentation kept in any medium are secure and that only authorized persons have access to them" (2014, B.6.b), a point that is carried through even when the counselor is no longer in practice.
- HIPAA regulations and any other state, local, or organizational requirements need to be considered when establishing a system of record keeping and maintenance.

Additional Resources

American Psychological Association. (n.d.). *Mental health progress notes*. https://www.apadivisions.org/division-31/publications/records/progress.aspx

Cameron, S., & turtle-song, i. (2002). Learning to write case notes using the SOAP format. *Journal of Counseling & Development*, 80, 290.

Freeburg, M. N., & McCaughan, A. M. (2008). HIPAA for dummies: A practitioner's guide. In G. R. Walz, J. C. Bleuer, & R. K. Yep (Eds.), *Compelling counseling interventions: Celebrating VISTAS' fifth anniversary* (pp. 305–312). Counseling Outfitters.

Knapp, S. J., & VandeCreek, L. D. (2006). Confidentiality, privileged communications, and record keeping. In *Practical ethics for psychologists: A positive approach* (pp. 111–128). American Psychological Association.

References

American Counseling Association. (2014). *ACA code of ethics*. https://www.counseling.org/Resources/aca-code-of-ethics.pdf

American Psychiatric Association. (2014). *Diagnostic and statistical manual of mental disorders* (5th ed.).

Baird, B. N. (2002). *The internship, practicum, and field placement handbook: A guide for helping professions* (3rd ed.). Pearson.

Barnett, J. E., & Johnson, B. W. (2014). *Ethics desk reference for counselors* (2nd ed.). Wiley.

Cameron, S., & turtle-song, i. (2002). Learning to write case notes using the SOAP format. *Journal of Counseling & Development*, *80*, 286–292.

Luepker, E. T. (2012). *Record keeping in psychotherapy and counseling: Protecting confidentiality and the professional relationship* (2nd ed.). Routledge.

Mitchell, R. W. (2007). *Documentation in counseling records: An overview of ethical, legal, and clinical issues* (3rd ed.). American Counseling Association.

Stolsmark, E. (2015). *Responding to a subpoena*. https://www.counseling.org/docs/default-source/ethics/ethics-columns/ethics_october_2015_subpoena.pdf?sfvrsn=ea22522c_4

U.S. Department of Health & Human Services. (2013). HIPAA administrative simplification: Regulation text. *§ 164.316 Policies and procedures and documentation requirements*.

Walsh, R. J., & Dasenbrook, C. (2005). *Meeting HIPPA requirements*. https://www.counseling.org/Kaplan/hipaa.pdf

Zhang, N., & Parsons, R. D. (2016). *Field experience. Transitioning from student to professional*. Sage.

SECTION IV

Clinical Mental Health Counseling as Profession

CHAPTER 11

Clinical Mental Health Counselor as Personal and Professional Identity

I was recently asked what I did. My automatic response was that I am a mental health counselor.

—Simone, a licensed professional counselor

The inquiry into what one does is somewhat commonplace in our culture. What stands out in Simone's response quoted above is that she highlighted her sense of being, her identity, and not merely her activities. This is a sign of a maturing sense of professional identity.

The concept of *identity* is not new to you. As applied to an individual, identity formation entails the development of an awareness and an expression of one's uniqueness. It is a process that defines each of us as both similar to and different from others. Understanding and embracing that which makes counseling unique, which distinguishes it from other mental health professions, is the foundation for our professional identity.

Counselors can be defined by the role they assume and enact. Counselors can be defined by membership within a specific organization. Counselors can be defined by state law, as would be the case when determining a licensed professional counselor, but perhaps an essential definition of counselor comes from the self-perception of the one identified as a counselor.

As you continue to grow in your professional identity, you will find it to be intricately tied to your personal identity. You, too, will respond to questions of "what you do" with responses that reference "who you are."

This chapter will help you begin to identify all that makes the profession of counseling unique among the helping professions and, in so doing, help to foster the development of your own professional identity.

After completing this chapter, the reader will be able to:

- Describe the characteristics that define a profession.
- Identify the factors that contribute to the uniqueness of counseling as a profession.
- Describe what is meant by a counselor's professional identity.
- Identify the components that contribute to one's professional identity.

Distinct Among the Helping Professions

To understand the uniqueness of counseling as a profession, we must first consider the elements or characteristics that define a profession.

The original meaning of *profession* is derived from the Middle English *profes*, an adjective meaning "having professed one's vows." The implication of this term, professional, is that those holding such a title make a public commitment to a high standard of performance, marked with integrity. For a professional, the goal is to provide quality work rather than mere economic gain (Freidson, 2001).

When attempting to discern the characteristics that define a profession, it is most often agreed that a profession is generally composed of a disciplined group of individuals who possess specialized knowledge and skills and who adhere to an agreed-upon set of ethical standards, having gained some public recognition (Australian Council of Professions, 2003). As reflected in Table 11.1, the elements most often employed as markers to define a profession are firmly rooted in the rich history and contemporary practice of mental health counseling. Thus, it is safe to state that counseling is, by definition, a profession.

TABLE 11.1 Defining Mental Health Counseling as a Unique Profession

DEFINING CHARACTERISTIC OF A PROFESSION	DESCRIPTION	HISTORICAL MARKERS
Based on specialized theoretical knowledge	Professionals render specialized services based on theory, knowledge, and skills that are most often peculiar to their profession and generally beyond the understanding and capability of those outside of the profession.	• Early 1900s: The founding of the National Vocational Guidance Association (NVGA) and the publication of *National Vocational Guidance Magazine* (to become the *Journal of Counseling and Development*) to encourage the pursuit of scholarly information to vocational guidance. • 1960s: The inclusion of psychological theories, particularly humanistic theories, to provide a theoretical framework for delivering mental health services to students. • 2000s: Highlighted the need and value for engaging in the research-based or empirically supported practice and the value of counseling.
Institutional preparation	Professions typically require a significant period of training and education, often under the supervision of senior members. Beyond initial training, professionals engage in ongoing professional development.	• The Council for Accreditation of Counseling and Related Education Programs (CACREP) was formed in 1981 and has articulated standards for the training and development of counselors, which now includes 60 semester hours and 700 supervised field experience hours. • The American Mental Health Counseling Association (AMHCA) created and revised its professional standards in 1993–94, 2003, and 2010–11 to reflect evolving practice requirements.
A professional organization of peers	Professionals see themselves as part of a community of like-minded individuals who put their professional standards above their individual self-interest or their employer's self-interest.	• In 1976, the AMHCA was created to provide a "home" for counselors who were employed in nonschool settings. While initially a division of ACA, AMHCA now stands as an independent association dedicated to the academic, internship, supervision, and licensure of clinical mental health counselors.

(Continued)

(*Continued*)

DEFINING CHARACTERISTIC OF A PROFESSION	DESCRIPTION	HISTORICAL MARKERS
Credentialing of practitioners	After completion of education and skills development, a professional is required to pass one or more exams that assure the person has attained a minimum level of knowledge.	• The National Board for Certified Counselors (NBCC) established criteria and process of counselors to earn board certification as a National Certified Counselor (NCC). • The NBCC establishes criteria and processes for counselors to earn board certification as Certified Clinical Mental Health Counselors (CCMHC).
Ethical constraints	Professionals are bound to a code of conduct or ethics specific to the distinct profession. Professionals also aspire toward a general body of core values centered upon uncompromising and unconflicted regard for the client's benefit and best interests.	• 1960s: The American Personnel and Guidance Association (now the ACA) published its first code of ethics, providing guidelines for ethical practice and ultimately protecting the public and increasing professionalism. These standards have and continue to be revised and in their latest iteration appear as the ACA code of ethics (2014). • The AMHCA articulated a code of ethics to guide members' practice in 2015.
Legal recognition		• Virginia became the first state to license professional counselors in 1976. Today all 50 states and District of Columbia and Puerto Rico have licensure.

Although this may be obvious, it is a starting point for considering the nature of this profession and the knowledge, skills, values, and worldviews held by those who embrace this as their calling and their profession.

The Nature of Professional Identity

A counselor's professional identity is the emerging sense of self as a professional and competency to perform within that professional role (Parsons & Zhang, 2012). Being able to articulate value and operate from a knowledge base, skill set, and philosophical perspective that distinguishes you from other helping professionals while aligning you with those self-identified as "counselors" is the core of one's professional identity (see Chapter 1).

There have been numerous attempts to define professional identity (e.g., Gray, 2001; Puglia, 2008; Weinrach et al., 2001), and although there is no one generally agreed-upon definition, the essence of professional identity is well depicted in the following description: "the possession of a core set of values, beliefs, and assumptions about the unique characteristics of one's selected profession that differentiates it from other professions" (Weinrach et al., 2001, p. 168).

Remley and Herlihy (2007) presented professional identity as reflecting the following six components: (1) knowledge and understanding of the profession's history, (2) knowledge and understanding of the philosophical foundations of the profession, (3) knowledge of the roles and functions of counselors and how they are similar and different from other mental health professions, (4) a sense of pride in the profession, (5) involvement in professional organizations and advocacy (i.e., professional engagement), and (6) knowledge and understanding of professional counselor ethics.

But "knowing" is not the same as "being." Calley and Hawley (2008) recommended a more active process for fostering the development of one's professional identity. They suggest that counselors actively identify with the distinct values of the counseling profession, engage in professional counseling associations, disseminate scholarship for and about the profession of counseling, utilize theoretical orientations that align with the values of the counseling profession, and obtain training, licensure, and certifications in the profession of counseling.

Many From One

At the broadest level counselors are one—sharing that which makes us unique among helping professionals as well as embodying a joint mission and vision. However, each counselor, while embracing a shared professional identity, does so in a way that reflects their diversity in both interests and practice. For those engaged in the profession, professional identity is a personal experience reflecting one's sense of calling and purpose and personal perspective on this particular helping profession. There is not one form or focus of counseling; there are many, and each specialization of service provided and population served further contributes to the evolving professional identities and uniqueness of the counselor so engaged.

This fact of many—reflecting both uniqueness and yet commonality—is reflected in the diversity of specialization existing within the divisions of the American Counseling Association (ACA). There are 18 divisions within the ACA, each organized around special interest and practice concerns. Some divisions address training and practice needs for those serving specific populations (e.g., Association for Child and Adolescent Counseling, International Association of Addictions and Offender Counselors). Other divisions attract counselors who share common interests in modes of service delivery (e.g., Association of Humanistic Counseling, Association of Specialist in Group Work). Other divisions have members interested in broader concerns that confront the current state and future direction of the counseling profession (e.g., Association of Counselor Education and Supervision, Association of Multicultural Counseling and Development). A more detailed description of each of the ACA divisions can be found at https://www.counseling.org/about-us/divisions-regions-and-branches/divisions.

The Professional Identity of Mental Health Counselors

As with all who align with counseling as their profession, mental health counselors share an identity that is grounded in an extensive history of the profession and reflects shared values and perspectives as well as goals, resources, and aspirations for the profession (Daniels, 2002). To this common core of values and goals held by all identified as counselors, those with a specialization as mental health counselors add to their professional identity the understanding of both psychopathology and wellness within a normal development framework to their professional identities (Gerig, n.d.).

With this as a perspective, clinical mental health counselors self-define as a counseling specialty, one that applies wellness and remedial approaches to the treatment of individuals and their related systems within relevant ecological contexts (Gerig, 2014). They strive to facilitate the growth of each person whose life challenges and experience exist along a continuum, ranging from relatively minor emotional distress to severe and persistent mental illness (Gerig, 2014; Granello & Witmer, 2013).

According to Gerig (n.a.), the paradigm from which clinical mental health counselors practice is based on three assumptions: (1) that mental health/wellness and mental illness/pathology lie on distinct but interacting dimensions, (2) persons must be viewed within their unique ecological contexts, and (3) the dimensions of wellness and pathology interact with and extend through the specific levels of ecological context. This paradigm's implications are significant in the formulation of a professional identity for a mental health counselor. The model, as discussed by Gerig (n.d.), points out that with their integration of wellness and pathology, clinical mental health counselors are uniquely positioned to serve in primary care or recovery-oriented settings. Additionally, the paradigm highlights the value clinical mental health counselors assign to the complex interaction of behavior and context, thus directing mental health counselors to employ ecological interventions engaging both direct service as well as indirect strategies such as consultation and advocacy.

The Need and Value of Our Professional Identity

The development and articulation of a counselor's professional identity are vital in that it serves both the individual counselors and the counseling profession (Gale & Austin, 2003; Myers et al., 2002). The issue of a counselor's professional identity addresses two distinct but related areas: (1) the identity of counseling as a unified profession (Kaplan & Gladding, 2011; Kaplan et al., 2014; Mellin et al., 2011) and (2) the development of individual's professional counselor identities (Auxier et al., 2003; Gibson et al., 2010). These two areas mutually inform one another with professional identity (Lile, 2017).

Value for the Profession of Counseling

The ACA (2009) has posited that developing a shared professional identity for counseling is critical to the future of this profession. The ACA has endorsed principles directly tied to counselor professional identity through the 20/20: A Vision for the Future of Counseling workgroup. Part of that vision declares that "sharing a common professional identity is critical for counselors" and "presenting ourselves as a unified profession has multiple benefits" (Kaplan & Gladding, 2011, p. 372).

Our profession is relatively young compared to other mental health professions such as psychiatry and psychology (Remley & Herlihy, 2007). As a profession, counseling is unique among the helping professions, and that uniqueness needs to be promulgated. The uniqueness of counseling as one of many mental health professions is that at its core counseling has a foundation within the humanistic theory (Hansen, 2003), strongly values contextual and culturally sensitive approaches (Kaplan et al., 2014; Mellin et al., 2011), and emphasizes empowering relationships that facilitate human development and wellness (Eriksen & Kress, 2006).

The articulation of a unified professional identity for counselors can strengthen the entire profession, enhance advocacy efforts, and provide standards for training and professional development (Calley & Hawley, 2008; Myers et al., 2002). Articulating the unique contributions of the counseling profession is not only essential to the argument for our profession's existence (Myers et al., 2002) but necessary in the fight to gain parity with and independent recognition from other mental health professions (Calley & Hawley, 2008).

Value for the Individual Mental Health Counselor

At the individual counselor level, the development of one's professional identity serves as a cognitive frame of reference to determine one's counseling role and responsibility (Brott & Myers, 1999). A professional identity serves as a template for what we do and similarly what we choose not to do as professional counselors. Our professional identity contributes to our sense of belonging—to being part of something larger than ourselves (i.e., our profession), as something unique that distinguishes who we are and what we do from others of similar helping professions (Heck, 1990, as cited in Pistole & Roberts, 2002). A strong counselor professional identity can increase ethical behavior, counselor wellness, and an accurate understanding of the counselor's scope of practice (Grimmit & Paisley, 2008; Ponton & Duba, 2009).

The profession's commitment to developing a counselor's professional identity, one reflecting a standard of training, is evident in the fact that the National Board for Certified Counselors (NBCC) will allow only graduates of CACREP-accredited programs to apply for the National Certified Counselor credential, starting in January 2022 (NBCC, 2014). Additional emphasis on counselors exhibiting a shared identity is found in the fact that The National Counselor Examination for Licensure and Examination (NCE; Loesch & Whittinghill, 2012), which is used in most states as the examination to obtain a counseling license, includes knowledge of the counseling profession in the professional orientation section.

Developing a Professional Identity

A counselor's professional identity forms and develops as they assimilate the professional knowledge, skills, and attitudes into their sense of self, as a person and as a professional. Just as one's personal identity develops over time, so, too, will a counselor's professional identity be shaped by their ongoing professional experiences.

It would seem that the more one becomes immersed in the profession—its research, its associations, its activities—the more the elements of a professional identity may take root. Certainly, the more one knows about the profession—its history, its philosophy, its place in contemporary society—the greater chance a professional identity will be claimed. But "knowing" is not the same as "being."

The formation of a counselor's professional identity requires integrating the profession's values, attitudes, and actions with those personally held values, beliefs, and actions (Lile, 2017). This is not an easy nor a quick process. Calley and Hawley (2008) recommended a more active process for fostering the development of one's professional identity. They suggest that counselors actively identify with the distinct values of the counseling profession, engage in professional counseling associations, disseminate scholarship for and about the profession of counseling, utilize theoretical orientations that align with the values of the counseling profession, and obtain training, licensure, and certifications in the profession of counseling. Gibson et al. (2010) posited that this process involved three transformational tasks: (1) the development of a personal definition of counseling, (2) the adoption of responsibility for professional growth, and (3) the recognition of professional identity as interlinked with larger systems (i.e., the professional counseling community and larger systems of practice).

The full realization of one's professional identity will undoubtedly take time. What makes the task even more daunting is that identity is something that becomes you and not something you simply espouse. Ours is not a profession in which you can put on a uniform and step in and step out of your role as a professional. Being a counselor demands that we embrace the values of diversity and respect and unconditionally value all peoples and present with integrity and authenticity. These characteristics cannot be put on at the beginning of our workday only to be removed when checking out of the office. As values guide our practice decisions, these traits need to be embodied in the counselor and not merely employed as a strategy or interpersonal skill. Therefore, the development of a counselor's professional identity cannot stand outside of that counselor's personal identity. For a professional identity to be claimed, it needs to be integrated, assimilated into the very substance of a counselor's view of self and the world.

The development of one's professional identity and the integration of that identity with one's view of self and the world takes time. It does not occur at graduation nor on the occasion of acquiring some credentials. It is the result of ongoing professional development, clinical experience, and reflection. Forming one's professional identity as a mental health counselor is genuinely developmental, taking shape across one's professional life span (Prosek & Hurt, 2014). One's identity as a professional counselor will take shape at the hands of continued education, experience as a practitioner, feedback, and immersion within the professional community (Gibson et al., 2010). But beyond contact, the development of an identity, the assimilation of the values and perspectives of the profession, requires self-reflection and a personal connection to that which is unique about the profession (Gale & Austin, 2003).

Exercise 11.1 invites you to gather data from those experiencing this evolution of professional identity.

Exercise 11.1 The Unfolding of a Professional Identity

Directions: The concept of professional identity and the process that moves one from a conceptual understanding of a profession to the assimilation of that profession's values into a personal view of self and the world is complex and very personal. While you are just beginning the journey in this developmental process, you may find it helpful to gain additional clarity from those at different stages in their professional development.

This exercise invites you to interview mental health counselors currently at different stages in their professional careers. For example, it may prove insightful to interview someone completing their first year of practice versus an individual with 5, 10, or 20 years of professional experience. The following are suggested questions; you should feel free to pose your own questions as well.

Suggested Questions

1. After experiencing life and the world of professional counseling, what if anything has surprised you about practice? About clients? About yourself?
2. Has your work as a professional counselor impacted your personal life? If so, how?
3. Has your work as a professional counselor impacted your view of self? Your opinion of others? Your view of the world?
4. What one piece of advice would you give to a person about the field of professional counseling?

Components of Counselor Professional Identity

Although specific competencies and training standards and curricula can be used to show a distinction between the professional training of a counselor vis-à-vis a psychologist or social worker, the distinction of the counselor's identity rests not in the knowledge base or skill set employed but the philosophy and values that guide practice decisions. For example, Sweeney (2001) noted that a counselor's professional identity is not based on the profession of counseling owning specific theories or techniques. As described in this text, counselors employ approaches that are identified as best practices and empirically supported, as do psychologists and social workers. Thus, it is not the knowledge or skill set that is key to the counselor's professional identity; rather, the distinction rests in the values that guide the employment of these shared mental health strategies and techniques.

The counselor's valuing of normal development, prevention, advocacy, wellness, and empowerment guide the counselor's unique perspective on and application of these strategies. It is the embodiment of these philosophical positions and values that distinguish counseling as a profession (Calley & Hawley, 2008; Puglia, 2008; Remley & Herlihy, 2014; Weinrach et al., 2001; Woo, 2013). As such, each counselor must understand and assimilate these values and perspectives into their own practice decision making. Table 11.2 highlights the uniqueness of a counselor's perspective when contrasted to social work and psychology.

TABLE 11.2 Views on Growth, Wellness, Prevention, and Empowerment

	COUNSELING	PSYCHOLOGY	SOCIAL WORK
Human growth and development	"Committed to enhancing human development through the life span" (ACA, 2014).	"Committed to increasing scientific and professional knowledge of behavior" (APA, 2016).	Presents with a broader focus "to enhance human well-being and help meet the basic human needs of all people" and "focus on individual well-being in a social context and the well-being of society" (NASW, 2017).
Target prevention services	"Counselors facilitate client growth and development in ways to foster the interest and welfare of clients and promote the formation of healthy relationships" (ACA, 2014). Prevention services are targeted to the person.	Employ a less directive approach to prevention. Psychologists "strive to help the public in developing informed judgments and choices concerning human behavior" (APA, 2016).	Focus on prevention in the context of local to global societies (NASW, 2017).
Wellness	"Counseling is a professional relationship that ... accomplish mental health, wellness, education, and career goals" (ACA, 2014).	In contrast to the empowerment focus of counseling, psychologists are called upon to safeguard wellness. "In their professional actions, psychologists seek to safeguard the welfare and rights of those with whom they interact professionally and other affected persons, and the welfare of animal subjects of research" (APA, 2016).	Social work takes a broader social/global perspective on wellness. "Social workers should promote the general welfare of society, from local to global levels, and the development of people, their communities, and their environments" (NASW, 2017).

(Continued)

(*Continued*)

	COUNSELING	PSYCHOLOGY	SOCIAL WORK
Empowerment (i.e., encouraging client autonomy self-advocacy and self-determination)	The ACA (2014) states the following as a core professional value: "honoring diversity and embracing a multicultural approach in support of the worth, dignity, potential, and uniqueness of people within their social and cultural contexts; promoting social justice."	Appears to focus less on the active process of empowerment as in reflecting the psychologists' provision of respect and dignity. "Psychologists respect the dignity and worth of all people, and the rights of individuals to privacy, confidentiality, and self-determination" (APA, 2016).	Similar to counseling, social work appears to value the empowerment of clients. "Social workers seek to enhance the capacity of people to address their own needs" (NASW, 2017).

Pride and the Merger of Personal and Professional Identities

Conceptualizing a profession as a unique, collective identity of shared values, beliefs, and assumptions contributes to the members' sense of pride and security (Daniels, 2002). In addition to knowing the history of our profession, the uniqueness of the values and perspectives that guide what we do—it is also essential to manifest a professional pride in being a mental health counselor.

Having a sense of pride in choosing counseling as a profession is a significant part of having a strong professional identity. Gray (2001), for example, defined counselor professional identity as "understanding and having a sense of pride in one's profession ... [that] is essential both for one's internal satisfaction with one's chosen career and for the continued societal recognition of the profession" (p. 12).

Your pride in becoming a counselor and working as a member of the counseling profession will contribute to your vocational satisfaction and position you to advocate for the profession and those we serve (Myers et al., 2002). The American Mental Health Counseling Association (AMHCA) encourages members to engage with local and national politics to increase the recognition of the profession and ensure equity of treatment among other mental health professions. The AMHCA's website (www.amhca.org/?page=advocacy) serves to keep counselors informed about contemporary issues and ways of getting involved in the promotion of the mental health counseling profession.

One final note. As you grow in your profession and develop your professional identity, you will realize that you *are* a counselor. Like Simone, whose quote opened this chapter, you will be able to respond to the question of "what you do" with an answer that reflects "who you are."

Keystones

- A profession is generally composed of a disciplined group of individuals who possess specialized knowledge and skills and who adhere to an agreed-upon set of ethical standards, having gained some public recognition.

- Essence of professional identity is well depicted in the following description: "the possession of a core set of values, beliefs, and assumptions about the unique characteristics of one's selected profession that differentiates it from other professions" (Weinrach et al., 2001, p. 168).
- Each member of the counseling profession shares a professional identity, one that is augmented by the uniqueness of their specialty area and the diversity in both interests and practice.
- The articulation of a unified professional identity for counselors can strengthen the entire profession, enhance advocacy efforts, and provide standards for training and professional development.
- A strong counselor professional identity serves as a cognitive frame of reference to determine one's counseling role and responsibility; it can increase ethical behavior, counselor wellness, and an accurate understanding of the counselor's scope of practice.
- One's identity as a professional counselor will take shape at the hands of continued education, experience as a practitioner, feedback, and immersion within the professional community.

Additional Resources

American Counseling Association: www.counseling.org

American Mental Health Counselors Association: www.amhca.org

Granello, D., & Young, M. E. (2012). *Counseling today: Foundations of professional identity.* MyHelpingLab Series. Merrill.

Nassar-McMillan, S., & Niles, S. C. (2010). *Developing your identity as a professional counselor: Standards, settings, and specialties.* Brooks/Cole.

References

American Counseling Association. (2009). *20/20 statement of principles advances the profession [News release].* https://www.counseling.org/PressRoom/NewsReleases.aspx?AGuid=4d87a0ce-65c0-4074-89dc-2761cfbbe2ec

American Counseling Association. (2010). 20/20—A vision for the future of counseling. http://counseling.org/20-20/definition.aspx

American Counseling Association. (2014). Code of ethics. https://www.counseling.org/Resources/aca-code-of-ethics.pdf

American Mental Health Counseling Association. (2011). *Standards for the practice of clinical mental health counseling.* http://www.amhca.org/assets/content/AMHCA_Standards_1-26-2012.pdf

American Psychological Association. (2016). Ethical principles of psychologists and code of conduct. https://www.apa.org/ethics/code/

Australian Council of Professions. (2003). *What is a profession?* https://www.professions.org.au/what-is-a-professional/

Auxier, C. R., Hughes, F. R., & Kline, W. B. (2003). Identity development in counselors-in-training. *Counselor Education & Supervision, 43,* 25–38.

Brott, P. E., & Myers, J. E. (1999). Development of professional school counselor identity: A grounded theory. *Professional School Counseling, 2,* 339–348. doi: 10.1002/j.1556-6676.2014.00124x

Calley, N. G., & Hawley, L. D. (2008). The professional identity of counselor educators. *The Clinical Supervisor, 27,* 3–16.

Daniels, L. G. (2002). The relationship between counselor licensure and aspects of empowerment. *Journal of Mental Health Counseling, 24*(3), 213.

Eriksen, K., & Kress, V. E. (2006). The DSM and the professional counseling identity: Bridging the gap. *Journal of Mental Health Counseling, 28,* 202–217.

Freidson, E. (2001). *Professionalism, the third logic: On the practice of knowledge.* University of Chicago Press.

Gale, A. U., & Austin, D. B. (2003). Professionalism's challenges to professional counselors' collective identity. *Journal of Counseling & Development, 81,* 3–10.

Gerig, M. S. (n.d.). *The professional identity of clinical mental health counselors.* https://www.dropbox.com/s/eaasn8378sw5bu3/ProfessionalIdentifyWP_MGFINAL.pdf?dl=0

Gerig, M. S. (2014). *Foundations for clinical mental health counseling: An introduction to the profession.* Pearson.

Gibson, D. M., Dollarhide, C. T., & Moss, J. M. (2010). Professional identity development: A grounded theory of transformational tasks of new counselors. *Counselor Education and Supervision, 50,* 21–38.

Granello, D., & Young, M. E. (2012). *Counseling today: Foundations of professional identity.* MyHelpingLab Series. Merrill.

Granello, P. F., & Witmer, J. M. (2013). The wellness challenge. In P. F. Granello (Ed.), *Wellness counseling* (pp. 2–10). Pearson.

Gray, N. D. (2001). The relationship of supervisor traits to the professional development and satisfaction with the supervisor of post-master's degree counselors seeking state licensure (Unpublished doctoral dissertation). University of New Orleans, LA.

Grimmit, M. A., & Paisley, P. O. (2008). A preliminary investigation of school counselor beliefs regarding important educational issues. *The Journal of Humanistic Counseling, 47*, 99–110.
Hansen, J. T. (2003). Including diagnostic training in counseling curricula: Implications for professional identity development. *Counselor Education & Supervision, 43*, 96–107.
Kaplan, D. M., & Gladding, S. T. (2011). A vision for the future of counseling: The 20/20 principles for unifying and strengthening the profession. *Journal of Counseling & Development, 89*, 367–372.
Kaplan, D. M., Tarvydas, V. M., & Gladding, S. T. (2014). 20/20: A vision for the future of counseling: The new consensus definition of counseling. *Journal of Counseling & Development, 92*, 366–372.
Lile, J. J. (2017). Forming a professional counselor identity: The impact of identity processing style. *The Journal of Counselor Preparation and Supervision, 9*(2). https://repository.wcsu.edu/cgi/viewcontent.cgi?article=1163&context=jcps
Loesch, L., & Whittinghill, D. (2012). *NCE technical manual for the national counselor exam* (Rev. ed.). National Board for Certified Counselors.
Mellin, E. A., Hunt, B., & Nichols, L. M. (2011). Counselor professional identity: Findings and implications for Counseling and interprofessional collaboration. *Journal of Counseling & Development, 89*, 140–147.
Myers, J. E., Sweeney, T. J., & White, V. E. (2002). Advocacy for counseling and counselors: A professional imperative. *Journal of Counseling & Development, 80*, 394–402.
Nassar-McMillan, S., & Niles, S. C. (2010). *Developing your identity as a professional counselor: Standards, settings, and specialties.* Brooks/Cole.
National Association of Social Workers. (2017). *Code of ethics.* https://www.socialworkers.org/About/Ethics/Code-of-Ethics/Code-of-Ethics-English
National Board for Certified Counselors. (2014). *Important announcement.* http://nbcc.org/assets/Change-announcement-flyer_2014.pdf
Parsons, R. D., & Zhang, N. (2013). *Becoming a skilled counselor.* Sage.
Pistole, M. C., & Roberts, A. (2002). Mental health counseling: Toward resolving identity confusions. *Journal of Mental Health Counseling, 24*(1), 1–19.
Ponton, R. F., & Duba, J. D. (2009). The *ACA code of ethics*: Articulating counseling's professional covenant. *Journal of Counseling & Development, 87*, 117–121.
Prosek, E. A., & Hurt, K. M. (2014). Measuring professional identity development among counselor trainees. *Counselor Education and Supervision, 35*, 284–293.
Puglia, B. (2008). The professional identity of counseling students in master's level CACREP-accredited programs (Unpublished doctoral dissertation). Old Dominion University.
Remley, T., & Herlihy, B. (2007) *Ethical, legal, and professional issues in counseling* (2nd ed.). Prentice Hall.
Sweeney, T. J. (2001). Counseling: Historical origins and philosophical roots. In D. C. Locke, J. Myers, & E. L. Herr (Eds.), *The handbook of counseling* (pp. 3–26). Sage.
Weinrach, S. G., Thomas, K. R., & Chan, F. (2001). The professional identity of contributors to the Journal of Counseling & Development: Does it matter? *Journal of Counseling and Development, 79*, 166–170.
Woo, H. (2013). *Instrument construction and initial validation: Professional Identity Scale in Counseling* (PISC) (Doctoral dissertation). Retrieved from ProQuest (UMI No. 3566722).

Ethical and Legal Issues Shaping the Profession

CHAPTER 12

> Fiduciary responsibility ... ours is a seriously responsible profession.
>
> —Ada, licensed professional counselor

Fiduciary responsibility: two words that highlight the responsibility and entrusted role that all counselors are given. *Fiduciary responsibility* refers to the obligation that one party has in relationship with another to act entirely on the other party's behalf and best interest. It is considered the highest standard of care, emphasizing that as mental health counselors we hold a legal and ethical relationship of trust with our clients. The ethical and legal standards that give form to this relationship are the focus of this chapter.

After reading this chapter, the reader will be able to:

- Explain the relationship between values, principles, and codes of ethics.
- Describe the values supporting the American Counseling Association's code of ethics.
- Describe the value of a code of ethics to the profession and the professional.
- Explain the nature of the relationship between the code of ethics and the law.

Ethics and Codes of Conduct

As noted in Chapter 12, one of the defining characteristics of a profession is the existence of a code or set of standards that guide practice. The establishment of a code of ethics signifies a profession's maturation and results from the evolution of a collective professional identity within the organization (Mabe & Rollins, 1986).

A code of ethics, regardless of the profession, provides a structure for articulating norms and expectations for practitioners. It serves as a benchmark against which the performance of the individual and the organization can be assessed (Parsons & Boccone, 2021). For counselors, knowing and acting per our professional code of ethics promotes our professionalism and protects our clients and ourselves from litigation.

Both the American Counseling Association (ACA, 2014) and the American Mental Health Counselors Association (AMHCA, 2020) have developed codes of ethics that inform and regulate the behavior of their members.

Counselors: Codes of Ethical Conduct

As is the case for all codes of ethical practice, our code of ethics reflects the values and moral principles collectively owned and espoused by the members of our counseling profession. Unlike legal mandates that can impact practice decisions, our ethical code is a moral guideline, not a legal one (Neukrug, 2000). This characteristic of ethical codes, of being moral rather than legal in nature, is evident in the current iteration of the ACA's (2014) code of ethics.

The ACA's code of ethics starts with identifying specific professional values that inform all counselors' practice, teaching, supervision, and research (Meyers, 2014). The values highlighted within the preamble of the ACA's code of ethics include (1) enhancing human development throughout the life span; (2) honoring diversity and embracing a multicultural approach in support of the worth, dignity, potential, and uniqueness of people within their social and cultural contexts; (3) promoting social justice; (4) safeguarding the integrity of the counselor–client relationship; and (5) practicing competently and ethically (ACA, 2014).

In turn, these professional values serve as the conceptual basis for the development of the principles that serve as the foundation for a counselor's ethical behavior and decision making. These principles of professional, ethical behavior, as identified in the Preamble of the ACA's code of ethics (2014), are as follows:

- *Autonomy*, or fostering the right to control the direction of one's life
- *Nonmaleficence*, or avoiding actions that cause harm
- *Beneficence*, or working for the good of the individual and society by promoting mental health and well-being
- *Justice*, or treating individuals equitably and fostering fairness and equality
- *Fidelity*, or honoring commitments and keeping promises, including fulfilling one's responsibilities of trust in professional relationships
- *Veracity*, or dealing truthfully with individuals with whom counselors come into professional contact

Although the code has formed these values and principles into statements of ethical behavior, the emphasis on values and principles highlights the fact that it is insufficient for counselors merely to know and be able to espouse the code; the values undergirding the specific principles must become part of the very substance of one's professional identity. The ethical counselor has personally embraced these values as ways of living ethically (Parsons & Boccone, 2021).

Given the importance of personalizing each of these values, there is value in reflecting on each as they manifest in your life. Exercise 12.1 invites you to take a moment to reflect on each and the degree to which you "own" the value as a source of guidance throughout your personal and professional decision making.

Exercise 12.1 Values Embodied

Directions: Review each of the values defined within the Preamble of the ACA's code of ethics and assess the degree to which these guide your decision making and actions, within both your professional and personal life.

DO YOU EMBRACE THE VALUE OF ...	HOW IS YOUR OWNERSHIP OF THESE VALUES EXPRESSED IN YOUR PERSONAL AND PROFESSIONAL DECISION MAKING?	WHAT ACTIONS COULD BE INCREASED, OR DECREASED, AS A WAY OF FULLY EMBODYING THESE VALUES IN YOUR PROFESSIONAL AND PRIVATE LIVES?
Enhancing human development throughout the life span?		
Honoring diversity ... and the dignity and worth of all people?		
Promoting social justice?		
Safeguarding the integrity of the counselor–client relationship?		
Practicing in a competent and ethical manner?		

Codes: Useful and Practical

The values, principles, and codes of conduct detailed within our codes of ethics (ACA, 2014; AMHCA, 2020) are inherently aspirational, serving as a reflection of the loftiest goals of professional practice. Being aspirational, however, does not mean they are less than useful.

As public pronouncements that constitute appropriate professional behavior, our codes of ethics publicly proclaim our values and principles that are key to our unique professional identities; they serve as a framework for the regulation of those in practice, and they help to protect our clients.

Our principles provide each practitioner with a scaffold for ethical and competent practice (Parsons & Boccone, 2021). As a standard, accepted by the members of our profession, the codes provide criteria against which practice decisions and actions can be judged. When confronted with choices, a practitioner can decide on the rightness and wrongness of each option (see Case Illustration 12.1).

CASE ILLUSTRATION 12.1 To Date or Not to Date?

Dr. Hanna Watson is a licensed professional counselor who vividly recalls her work with Juan, a young, aspiring lawyer, who at the time of her contact, presented with extreme anxiety and panic attacks. Her work with Juan proved quite successful, and she terminated the professional relationship, having her last follow-up contact 6 years before the current situation.

Dr. Watson was attending a professional workshop, with several colleagues, on the topic of "Counseling and the Law." To her surprise, she found that Juan (her previous client) was one of the main presenters. Throughout the weeklong training, Dr. Watson found herself more frequently engaging with Juan, professional to professional. What began as conversing over legal issues and topics, most often

(Continued)

(*Continued*)

occurring during workshop breaks, soon morphed into meetings with Juan and other presenters in small group lunches and even drinks after the day's presentation.

On the morning of the final day of the workshop, Juan asked Dr. Watson if it would appropriate for him to call her and maybe "get together." Although the invitation was very enticing to Dr. Watson, she became concerned about the ethics of dating a previous client and the potential that this may pose as a boundary violation.

During the day, Dr. Watson consulted with her colleagues about the appropriateness of accepting this invitation. Everyone agreed that it was a bit unusual and that this might be something to which to be cautious given the nature of their previous relationship. To test the "appropriateness" of accepting the invitation, they turned to the American Counseling Association's code of ethics:

> *Sexual and/or romantic counselor-client interactions or relationships with former clients, their romantic partners, or their family members are prohibited for a period of 5 years following the last professional contact. (ACA, 2014, Principle A.5.c)*

Besides reviewing the ACA standards, she decided to consult the AMHCA's code of ethics (2020) to gain additional clarity around this issue. She found that the AMHCA's code of ethics, Principle I.A.4.b, states:

> *CMHCs should not knowingly enter into a romantic or sexual relationship with a former client. If a CMHC chooses to enter into such a relationship, the burden to demonstrate that neither coercion nor harm to the client has transpired is on the CMHC and not the former client.*

Although it appears that there is nothing explicitly unethical about accepting an invitation to go out with Juan, since her last professional contact with him was more than 6 years ago, it would be helpful for Dr. Watson to consider her previous professional relationship with Juan and consider whether there is anything that might suggest a vulnerability to be harmed if their relationship failed to develop. The colleagues also suggested she consider the potential for exploitation by either party. As a result of their discussion, Dr. Watson decided to meet with Juan and share her concerns before deciding to move forward with the development of their relationship.

Multiple Codes

Professional counseling comes in varied forms of specialization (see Chapter 12). In addressing a specific area of service or the uniqueness of the populations served, each specialized area of counseling will develop its ethical codes. Codes developed by the ACA (2014) and the AMHCA (2020) appear to be the most directly relevant for those engaging as mental health counselors. These codes generally reflect the same principles guiding ethical practice.

The ACA code of ethics (2014) consists of a preamble, a purpose statement, and nine sections addressing specific ethical behavior (see Table 12.1).

TABLE 12.1 ACA Code of Ethics (2014): Specific Areas of Ethical Behavior

Section A: The Counseling Relationship. Section highlights the counselor's primary responsibility to respect the dignity of their clients and promote client welfare. Areas covered include: informed consent, avoiding harm and imposing values, prohibited noncounseling roles and relationships, managing boundaries and professional relationships, fees and business practices, termination and referral, and client neglect and abandonment.

Section B: Confidentiality and Privacy. Respecting the rights of client privacy is the focus of this section. Standards address issues governing disclosure of confidential information and navigating confidentiality when working with families or groups.

Section C: Professional Responsibility. This section discusses the standards of training, credentialing, and professional competences.

Section D: Relationships With Other Professionals. Highlights the need to maintain professional standards when engaging with colleagues, employers, employees, and consultees.

Section E: Evaluation, Assessment, and Interpretation. This section directs counselors to engage specific principles for ethical and cultural sensitivity to the use of assessment techniques. The role and responsibilities of counselors in establishing adequate assessment conditions and performing forensic evaluations are also presented.

Section F: Supervision, Training, and Teaching. These standards set guidelines regarding supervisor and counselor educator competence, relationships with current and former supervisees and students, and the use of case illustrations and innovative techniques, and responsibilities associated with field placements. Supervisors are directed to ensure the welfare of clients treated by trainees and monitor the performance of the supervisee.

Section G: Research and Publication. This section addresses specific ethical issues when involved with human participant research.

Section H: Distance Counseling, Technology, and Social Media. The need for counselor knowledge and competence in the use of technology and its application is the focus of this section. The need to employ measures such as encryption to ensure client privacy is discussed as is the effect of distance counseling approaches and the need for special attention to informed consent, confidentiality, client verification and security of health-related information.

The codes of ethics articulated by the AMHCA (2020) reflect the unique needs of the clinical mental health counseling profession. As is true for the ACA code of ethics (2014), the AMHCA code begins with a preamble, followed by six sections of detailed guidance to clinical mental health counselors (see Table 12.2).

TABLE 12.2 AMHCA Code of Ethics (2020)

i. **Commitment to Clients.** This section addresses issues of counselor–client relationships, the counseling process, counselor responsibility and integrity, assessment and diagnosis, record keeping, fee arrangements and bartering, and other roles.

ii. **Commitment to Other Professionals.** This section addresses issues of relationships with colleagues and clinical consultation.

iii. **Commitment to Students, Supervisees, and Employee Relationships.** This section addresses issues regarding relationships with students, interns, and employees; commitment for clinical supervision; and confidentiality of clinical supervision.

iv. **Commitment to the Profession.** Areas covered include teaching, research and publications, and service on public or private boards and other organizations.

v. **Commitment to the Public.** Directs members in regards to public statements; marketing.

vi. **Resolution of Ethical Problems.** Members are encouraged to employ recognized procedures for ethical decision making to resolve ethical conflicts.

Both codes of ethics serve as guidelines for ethical conduct and practice. The codes share similar structures and positions on general themes of ethical conduct. For example, both codes emphasize respecting the dignity and promoting the welfare of the client (see ACA, 2014, Section A; AMHCA, 2020, Section A).

Although some differences do exist (see Table 12.3), these tend to be more a matter of presentation than substance. Both codes direct counselors to embrace their ethical and moral obligations as fiduciaries in the service of their client's welfare.

TABLE 12.3 Comparison of Selected Standards

PROFESSIONAL STANDARD	AMERICAN COUNSELING ASSOCIATION (2014)	AMERICAN MENTAL HEALTH COUNSELING ASSOCIATION (2020)
Competency	**C.2.a Boundaries of Competence:** Counselors practice only within the boundaries of their competence, based on their education, training, supervised experience, state, and national professional credentials, and appropriate professional experience.	**C.1 Competence:** The maintenance of high standards of professional competence is a responsibility shared by all CMHCs in the best interest of the client, the public, and the profession. **C.1.b**: CMHCs provide only those services and use only those techniques for which they are qualified by education, training, or experience.
Informed consent	**Section A: The Counseling Relationship** **A.2.a Informed Consent:** Counselors have an obligation to review in writing and verbally with clients the rights and responsibilities of both the counselor and the client. Informed consent is an ongoing part of the counseling process, and counselors appropriately document discussions of informed consent throughout the counseling relationship.	**B.1.2 Informed Consent:** Clients have the right to understand what to expect in counseling and the freedom to choose whether and with whom they enter a counseling relationship. **B.1.2.a:** CMHCs provide information that allows clients to make an informed decision about selecting a provider.
Confidentiality	**Section A: The Counseling Relationship** **A.2.b Types of Information Needed:** Clients have the right to confidentiality and to be provided with an explanation of its limitations (including how supervisors and/or treatment team professionals are involved); to obtain clear information about their records; to participate in the ongoing counseling plans; and to refuse any services or modality change and to be advised of the consequences of such refusal. **B.1.b Respecting Client Rights:** Counselors respect the privacy of prospective and current clients. Counselors request private information from clients only when it is beneficial to the counseling process. **B.1.c Respect for Confidentiality:** Counselors protect the confidential information of prospective and current clients. Counselors disclose information only with appropriate consent or with sound legal or ethical justification.	**I.A.2 Confidentiality:** CMHCs have an obligation to safeguard information about individuals obtained in the course of practice, teaching, and research. **I.A.2.a:** Confidentiality is a right granted to all clients of mental health counseling services.

Boundaries	**A.6.b Extending Counseling Boundaries:** Counselors consider the risks and benefits of extending current counseling relationships beyond conventional parameters. **A.5.d Friends or Family Members:** Counselors are prohibited from engaging in counseling relationships with friends or family members with whom they have an inability to remain objective. **A.5.a Sexual and/or Romantic Relationships Prohibited:** Sexual and/or romantic counselor–client interactions or relationships with current clients, their romantic partners, or their family members are prohibited. **A.5.c Sexual and/or Romantic Relationships With Former Clients:** Sexual and/or romantic counselor-client interactions or relationships with former clients, their romantic partners, or their family members are prohibited for a period of 5 years following the last professional contact.	**I.A.3.a Dual/Multiple Relationships** CMHCs make every effort to avoid dual/multiple relations with clients that could impair professional judgment or increase the risk of harm. **I.A.4.a:** Romantic or sexual relationships with clients and their immediate family are strictly prohibited. CMHCs do not counsel persons with whom they have had a previous sexual relationship. **I.A.4.b:** CMHCs should not knowingly enter into a romantic or sexual relationship with a former client. If a CMHC chooses to enter into such a relationship, the burden to demonstrate that neither coercion nor harm to the client has transpired is on the CMHC and not from client.

Guides to Decision Making

Ethical concerns are rarely, if ever, clear cut. Selecting the right or most appropriate course of action can be challenging. For example, how should a counselor respond when a very appreciative client offers a very expensive gift as a sign of that appreciation? Is it appropriate to accept? How might a failure to accept impact the client or the therapeutic relationship? Are gift giving and gift reception enabling the maintenance of a less than healthy need, or might it reflect the client's culture and cultural values?

Knowing the ethical principles that are provided to guide professional decisions and actions and employing a useful, ethical decision-making model can assist the counselor in selecting a course of action that is most beneficial to the client and the therapeutic relationship. Although the directive for a counselor to engage in ethical practice is clear, the "how" of fulfilling that directive is not as clear.

In its statement of purpose, the ACA code of ethics (2014) states that counselors are expected to use a credible decision-making approach to resolving dilemmas:

> When counselors are faced with ethical dilemmas that are difficult to resolve, they are expected to engage in a carefully considered ethical decision-making process.

Although directed to employ decision-making approaches to resolving ethical dilemmas, no one decision-making model is set as a standard to be useful in all situations. There appears to be more than 30 ethical decision-making models currently available (Cottone & Clause, 2000). In selecting the approach to the applications of our professional ethics, it is essential, regardless of the model employed, to use one "that can bear public scrutiny in its application" (ACA, 2014, p. 3).

Parsons and Boccone (2021) integrated key elements from many traditional approaches to ethical decision making (see Forester-Miller & Davis, 2016; Garcia et al., 2003; Tarvydas, 2012) and articulated an eight-step approach to ethical decision making. The specific steps and sample questions that should be considered at each point in the process are presented in Table 12.4.

TABLE 12.4 Ethical Decision Making: Steps and Guiding Questions

Step 1: Preparation for ethical practice.

Before encountering an ethical dilemma, counselors need to have a fundamental understanding of the ethical and legal standards guiding practice. It is also essential to have an awareness of one's values and worldview as they align with these standards.

- Am I knowledgeable of the latest code of ethics?
- Is the latest version of the code of ethics available?
- Am I familiar with some of the contemporary challenges to ethical practice?
- Am I aware of my values, prejudices, bias, and view of self and others?
- Am I aware of those areas of need or self-interest that may come under challenge in an ethical dilemma?

Step 2: Identify the problem.

It is crucial to identify the nature of the issue, the expanse of stakeholders involved, and the potential impact on each participant.

- What are the facts of the situation?
- Is this a personal problem?
- Is this a clinical problem?
- Is this a legal problem?
- Is this an ethical problem?
- Is it more than one of the above?
- Is legal advice needed?
- How might the problem be viewed by one having a different worldview?

Step 3: Formulation of ethical concern.

With a more definite sense of the issue being confronted, the counselor should refer to the ethical standards (e.g., ACA, 2014; AMHCA, 2020) to identify the specific principles applicable to this issue.

- How might the dilemma relate to specific principles listed in the professional code of ethics?
- How might the dilemma relate to institutional policies of the context in which you experienced the dilemma?
- How might the dilemma relate to your values?
- How might the dilemma be related to your worldview?
- Does the dilemma tap into your personal needs, biases, or prejudices?

Step 4: Determine the nature and dimensions of the dilemma.

It is essential to revisit the potential impact this issue may have on the client and the family, community, and even the institution in which one works. It is vital to examine the issue in light of counseling's foundational principles.

- What implications might this have for the principle of autonomy?
- What implications might this have for the principle of nonmaleficence?
- What implications might this have for the principle of beneficence?
- What implications might this have for the principle of justice?
- What implications might this have for the principle of fidelity?
- What are the possible impacts of this dilemma on all stakeholders?

Generate potential courses of action.

- Have you brainstormed possible courses of action (being nonjudgmental as to feasibility)?
- Have you engaged a colleague in the process?

Step 5: Generate potential courses of action.

Brainstorming potential courses of action is the next step, and often engaging colleagues or supervisors may prove helpful.

- Am I resisting judging or evaluating ideas?
- Is the goal to create several options—thinking out of the box?
- Am I thinking broadly and creatively?

Step 6: Assessment of options.

With a variety of approaches identified, each should be assessed in terms of cost/benefits and feasibility of implementation.

- What is the possible impact (both positive and negative) of each course of action on the client (e.g., physical, psychological, social realms)?
- What is the possible impact on the principles of doing no harm and promoting the client's welfare?
- What is the possible impact (both positive and negative) of each course of action on other stakeholders (family, friends, coworkers)?
- What is the possible impact (both positive and negative) of each course of action on the client's community?
- What is the possible impact (both positive and negative) of each course of action on the counseling profession's public view?
- How will the option look to others once it is known?
- Would this option be applied to others within similar circumstances?
- Would this option be recommended to a colleague in a similar situation?

Step 7. Selection and implementation.

While selecting and implement a course of action, it is crucial to remain open to additional information and adjust accordingly.

- Are the needed resources available for the implementation of the selected course of action?
- Is there a set plan or steps in place to support implementation?

Step 8. Documentation.

As a means of establishing a base of accountability, the counselor should document the steps taken along with the outcome experienced.

- Have I recorded the decisions I have made and the resources I may have employed in making those decisions?
- Does my documentation adequately convey my desire to tend to the welfare of my client while adhering to laws and regulations governing my practice?
- Is the confidentiality of my client maintained even when documenting the issues and the dilemmas I encountered?

Source: Adapted from Richard D. Parsons and Peter J. Boccone, "Questions-Guiding Ethical Decision Making," *Ethical Decision Making: A Guide for Counselors in the 21st Century*, pp. 36–37. Copyright © 2020 by Cognella, Inc. Reprinted with permission.

The Legal Connection

A profession's code of ethical conduct can often give form to, and be shaped by, legislation. Although laws governing practice are generally supportive of the profession's monitoring of its members' behaviors, there are situations, such as licensing requirements, where the law may supplement the aspirations found within the code of ethics. There are also circumstances, however, where the forces of the law have actively given shape to practice, as is the case of mandated reporting and duty to warn.

Our current practice of providing clients with informed consent—especially with an articulation of the limits of confidentiality—is a direct reflection of the impact that the legal system can have on professional standards. This focus on limited confidentiality reflects the findings of a landmark decision in *Tarasoff v. The Regents of the University of California* (1976) (see Case Illustration 12.2).

CASE ILLUSTRATION 12.2 Tarasoff Summary

The case of Tarasoff v. The Regents of the University of California involved Prosenjit Poddar, a University of California graduate student; Tatiana Tarasoff, a woman he met at a dance class with whom he became infatuated; and his therapist, Lawrence Moore, a psychologist at Berkeley's Cowell Memorial Hospital. Mr. Poddar presented as depressed and obsessed about Tarasoff and began stalking her. In his final session with Dr. Moore, he revealed that he intended to kill Tatiana. Having diagnosed him with an acute paranoid schizophrenic reaction, Dr. Moore notified campus police, suggesting he be placed in a psychiatric hospital for observation. After a brief detention, Poddar was released. He did not return to therapy and once again began to stalk Tarasoff. On October 27, 1959, he stabbed her to death.

In this case, although informing campus police about the risk factor Poddar presented, Dr. Moore did not inform Tarasoff or her family. Tarasoff's parents sued Dr. Moore and the university. Although this case was initially dismissed on the grounds that the doctor had met his duty to warn, upon appeal the U.S. Supreme Court in 1974 found that mental health professionals do have a duty to warn clearly identified potential victims.

Given the potential impact on both the services we provide and those in need to access our services, all counselors need to remain advocates for the profession. Both the ACA and the AMHCA are engaged in government affairs and public policy agenda and invite all members to participate (see the websites listed in the Additional Resources).

Keystones

- A code of ethics, regardless of the profession, provides a structure for the articulation of norms and expectations for practitioners.
- Our codes call us to (1) embrace the inherent worth and dignity of each client; (2) respect each client's uniqueness, autonomy, and right to self-determination; (3) honor human growth and development; and (4) respect the diversity within our clientele.
- The law is generally supportive or neutral, with both the code and the law mutually impacting each other.
- Counselors are expected to be familiar with a credible model of ethical decision making, one that can bear public scrutiny.

Additional Resources

American Counseling Association. (2014). *ACA code of ethics.*

American Counseling Association. (2020). *Government affairs and public policy agency 2020.* https://www.counseling.org/docs/default-source/government-affairs/government-affairs-and-public-policy-2020-agenda.pdf?sfvrsn=5fd25e2c_4

American Mental Health Counselors Association. (n.d.). *AMHCA's policy agenda.* https://www.amhca.org/advocacy/policyagenda

Dobrin, A. (2012). Why ethics is hard. *Psychology Today.* https://www.psychologytoday.com/us/blog/am-i-right/201202/why-ethics-is-hard

Fisher, M. A. (2005). *Ethical decision-making model.* Center for Ethical Practice. http://www.centerforethicalpractice.org/publications/models-mary-alice-fisher-phd/ethical-decision-making-model/

Parsons, R. D., & Boccone, P. J. (2021). *Ethical decision making: A guide for counselors in the 21st century.* Cognella Academic Press.

Parsons, R. D., & Dickinson, K. L. (2017). *Ethical practice in the human services.* Sage.

Sisti, D. A., Caplan, A. L., & Rimon-Greenspan, H. (2014). *Applied ethics in mental health care: An interdisciplinary readers.* MIT Press.

References

American Counseling Association. (2014). *ACA code of ethics*. https://www.counseling.org/knowledge-center/ethics

American Mental Health Counselors Association. (2020). *AMHCA code of ethics*. https://www.amhca.org/HigherLogic/System/DownloadDocumentFile.ashx?DocumentFileKey=24a27502-196e-b763-ff57-490a12f7edb1&forceDialog=0

Cottone, R. R., & Claus, R. E. (2000). Ethical decision-making models: A review of the literature. *Journal of Counseling and Development, 78*, 39–45.

Forester-Miller, H., & Davis, T. E. (2016). *Practitioner's guide to ethical decision making* (Rev. ed.). http://www.counseling.org/docs/default-source/ethics/practioner's-guide-to-ethical-decision-making.pdf

Garcia, J. G., Cartwright, B., Winston, S. M., & Borzuchowska, B. (2003). A transcultural integrative model for ethical decision making in counseling. *Journal of Counseling & Development, 81*(30), 268–278.

Mabe, A., & Rollins, S. (1986). The role of a code of ethical standards in counseling. *Journal of Counseling & Development, 64*, 294–297.

Meyers, L. (2014). A living document of ethical guidance. *Counseling Today*. http://ct.counseling.org/2014/05/a-living-document-of-ethical-guidance/

Neukrug, E. (2000). *Theory, practice, and trends in human services: An introduction to an emerging profession* (2nd ed.). Wadsworth/Thomson Learning.

Parsons, R. D., & Boccone, P. J. (2021). *Ethical decision making: A guide for counselors in the 21st century*. Cognella Academic Press.

Tarasoff v. The Regents of the University of California, 551 P.2d 334 (Cal.Sup.Ct., 1976).

Tarvydas, V. M. (2012). Ethics and ethical decision-making. In D. R. Maki & V. M. Tarvydas (Eds.), *The professional practice of rehabilitation counseling* (pp. 339–379). Springer Publishing.

CHAPTER 13

Professional Development

Beyond a Graduate Degree

What are all those initials after her name?

—Brianna, a graduate student

Brianna's question was in response to seeing one of her professors list her name followed by PhD, LPC, NCC, LPCMH, and ACS. This extensive list of letters supporting a professor's name could be viewed as quite an alphabet soup but one of which her professor is quite proud. Each of these initials represents her professor's level of education, training, experience, and specialized knowledge and skill set.

Perhaps for a student entering a graduate program in mental health counseling the focus is solely on achieving the degree at the end of the program. The acquisition of a master's degree is certainly something to celebrate. A master's degree is necessary for entry into the profession. With a diploma in hand, this graduate can then engage in professional practice under the supervision of a qualified mental health professional.

A graduate degree is necessary, but not sufficient, if one is to grow in the profession and work in the area of mental health services they desire. As suggested by the many initials following Brianna's professor's name, counselors can and do pursue additional education following graduate school. This chapter addresses the academic preparation necessary to become a mental health counselor as well as the "what," "why," and "how" of professional development and the acquisition of certifications in specialized areas as well as professional licensing.

Upon completion of this chapter, the reader will be able to:

- Explain the role and function of CACREP.
- Describe how registry, certification, and licensure differ.
- Explain the problem of portability.
- Describe current efforts to address the challenge of portability.

Graduate Training: A First Step

According to the American Mental Health Counseling Association (AMHCA), prior to calling yourself a clinical mental health counselor, you will need to satisfy several educational requirements and training standards. Clinical mental health counselors have as a foundation for their professional development a master's degree in counseling.

In the past, the nature of that training and degree varied from institution to institution but most often provided a foundational skill set distinct from other behavioral health disciplines. Historically, clinical mental health degree programs varied in length and design, across institutions. However, to unify the training process, the AMHCA, in 2016, delineated specific curricular experiences and a required minimum of a 60-semester-hour program as a standard for clinical mental health training.

As a specialty area of counseling, clinical mental health counselors are expected to have knowledge and expertise that goes beyond that considered fundamental for the general practice of professional counseling (American Counseling Association [ACA], 2004; Myers & Sweeney, 2001). Currently, the national standards for clinical mental health counselors' training are established by the Council for Accreditation of Counseling and Related Educational Programs (CACREP, 2016).

The general curricular model established by CACREP consists of three broad components: a common core curriculum, standards for the specializations, and professional practice experiences. Standards associated with the foundations, contextual dimensions, and practice of clinical mental health counseling helps ensure that students intending to specialize as clinical mental health counselors are equipped with the knowledge and skills needed to address a wide variety of circumstances within the context of clinical mental health counseling (CACREP, 2016). The specific standards for both "core" and "specialty" are listed in Chapter 1.

CACREP sets standards for and renders accreditation decisions on the following programs: addiction counseling; career counseling; clinical mental health counseling; clinical rehabilitation counseling; college counseling and student affairs; marital, couple, and family counseling; school counseling; and counselor education and supervision (doctoral level only). CACREP standards are employed to assess the overall quality of the learning environment, its administrative structure, and organization; the program's objectives, curriculum, and clinical instruction; the faculty and staff; program organization and administration; and evaluation procedures.

The number of programs seeking CACREP accreditation continues to grow. Many states are now requiring clinical mental health counselors seeking licensure to have been graduates of an institution accredited by CACREP. Although research is needed to test any claims for the superiority of clinical training obtained in CACREP-approved programs, it is clear that graduating from a CACREP-accredited program supports professional credibility for the graduate and facilitates their entry into the licensing and credentialing processes.

Credentialing

Credentialing refers to a formalized process of obtaining, verifying, and assessing the qualifications and competence of an individual by a third party with the relevant authority to issue such credentials. There are various levels of credentials that a counselor can seek following the acquisition of a master's degree; these include registry, certification, and licensure.

During the credentialing process, the applicant must provide documentation supporting their educational background, training, clinical experience, and licensure status. The types of documentation required can vary across and within the various types of credentialing. Students would do well to understand the types of credentials available and be sure that their curriculum fulfills the academic requirements of the relevant credentialing bodies.

Registry Listing

Applying for listing upon a registry is a relatively simple and minimally demanding process. Being listed on a registry allows a mental health counselor to share information with the marketplace in support of receiving referrals.

Being accepted for a registry is a statement that the individual has completed requirements mandated for the practice of mental health counseling. For example, some states have created registries for mental health professions identifying those who have met standards for counseling with a specific population (e.g., bilingual) or serve specialty areas of practice (e.g., eating disorders). For example, New York State (http://nymhca.macusa.net:591/nymhca/search.htm) provides a search engine that allows consumers to enter their location or specialty sought and be provided with a listing of counselors that are on the registry.

Being listed on a registry is not an endorsement or certification of one's competencies. It is merely a statement that one has met the minimal standards for recognition in this field of practice.

Certifications and Specializations

Certification is a process that is more stringent than that employed with registration. It is a process typically created by a profession or a specific group within a profession to identify those individuals who have met specific professional qualifications. Earning certification is evidence that a counseling professional possesses specialized expertise in a subset of the field. In many cases, certifications focus on niche areas that do not confer licenses. For example, a counselor may seek certification for treating an identified population, as would be the case of certification as an addictions counselor, or a counselor may wish to be certified in the use of specific techniques, such as eye movement desensitization and reprocessing (EMDR). The process, which is voluntary, requires the applicant to document meeting or exceeding the minimum standards for practice as set by the profession.

Certification often proves attractive for marketing to potential clients and entry into specific forms of employment. Including a certification on a resume may entice prospective employers looking for those who demonstrate expertise and a commitment to a particular area of the field. Counselor certification leads to increased opportunities for career advancement and professional development.

Certification allows the individual to employ a title or associate a set of credentials with their name. Certification is one way that counselors enhance their expertise, assert their professional identity, and bolster their resume (Paterson, 2006). Achieving certification enhances a counselor's professional reputation and credibility.

A Wide Array of Certifications

Numerous certifications are available (see Table 13.1). Each certification designates the training and experience requirements for that unique certification. Certifications are offered at the state and national levels. National and international certifications validate the level of knowledge, training, and expertise to clients, employers, and the public. National certifications can be acquired through the National Board of Certified Counselors (NBCC) and the AMHCA.

TABLE 13.1 Sample of Certification in Specialization

Approved Clinical Supervisor (ACS). The ACS credential ensures that mental health professionals have met national supervision standards and encourages the professional growth of clinical supervisors.
American Association of Sexuality Educators, Counselors, and Therapists (AASECT) Certified Sex Therapist. To become a Certified Sex Therapist, licensed clinicians must obtain specific core knowledge and AASECT-supervised clinical experience.
Certified Cognitive-Behavioral Therapist (CCBT). To become a CCBT, applicants must have a master's or doctoral degree in psychology, counseling, or related field, 6 years of postgraduate experience providing CBT, letters of recommendation, and successful completion of an introductory certification program in CBT. Certified Cognitive-Behavioral Group Therapist (CBGT) certification is also available.
Certified Clinical Mental Health Counselor (CCMHC). A specialty certification for counselors in clinical mental health earned in addition to the NCC credential by completing additional clinical client contact hours and passing the National Clinical Mental Health Counseling Examination.
Certified Eating Disorders Specialist (CEDS). Professionals who demonstrate clinical expertise through education, experience, and examination are eligible for certification as a CEDS.
Certified Group Psychotherapist (CGP). This international certification is offered to master's-level clinicians who meet internationally accepted criteria of education, training, and experience in group psychotherapy.
Certified Rehabilitation Counselor (CRC). This internationally recognized certification aims to set the standard of quality rehabilitation counseling for clinicians working to support individuals with disabilities.
Dialectical Behavior Therapist (DBT). Candidates must be licensed as a psychologist, counselor, or in a related field and must complete DBT educational criteria, skills training, educational requirements, and supervised clinical hours.
Equine Assisted Psychotherapist (EAGALA). The EAGALA model requires a cofacilitating team that must include a mental health professional and an equine specialist professional in all settings. The mental health professional must have a degree in psychology, counseling, or a related field and be under a governing board or association that they are accountable to hold up standards of practice.
Eye Movement Desensitization and Reprocessing (EMDR). Licensed clinicians with 2 years of experience in their field who have completed an approved training program, clinical sessions, consultation, and continuing education in EMDR are eligible to work toward certification in EMDR.
Licensed Marriage and Family Therapist (LMFT). To become licensed in this core mental health profession, therapists must graduate from an accredited program, gain supervised clinical experience, and pass the state licensing exam.
Music Therapist, Board Certified (MT-BC). Music therapists are eligible to become board certified after completing the academic and clinical training requirements identified by the American Music Therapy Association and passing the board certification examination.
National Certified Addiction Counselor, Level I (NCACI). Certified or Licensed Substance Use Disorder Counselors with 3 years of supervised experience, continuing education, and a passing score on the national examination for Level 1 are eligible to apply for NCACI.
National Certified Addiction Counselor, Level II (NCACII). The NCACII is a step up from NCACI because applicants must also have a bachelor's degree and at least 5 years of supervised experience as a Substance Use Disorder Counselor.
National Certified Counselor (NCC). The NCC certification is offered to clinicians who have completed an eligible master's program, postgraduate supervised clinical experience, and passed the National Counselor Exam.
National Certified School Counselor (NCSC). A specialty credential for counselors who work in schools with students, parents, and teachers.
Registered Expressive Arts Therapist (REAT). Clinicians with a master's or doctoral degree and one of five combinations of clinical work and arts involvement can work toward becoming an REAT.
Registered Play Therapist (RPT). Licensed mental health professionals with core coursework, supervised clinical experience, and training in play therapy are eligible to work towards an RPT.

State certifications often serve as the portal for entry into professional practice, as would be the case, for example, for states requiring special certification for school counseling positions.

NBCC Certifications

The NBCC offers three of the most commonly sought counselor certifications, the National Certified Counselor credential, the Master Addictions Counseling certification, and the Clinical Mental Health Counselor certification.

National Certified Counselor

Perhaps the most widely recognized national counseling certification is the NBCC's National Certified Counselor (NCC) credential (Schweiger et al., 2011). Counselors seeking the NCC credential must document holding a degree from either a CACREP-accredited counseling program or a master's-level program in counseling with a minimum of 48 graduate-level semester hours or 72 quarter hours, engaging in a minimum of 100 hours of counseling supervision, completing a minimum of 3,000 clock hours of postmaster's counseling experience within 24 months, demonstrating satisfactory performance on the National Counselor Examination (NCE), and ensuring that their behavior adheres to the standards identified in the NBCC's code of ethics. Of particular note is that beginning January 1, 2022, individuals applying for the NCC credential will have to hold a graduate degree from a CACREP-accredited counselor education program.

According to the NBCC website (https://www.nbcc.org/resources/nccs/marketyourself), acquiring the NCC is a public statement to colleagues, clients, and employers that the holder of the credential has met high national standards for professional counseling. Obtaining such a credential lets consumers know that the holder is committed and dedicated to quality services and invested in continuing education and ongoing professional development. Additionally, having the NCC serves as a springboard for the acquisition of additional certifications in specialty areas.

Master Addictions Counseling Certification

Another certification often sought by those in clinical mental health counseling is the Master Addictions Counseling, or MAC, certification. MAC certification was created jointly by the ACA, specifically the International Association of Addiction and Offenders Counselors (IAAOC), and the NBCC. The certification signifies that a counselor has specialized training and experience in the treatment of substance abuse and dependence. Counselors holding the MAC credential are eligible to seek Substance Abuse Professional (SAP) status through the U.S. Department of Transportation (U.S. DOT). With SAP credentialing, a counselor is recognized as being able to evaluate employees who have violated a Department of Transportation drug and alcohol program regulation and make recommendations concerning education, treatment, follow-up testing, and aftercare (U.S. DOT, 2020).

To achieve the MAC from the NBCC, a counselor must first be an NCC. In addition to holding NCC certification, one must be able to document a minimum of 12 semester hours of graduate coursework in addictions counseling, including drug terminology, theories of addictions, and addictions treatment methods. Up to six semester hours of coursework in group counseling (limit three semester hours) and/or family counseling (limit three semester hours) may be included.

There is provision for those seeking certification by way of continuing education hours. In this case, a total of 500 continuing education hours of addictions-specific continuing education can be substituted for the coursework. Beyond coursework, candidates must document 3 years of supervised experience as an addictions counselor at no fewer than 20 hours per week. Two of the three years must have been completed after the counseling master's degree was conferred. Finally, all applicants are required to pass the Examination for Master Addictions Counselors (EMAC).

The Association for Addiction Professionals (NAADAC; https://www.naadac.org) is composed of addiction counselors, educators, and other addiction-focused healthcare professionals who specialize in addiction prevention, treatment, recovery support, and education. It also provides independent certification for the MAC. The eligibility requirements are (https://www.naadac.org/mac):

- Master's degree or higher in substance use disorders/addiction and/or related counseling subjects (social work, mental health counseling, marriage and family, psychology, medical doctor) from a regionally accredited institution of higher learning.
- Current credential or license as a substance use disorders/addiction counselor or professional counselor (social worker, mental health, marriage and family therapist, psychologist, medical doctor, LAP-C) issued by a state or credentialing authority.
- At least 3 years of full-time or 6,000 hours of supervised experience as a substance use disorders/addiction counselor.
- At least 500 contact hours of education and training in substance use disorders/addiction.
  - Must include at least 6 hours of ethics training within the last 6 years.
  - Must include at least 6 hours of HIV/other pathogens training within the last 6 years.
- A passing score on one of the following exams:
  - MAC exam through NCC AP.
  - eMAC exam through the NBCC.
  - AADC exam through the International Certification & Reciprocity Consortium (IC & RC).

Certified Clinical Mental Health Counselor

Certification as a Certified Clinical Mental Health Counselor was established in 1993 through joint efforts of the National Academy of Clinical Mental Health Counselors (NACMH) and the NBCC. CCMHC sets uniform standards of competency for those identified as clinical mental health counselors. To become certified as a Clinical Mental Health Counselor one needs to hold a degree from either a CACREP-accredited counseling program or a master's-level program in counseling with a minimum of 60 graduate-level semester hours or 90 quarter hours, document a minimum of 100 hours of counseling supervision, complete a minimum of 3,000 clock hours of postmaster's clinical client contact within 24 months, demonstrate satisfactory performance on the National Clinical Mental Health Counseling Examination (NCMHCE), provide a video or audio recording of a clinical session, and ensure that their behavior adheres to the standards identified in the NBCC's Code of Ethics.

One of the benefits of this certification is that it opens doors to insurance carriers and third-party payers that are closed to those without such certification (Litchfield & Watson, 2009).

American Mental Health Counseling Association

The AMHCA offers qualified mental health counselors (CMHCs) three professional development certifications:

- Certification–Clinical Mental Health Counseling Specialist
- Certification–Diplomate in Advanced Clinical Mental Health Counseling Practice
- Certification–Fellow in Clinical Mental Health Counseling Education and Research

The AMHCA credentials are for licensed clinical mental health counselors who are currently practicing. An AMHCA credential/specialty certification signifies that the holder has met the highest standards developed in the clinical mental health counseling profession nationally in addition to having experience and supervision working with specific populations. Each credential has its criteria. Application requirements can be found at www.amhca.org/career/credential/apply.

Licensure

Within the counseling profession, state licensure stands as the most prestigious credential to obtain. Unlike certification, which is trade sanctioned and granted by individual professional guilds (e.g., NBCC), licensure is a government-sanctioned credential issued by state licensing boards.

Licensure is a statutory process providing regulatory power to the state. As a legal process, licensure governs and regulates the use of a professional title (e.g., Licensed Mental Health Counselor, Licensed Professional Counselor), as well as the scope of practice in that state (i.e., an identified set of techniques and practices that is limited to those professionals holding the counselor license). Essentially, licensure laws spell out who can legally use the term *licensed counselor* and provide counseling services in a state.

Licensure laws also allow states to specify the precise requirements for licensure within the particular state. These include requirements for education, clinical experience and supervision, the examination of applicants, continuing education, and licensure fees.

A clinical mental health counselor who is licensed can legally use the specific professional title accepted by that state and engage in the activities (i.e., the scope of practice) of the profession defined by the law. The value of licensure is that it not only regulates the use of title but regulates the actual practice of the profession, thus contributing to the unique identity of that profession (Corey et al., 2015).

Portability

All 50 states, as well as Puerto Rico, the District of Columbia, and Guam, provide for licensure for mental health counselors. However, there is no single national standard, and thus requirements for licensure vary from state to state. Because there is no one unified licensure law, it is vital to understand and practice within the parameters of the state law in which one is providing services.

Information on the licensure requirements and articulation of the allowable scope of practice can be gathered by contacting the licensure board in the state in which a counselor intends to practice. These licensing boards are typically charged with the development of administrative rules regarding professional practice, the application for and renewal of licenses, the approval of providers of continuing education, the administration of licensure exams, and the enforcement of the ethics code. NBCC provides an accessible directory that allows a counselor to click on any state of interest to gain contact regarding licensure in that state (www.nbcc.org/directory).

The failure to have a single standard for identifying educational requirements for licensure, or the scope of practice, and even a common licensure title have led to market confusion and issues with counselors moving licenses from one state to another (i.e., portability issues). As it currently stands, counselors who move between or practice in more than one state must obtain a license in each state where they want to offer services.

A congressional report addressing issues in health care noted that "Overcoming unnecessary licensure barriers to cross-state practice is seen as part of a general strategy to expedite the mobility of health professionals to address workforce needs and improve access to health care services, particularly in light of increasing shortages of healthcare professionals" (Wakefield, 2013, p. 5).

Although this statement initially focused on concerns in the provision of physical health care, the same utility and value of portability and the removal of unnecessary licensure barriers to cross-state practice apply to mental health services and counseling practitioners. All major professional counseling-related organizations agree that establishing a system of portability is a top priority.

The issue of portability is complicated. Establishing portability is challenged by varying philosophical orientation among the professional associations and issues of state's autonomy in the regulation of professional practice within their boundaries. One major impediment has to do with degree requirements, including required hours, coursework, clinical training hours, and even professional identity, that have been specified by the states.

Portability requires that professional counseling organizations establish a uniform educational and training requirement for portability. With different state codes and substantial interstate politics, achieving portability is difficult.

The Department of Defense provided a significant push toward acceptance of portability and the establishment of an educational standard for practitioners by approving licensed mental health counselors' services to TRICARE beneficiaries. TRICARE (2011) is the primary healthcare program of the U.S. Department of Defense, providing civilian healthcare benefits to military personnel, retirees, their dependents, and some members of the military reserve.

The rule specified that all providers would have to have passed the Clinical Mental Health Counselor Exam (CMHCE) and be licensed at the highest tier in their respective states. The wording employed in this policy reflected the CACREP standards for Clinical Mental Health Counseling and the AMHCA Standards for the Practice of Clinical Mental Health Counseling (AMHCA, 2015) and begin to provide a national statement regarding educational requirements. As of January 2021, these criteria will be amended to require applicants to have graduated from a CACREP-approved clinical mental health counseling program.

As noted, although addressing educational requirements, the rule refers only to those seeking recognition by TRICARE and even then defers to state standards for licensing, standards that can vary.

National Portability Taskforce

Four organizations—the American Association of State Counseling Boards (AASCB), the Association of Counselor Education and Supervision (ACES), the AMHCA, and the NBCC—joined forces as the

National Portability Taskforce (see https://www.amhca.org/advocacy/portability). The initiative's overarching goal is to move the counseling profession toward unified education standards, exam requirements, and years of postgraduate experience.

It is believed that improved portability will help reduce the variability in the counselor licensure process and requirements and will facilitate cross-state practice and movement. Such portability will allow a licensed professional counselor to provide ethical services across the country and create a network of reciprocal relationships across the country. In this era of distance counseling, the need for portability is even more evident. The taskforce identified the following as valuable outcomes of portability:

- Significantly increase public access to qualified care.
- Establish minimum standards for safe practice.
- Reduce administrative burdens for state regulatory boards and licensees.
- Create consistency in licensure standards across state lines.
- Ensure protection of the public and the continued development of the profession.

The taskforce's efforts attempted to show respect for the state autonomy and each state's fundamental right to regulate professional practice within its boundaries. Even with this sensitivity, the taskforce highlighted the value of portability to the protection of the public. Through the hard work and collaboration of the task force, the National Counselor Licensure Endorsement Process (NCLEP 2.0, 2017; https://www.amhca.org/advocacy/portability/portability2017) was created.

The National Counselor Licensure Endorsement Process (NCLEP 2.0) is designed to facilitate efficient review of licensure requirements and the mobility of licensed professionals. NCLEP 2.0 reflects significant progress towards profession unification and portability of licensure. The recommendations presented in NCLEP 2.0 are supported by CACREP and are complimentary to the ACA's development and promotion of a counseling interstate compacts.

NCLEP 2.0 outlines two pathway options for meeting standards of endorsement. Option 1 requires applicants to meet current standards for endorsement adopted by the receiving state counseling licensure board. Option 2 provides for applicants who have been actively licensed as a mental health counselor for at least 3 years before the date of application for licensure endorsement. It further requires that applicants are currently in good standing with no pending disciplinary action and have completed a jurisprudence or equivalent exam and background checks as required by the state regulatory body (if required by the originating state).

Under option 2, applicants must also comply with one of the following: (a) has maintained a license to practice independently that was awarded on or before December 31, 2014; (b) possesses the NCC credential as issued by the NBCC; or (c) possesses a graduate-level degree in counseling from a regionally accredited program (if the degree is awarded on or after January 1, 2025, then possesses a graduate-level degree from a CACREP-accredited program).

American Counseling Association–Interstate Compacts

Although NCLEP 2.0 reflects a coming together of many within the counseling professions, the development of portability legislation remains the responsibility of the state licensing boards. To this end, the ACA announced in 2018 that it would begin partnering with the National Center for Interstate Compacts (NCIC) to move legislation toward portability legislation.

The NCIC is a policy program developed by the Council of State Governments (CSG) to assist states in developing interstate compacts, which are contracts between states. NCIC serves as an information clearinghouse, a provider of training and technical assistance, and a primary facilitator in assisting states in reviewing, revising, and creating new interstate compacts to solve multistate problems. The hope is that such partnering will facilitate the adoption of portability laws across the nation.

Ongoing Professional Development

Upon completion of a graduate program and the reception of a master's degree, a counselor may have little desire to seek certification or licensing. Regardless of an interest in further credentialing, all mental health counselors must commit to ongoing professional development in the form of continuing education and supervision. Professional development is not only practical, given the rapid advances in our profession, but it is also an ethical mandate.

As discussed in Chapter 6, ours is still a young profession that reflects a level of artistry grounded in science. The expanding research on the factors affecting mental health and wellness, along with new and innovative treatment approaches, requires that counselors stay abreast of these data and continue to develop their knowledge and skill.

The ACA (2014) is clear in its ethical mandate to its members:

> Counselors recognize the need for continuing education to acquire and maintain a reasonable level of awareness of current scientific and professional information in their fields of activity. Counselors maintain their competence in the skills they use, are open to new procedures and remain informed regarding best practices for working with diverse populations. (C.1.a)

The AMHCA is even more specific in its ethical directives. AMHCA members are mandated to "Maintain knowledge of relevant scientific and professional information related to the services rendered and recognize the need for ongoing education" (AMHCA, 2020, C.1.c). Additionally, AMHCA members are directed to be "responsible for continuing education and remaining abreast of current trends and changes in the field, including the professional literature on best practices" (AMHCA, 2020, C.1.n). Ethical mental health counselors will "seek appropriate workshops, supervision, and training to familiarize themselves with assessment techniques and the use of specific assessment instruments" (AMHCA, 2020, D.e.a).

It is clear that ongoing professional development is not merely a nice idea—it is essential to a counselor's ethical and effective practice.

Keystones

- Clinical mental health counselors have as a foundation for their professional development a master's degree in counseling.
- CACREP establishes the national standards for the training of clinical mental health counselors.

- Credentialing refers to a formalized process of obtaining, verifying, and assessing the qualifications and competence of an individual by a third party with the relevant authority to issue such credentials.
- Three levels of credentialing include registry, certification, and licensure.
- Being accepted for a registry is a statement that the individual has completed requirements mandated for the practice of mental health counseling.
- Earning certification is evidence that a counseling professional possesses specialized expertise in a subset of the field.
- Perhaps the most widely recognized national counseling certification is the National Certified Counselor (NCC) credential offered through the NBCC.
- The Master of Addiction (MAC) and the Clinical Mental Health Counselor (CMHC) certifications are also provided through the NBCC.
- The AMHCA offers qualified mental health counselors (CMHCs) three professional development certifications (NACMH) and the NBCC. CCMHC establishes uniform standards of competency for those identified as clinical mental health counselors.
- Licensure is a government-sanctioned credential issued by state licensing boards through which states regulate the of a professional title (e.g., licensed mental health counselor, licensed professional counselor) as well as the scope of practice in that state (i.e., an identified set of techniques and practices that is limited to those professionals holding the counselor license).
- Each state creates its standards for licensure, thus creating a portability problem, allowing one to carry their license across state lines.
- The AASCB, the ACES, the AMHCA, and the NBCC joined forces as the National Portability Taskforce to establish standards of educational requirements for licensure, a common title, and a clear articulation of the scope of practice. Their work resulted in the National Counselor Licensure Endorsement Process (NCLEP 2.0).
- The ACA has partnered with the NCIC in an attempt to move state legislation toward portability legislation.

Additional Resources

- **American Association of State Counseling Boards**
  www.aascb.org
- **American Counseling Association**
  www.counseling.org
- **American Mental Health Counselors Association**
  www.amhca.org
- **Council for the Accreditation of Counseling & Related Educational Programs**
  www.cacrep.org
- **National Board of Certified Counselors:**
  www.nbcc.org

References

American Counseling Association. (2004). *Definition of professional counseling specialty.* https://www.counseling.org/news/updates/2004/07/26/definition-of-professional-counseling

American Counseling Association. (2014). *ACA code of ethics.* https://www.counseling.org/Resources/aca-code-of-ethics.pdf

American Mental Health Counselors Association. (2015). *Standards for the practice of clinical mental health counseling.*

American Mental Health Counselors Association (2020). *AMHCA code of ethics.* https://www.amhca.org/HigherLogic/System/DownloadDocumentFile.ashx?DocumentFileKey=24a27502-196e-b763-ff57-490a12f7edb1&forceDialog=0

Corey, G., Corey, M. S., Corey, C., & Callanan, P. (2015). *Issues and ethics in the helping professions* (9th ed.). Brooks/Cole.

Council for Accreditation of Counseling and Related Educational Programs (CACREP). (2016). *CACREP standards.* https://www.counseling.org/resources/library/ERIC%20Digests/2001-09.pdf

Litchfield, M., & Watson, J. C. (2009). Mental health counseling. In American Counseling Association (Ed.), *The ACA encyclopedia of counseling* (pp. 101–103). American Counseling Association.

Myers, J. E., & Sweeney, T. J. (2001). Specialties in counseling. In D. C. Locke, J. E. Myers, & E. L. Herr (Eds.), *The handbook of counseling* (pp. 43–54). Sage.

National Counselor Licensure Endorsement Process. (2017). *NCLEP 2.0.* (https://www.amhca.org/advocacy/portability/portability2017.

Paterson, J. (2006). *Sorting out certification.* Counseling Today. https://ct.counseling.org/2006/10/sorting-out-certification/

Schweiger, W. K., Henderson, D. A., McCaskill, K., Clawson, T. W., & Collins, D. R. (2011). *Counselor preparation: Programs, faculty, trends* (13th ed.). Routledge.

TRICARE: Certified Mental Health Counselors. (2011, December). *Federal Register, 76,* 80741–80744.

U.S. Department of Transportation. (2020). *Substance abuse professionals (SAP).* https://www.transportation.gov/odapc/sap

Wakefield, M. (2013). *Health licensing board report to Congress.* www.hrsa.gov/ruralhealth/about/telehealth/licenserpt10.pdf

CHAPTER 14

Self-Care and Wellness

What is to give light must endure burning.

—Viktor Frankl (1963)

As suggested in the Frankl quote, one cannot engage in the depth of relationship with deep empathy, which is the hallmark of our profession, without "enduring burning." Mental health counselors are called to journey with others who may be experiencing extreme distress and emotional upheaval. The process of entering this experience with one's client can come at a cost. "The stresses encountered by a counselor stem from both the nature of the work and the role expectation of the profession" (Evans & Villavisanis, 1997, p. 342).

Mental health professionals may experience an increased likelihood of adverse psychological outcomes because of their work (Figley, 2002; Sabin-Farrell & Turpin, 2003). The physical, social, and even spiritual drain on mental health counselors can be significant. For example, one study reported that more than 63% of those surveyed stated that they knew a colleague who was impaired to the degree that it could negatively impact their practice (American Counseling Association [ACA], 2010). The increased awareness of the stress and strain encountered by counselors moved the American Counseling Association (ACA) to organize a taskforce to enhance the wellness of professional counselors (ACA, 2010). The ACA has a clear commitment to providing for the health and well-being of its members while at the same time encouraging its members to do the same (see ACA, 2014, C.2.g). This chapter reviews conditions that place counselors' wellness at risk and the steps necessary to reduce the possibility of experiencing professional burnout, compassion fatigue, or secondary traumatization.

Upon completion of this chapter, the reader will be able to:

- Describe the nature of burnout, compassion fatigue, and secondary (vicarious) traumatization.
- Explain the factors that contribute to the development of burnout, compassion fatigue, and secondary (vicarious) traumatization.
- Describe steps to be taken to prevent and, when necessary, intervene with burnout, compassion fatigue, and secondary (vicarious) traumatization.

A Profession That Can Challenge a Counselor's Well-Being

Mental health counselors are tasked with providing services that address the needs of their clients. This exclusive focus on another's struggles can negatively impact the counselor's own well-being.

The cumulative effect of engaging with human suffering can take its toll on the counselor (Webb, 2011). To expect that a counselor can journey with those experiencing personal suffering and remain immune to its impact is, according to Remen (1996), as unrealistic as expecting to be able to walk through water without getting wet.

Studies have described high rates of emotional exhaustion experienced by those providing mental health services (Oddie & Ousley, 2007; Rohland, 2000; Siebert, 2005). For example, Oddie and Ousley (2007) reviewed several studies and found that a range of 21% to 48% of general mental health workers gave claim to having experienced high emotional exhaustion. Others have reported on the high rates with which counselors experience anxiety and depression and reduction in self-esteem (Butler & Constantine, 2005; Tyssen et al., 2001).

These conditions are not only detrimental to the health and well-being of the counselor but can impact their practice decisions. Counselors who lack an awareness of these threats to their health and well-being and thus fail to engage in self-care not only place themselves at risk but risk making poor professional judgments, such as misdiagnosis, inadequate treatment planning, or abuse of clients (Rudolph et al., 1997).

The Future: Perhaps Even More Challenging

Conditions such as heavy caseloads, complex and multifaceted presenting concerns, and restrictions imposed by outside forces such as third-party payers have been found to increase the stress and distress experienced by mental health providers. Sadly, these conditions will only increase in the future, thus proving even more challenging to counselors' well-being.

Data suggest the future will see a significant increase in the demand for mental health services. According to the National Alliance of Mental Health (2019), 1 in 5 adults in the United States experience mental health illnesses, and about 1 in 25 experience serious mental health illnesses in a given year. Although the demand for mental health services is apparent, studies have shown that reduced availability of service providers will result not only in many consumers failing to get the services needed but that counselors will be overloaded by the sheer number needing care (Han et al., 2017). This gap between those needing mental health services and those who can provide them is predicted to widen by 2025 (Health Resources and Services Administration [HRSA], 2015). The immediate implication of these data is that more will be expected from those providing mental health services, and that "more" will challenge those providers' well-being. Excessive caseloads impact a counselor's ability to provide quality care (Hoge et al., 2013) and attack the very emotional and physical well-being of the counselor.

The increased stress comes not only from the expanding caseloads but by the very nature of the cases being seen. Counselors see an increasing number of clients who present with more complex and complicated issues, including comorbid or co-occurring mental health issues, with many having experienced significant life trauma. This last point is particularly concerning because research has found that counselors' interactions with traumatized clients "can be disruptive and painful for the helper and can persist for months or years after work with traumatized persons" (McCann & Pearlman, 1990, p. 133). High exposure to traumatized clients can negatively affect a counselor's ability to remain emotionally present and compassionate with clients (Bowen & Moore, 2014) and can increase the risk of secondary trauma for the counselor (Baird & Kracen, 2006; Craig & Sprang, 2010; Sprang et al., 2007).

Burnout, Compassion Fatigue, and Secondary (Vicarious) Trauma

The physical and emotional drain that some counselors experience takes the form of counselor burnout, compassion fatigue, and secondary (vicarious) trauma. All counselors need to understand the nature of these conditions and the factors that place a counselor at risk and the steps necessary to reduce the potential of experiencing these conditions.

Burnout

The term *burnout*, which originally referred to developing exhaustion associated with the accumulating stress of one's work, was first introduced into the scientific literature in 1974 (Freudenberger, 1974). Burnout is "a state of physical, emotional, and mental exhaustion caused by long-term involvement in situations that are emotionally demanding" (Pines & Aronson, 1988, p. 9). Burnout can occur when a helping professional's caseload and expectations repeatedly exceed their capacity to meet such requirements (Maslach, 1982).

Burnout is insidious and develops over time. Symptoms tend to progress, moving from mild to severe and from acute to chronic (Hamann & Gordon, 2000). Given this developmental nature of burnout, it can go unnoticed until it is well entrenched and damaging to the counselor as well as their clients.

The progression can move a counselor from feelings of apathy about work and clients to their development of strong negative feelings and attitudes toward their clients. With increasing detachment from their clients, counselors will often employ processes of dehumanizing the client, such as labeling the client as "my 4 o'clock" or "the complainer." Such a process is the counselor's attempt to minimize the emotional drain (Maslach et al., 2001).

As burnout continues to develop, the counselor can feel helpless and hopeless about the work they are doing and thus experience discouragement. Counselors may increase distancing from the client and develop disbelief in the effectiveness of what they do. The impact of burnout is such that it prevents the counselor from ethically and effectively providing services and meeting clinical responsibilities (Fothergill et al., 2004; Lee et al., 2010; Morse et al., 2012).

Compassion Fatigue

"Compassion is feeling and acting with deep empathy and sorrow for those who suffer" (Stamm, 2002, p. 107). Mental health professionals possessing the skills of compassion and empathy will tend to be more effective than those who lack these skill areas (Bowen & Moore, 2014).

The experience of compassion and empathy, although beneficial to our clients, can come at a cost for the professional counselor. Compassion fatigue is a phenomenon in the mental health field that is getting more and more attention (Adams et al., 2006; Bowen & Moore, 2014; Harr & Moore, 2011; Smart et al., 2014). The somewhat irony of this situation is that the qualities that make counselors effective with their clients—qualities such as empathy, compassion, and caring—may also leave them vulnerable to such adverse outcomes as compassion fatigue (Figley, 1995; Lawson et al., 2007). While our empathy allows us to understand our clients' stories more fully, it also can result in our absorbing their distress and suffering.

Compassion fatigue, like burnout, impacts the counselor's ability to be empathic. Unlike burnout, however, compassion fatigue has a sudden onset, most often coming with little warning. Counselors experiencing empathy fatigue will report experiencing physical and emotional exhaustion. In addition, compassion fatigue often results in an impaired ability to concentrate (cognitive symptom), an increase in feelings of sadness, guilt, or anxiety (emotional impact), and changes in eating and sleeping patterns (behavioral effects). Further, those with compassion fatigue often report experiencing increased aches and pains (somatic symptoms), evidence of increasing mistrust and isolation (interpersonal aspects), reduction in work efficiency and effectiveness, and a change in their fundamental values and beliefs (spiritual impact).

It appears counselors who are under high levels of stress within their personal lives and those who have a history of personal trauma, as well as those who overly conscientious, somewhat perfectionistic, and who have low levels of social support, tend to be at higher risk experiencing compassion fatigue (Meadors & Lamson, 2008).

Secondary (Vicarious) Trauma

As suggested by the name, secondary trauma presents with symptoms similar to those of primary trauma with less intensity (Catanese, 2010). Symptoms of posttraumatic stress disorder (PTSD) such as intense images, feelings of sadness and irritability, and profound changes in the counselor's core sense of self have been reported (Catanese, 2010; Pearlman & Saakvitne, 1995).

Secondary traumatization is the result of exposure to the explicit and often graphic accounts of clients' traumatic experiences (Bride, 2004; Dunkley & Whelan, 2006). Like burnout, secondary (vicarious) traumatization develops over time. Counselors who are continually exposed to the traumatic hurts and pains of their clientele might find that their sense of safety and trust and even their self and worldviews have been altered (Sabin-Farrell & Turpin, 2003; Pearlman & Saakvitne, 1995).

With data suggesting that between 82% and 94% of clients seeking treatment had experienced some form of trauma (Bride, 2004), counselors will likely be exposed to the traumatic experiences of their clients at some point in their professional careers. Studies have shown that higher exposure rates to traumatized clients resulted in higher rates of secondary trauma (Craig & Sprang, 2010; Sprang et al., 2007). Dunkley and Whelan (2006) estimated the prevalence rate of vicarious traumatization to be 45.9% among counselors.

As is true for burnout and compassion fatigue, empathy and deep interpersonal engagement with distressed clients is a primary contributor to the development of secondary trauma (Trippany et al., 2004). Table 14.1 provides descriptions of personal and contextual factors that may increase a counselor's risk of experiencing secondary (vicarious) traumatization (Perlman & McKay, n.d.).

TABLE 14.1 Factors that Contribute to Counselor Secondary (Vicarious) Traumatization

THE HUMANITARIAN WORKER	THE SITUATION	THE CULTURAL CONTEXT
• An avoidance personality and coping style • Personal history with trauma • Current life stress and heavy demands • Limited social support • Limited spiritual resources providing life meaning • Unrealistic work expectations and problems with boundaries	• The professional role, work setting, and exposure—high workload, long engagement without rest, clients with trauma experiences • Limited agency support/time off • Serving populations affected by disaster, violence, and chronic deprivation and injustice	• Cultures of intolerance to those struggling to reclaim dignity • Cultural styles of expressing distress and extending and receiving assistance are difficult to understand • The culture of humanitarian work of subtly promoting over self-reliance and resistance to seeking assistance

Source: Adapted from Pearlman, L. A., & McKay, L. (n.d.). *Understanding and addressing vicarious trauma*. https://headington-institute.org/files/vtmoduletemplate2_ready_v2_85791.pdf

Finding Balance: Wellness

Just as counselors attend to their clients' well-being, it is crucial for them to monitor and assess their own levels of health and well-being. Counselors need to find a balance between emotional involvement with their clients and the ability to gain emotional distance (Skovholt & Trotter-Mathison, 2016). It is a "paramount necessity of carefully nurturing and regulating the self and ensuring the development of a self-protective, self-healing, and self-soothing way of being as a professional and as a full human being" (Danieli, 1996, p. 200).

Researchers have found that the introduction and utilization of career-sustaining behaviors might reduce the risks related to secondary trauma stress, compassion fatigue, and burnout (Lawson et al., 2007; Lawson & Myers, 2011). The employment of self-care and career-sustaining behaviors, such as maintaining a leisure mindset, a leisure space, spending time with family and friends, and maintaining a sense of humor, are not merely good ideas but are steps to be taken to ensure a counselor's ability to provide effective and ethical services (Grafanaki et al., 2005; Stevanovic & Rupert, 2004).

The ACA code of ethics states: "Counselors engage in self-care activities to maintain and promote their own emotional, physical, mental, and spiritual well-being to best meet their professional responsibilities" (ACA, 2014, Section C: Professional Responsibility, Introduction). It is not sufficient for counselors to address their health and well-being when it is in jeopardy. Implicit in the ACA ethical directive is the call for counselors to intentionally employ self-care and wellness strategies as part of their lifestyle.

Wellness

Wellness is a multidimensional concept and thus calls for plans that facilitate balanced growth across the physical, emotional, intellectual, social, spiritual, and psychological dimensions of one's life (e.g., Adams et al., 2000; Roscoe, 2009).

Physical Health

It is certainly not a revelation to state that physical activity promotes general health and reduces the development of chronic illnesses (Reiner et al., 2013; Warburton et al., 2006). Research also supports the value of physical activity to the promotion of overall mental health (White et al., 2017). This point is especially important given the very sedentary nature of the counseling profession.

Although understanding the value of exercise, most practitioners will cite caseloads, schedules, and a multitude of professional tasks that inhibit their ability to increase their physical activities. Sadly, these are realities. However, as the saying goes, every little bit helps. Thus, although intense exercise may not be possible, even moderate physical activities such as walks (at lunch or after work) can support one's health.

In addition to exercise, one must attend to healthy eating. "Good nutrition is the bedrock of human well-being ... [which] enables optimal brain and immune system development and functioning" (Fanzo et al., 2015, p. 639). Maintaining healthy eating might even be more challenging for many practitioners. Tight schedules and multiple commitments and meetings often invite the counselor to "grab something on the go." Taking time to plan meals and schedule time to eat without competing activities (e.g., phones, internet, paperwork, etc.) should be a part of a counselor's intentional plan for wellness.

Connecting

Counseling, with its commitment to client privacy and confidentiality, can become a very isolating experience for the counselor. Unlike other professions, counselors cannot readily share stories of their success or lament about difficulties or simply vent about work-related frustrations to friends or loved ones.

The experience of professional isolation needs to be combated with intentional plans to connect socially. Whether it is dinner out, movie night, or an activity such as a book club or a church choir, developing and maintaining strong, healthy relationships outside of the professional world fosters a broader perspective on life (one not constricted to the world of work) and offers opportunities for healthy distraction and enjoyment.

Centering Self

The idea of leaving work at work is a wonderful directive for living a healthy life. Many counselors, however, find that this directive is hard to implement. The past 20 years have seen increased recognition of the value of mindfulness practice for promoting wellness (e.g., Campbell et al., 2017; Rothaupt & Morgan, 2007). Research has demonstrated the value of mindfulness practice as a prophylactic for the stress that is often associated with burnout (Cohen & Miller, 2009; Shapiro et al., 2007), as well as an intervention for decreasing burnout levels (Goodman & Schorling, 2012; Rothaupt & Morgan, 2007). Jacob and Holzer (2016) found that those clinicians with higher self-reported mindfulness qualities had significantly lower levels of self-reported vicarious traumatization. These authors suggest that trauma-focused counselors should engage in mindfulness activities routinely to increase awareness of internal processes and decrease the likelihood of vicarious traumatization due to exposure to clients' trauma-related narratives.

While having both curative and preventive value for counselors, a counselor's engagement with mindfulness practice has been associated with better service for clients. Mindfulness practice has been associated with the increase in a counselor's competency and ability to conceptualize cases (Campbell et al., 2017; Escuriex & Labbe, 2011) and reduce burnout (Rothaupt & Morgan, 2007).

Addressing Risk Factors

In addition to engaging in an intentional plan of wellness, counselors need to identify and modify conditions that increase the risk of burnout, compassion fatigue, and secondary trauma. Counselors need to be realistic in the standards and expectations they set and be mindful of times of excessive stress because these can contribute to experiences such as compassion fatigue (Meadors & Lamson, 2008). Counselors need to address the systemic issues that may be eroding their health and wellness. Given the research highlighting the negative impact of excessive caseloads, long hours, and imposed isolation on a counselor's health and wellness (Schaufeli, 2003), focusing on the system and work environment is a fertile ground for prevention planning.

Intervention

Counselors experiencing stress, distress, or impairment may not be able to offer high-quality services to clientele and experience a decline in their quality of life (Lawson et al., 2007). Counselors in the grips of burnout, compassion fatigue, or secondary (vicarious) traumatization need to experience interventions that help with the healing process. To be most effective, interventions need to be at the earliest point possible. This requires counselors to not only be aware of and on the lookout for symptoms or signs but also engage in the process of self-monitoring.

Signs of Trouble

EXHAUSTION! The experience of low energy, chronic fatigue, and exhaustion may be some of the earliest signs that a counselor is in trouble. Other physical symptoms such as sleep difficulties, headaches, and gastrointestinal problems may also be harbingers of burnout, compassion fatigue, or secondary traumatization. Additionally, the development of a cynical, negative attitude (Maslach, Schaufeli, & Leiter, 2001) and emotions ranging from boredom, moodiness, annoyance, and frustration to feelings of depression, anxiety, helplessness and hopelessness (Lambie, 2002; Maslach, Schaufeli, & Leiter, 2001) all serve as signs of a counselor in trouble.

Self-Monitoring

The possibility of falling within the grips of burnout, compassion fatigue, or vicarious trauma is such that each counselor needs to maintain a process of self-assessment and self-monitoring. Counselors might have difficulty recognizing the specific impacts of expressing compassion and empathy (Bowen & Moore, 2014), and as such, a routine of self-monitoring might be of value.

Self-monitoring can be as simple as periodically reviewing the symptoms associated with these conditions or employing a more standardized instrument. Table 14.2 provides a sampling of such instruments.

TABLE 14.2 Standardized Instruments for Monitoring Burnout, Compassion Fatigue, and Secondary Trauma

CONDITION	INSTRUMENT DESCRIPTION
Burnout	The Maslach Burnout Inventory (http://www.mindgarden.com/products/mbi.htm) is a commonly used instrument measuring burnout. It has been configured to assess three dimensions of burnout: emotional exhaustion, depersonalization, and personal accomplishment (Maslach et al., 2009).
Compassion Fatigue	Measures currently employed to assess compassion fatigue include the Compassion Fatigue Self-Test (CFST; Figley & Stamm, 1996) and the Compassion Fatigue Scale (CFS-R; Adams et al., 2008).
Secondary (vicarious) trauma	The Traumatic Stress Institute Belief Scale–Revision L (TSI-BSL) is an 80-item questionnaire measuring levels of disruption among five separate domains of safety, trust, control, esteem, and intimacy (Jenkins & Baird, 2002). The Traumatic Stress Institute Life Events Checklist (TSI-LEC) attempts to identify the added vulnerability that an individual professional might have to the onset of vicarious trauma due to the personal trauma that may have occurred throughout their own lives (Bride et al., 2007).

One of the most popular self-monitoring instruments providing an assessment of potential burnout, compassion fatigue, and secondary trauma is the Professional Quality of Life (ProQOL) scale (Stamm, 2012a). ProQOL, Version 5 (Stamm, 2012a) is available at http://www.proqol.org/uploads/ProQOL_5_English.pdf. This measure can be used at regular intervals to track changes over time, especially when strategies for prevention or intervention are being tried. It is suggested that you take the self-scoring measure found in Table 14.3 to gauge your state of well-being.

TABLE 14.3 ProQOL Version 5 Self-Score

Compassion Satisfaction and Compassion Fatigue (ProQOL) Version 5 (2009)

When you **help** people you have direct contact with their lives. As you may have found, your compassion for those you **help** can affect you in positive and negative ways. Below are some questions about your experiences, both positive and negative, as a **helper**. Consider each of the following questions about you and your current work situation. Select the number that honestly reflects how frequently you experienced these things in the *last 30 days*.

1 = NEVER	2 = RARELY	3 = SOMETIMES	4 = OFTEN	5 = VERY OFTEN

_______ 1. I am happy.

_______ 2. I am preoccupied with more than one person I **help**.

_______ 3. I get satisfaction from being able to **help** people.

_______ 4. I feel connected to others.

_______ 5. I jump or am startled by unexpected sounds.

_______ 6. I feel invigorated after working with those I **help**.

_______ 7. I find it difficult to separate my personal life from my life as a **helper**.

_______ 8. I am not as productive at work because I am losing sleep over traumatic experiences of a person I **help**.

_______ 9. I think that I might have been affected by the traumatic stress of those I **help**.

_______ 10. I feel trapped by my job as a **helper**.

_______ 11. Because of my helping, I have felt "on edge" about various things.

_______ 12. I like my work as a **helper**.

(*Continued*)

(*Continued*)

	1 = NEVER	2 = RARELY	3 = SOMETIMES	4 = OFTEN	5 = VERY OFTEN

_____ 13. I feel depressed because of the traumatic experiences of the people I **help**.

_____ 14. I feel as though I am experiencing the trauma of someone I have **helped**.

_____ 15. I have beliefs that sustain me.

_____ 16. I am pleased with how I am able to keep up with **helping** techniques and protocols.

_____ 17. I am the person I always wanted to be.

_____ 18. My work makes me feel satisfied.

_____ 19. I feel worn out because of my work as a **helper**.

_____ 20. I have happy thoughts and feelings about those I **help** and how I could help them.

_____ 21. I feel overwhelmed because my case work load seems endless.

_____ 22. I believe I can make a difference through my work.

_____ 23. I avoid certain activities or situations because they remind me of frightening experiences of the people I **help**.

_____ 24. I am proud of what I can do to **help**.

_____ 25. As a result of my **helping**, I have intrusive, frightening thoughts.

_____ 26. I feel "bogged down" by the system.

_____ 27. I have thoughts that I am a "success" as a **helper**.

_____ 28. I can't recall important parts of my work with trauma victims.

_____ 29. I am a very caring person.

_____ 30. I am happy that I chose to do this work.

Based on your responses, place your personal scores below. If you have any concerns, you should discuss them with a physical or mental health care professional.

Compassion Satisfaction: _____

Compassion satisfaction is about the pleasure you derive from being able to do your work well. For example, you may feel like it is a pleasure to help others through your work. You may feel positively about your colleagues or your ability to contribute to the work setting or even the greater good of society. Higher scores on this scale represent a greater satisfaction related to your ability to be an effective caregiver in your job.

If you are in the higher range, you probably derive a good deal of professional satisfaction from your position. If your scores are below 23, you may either find problems with your job, or there may be some other reason—for example, you might derive your satisfaction from activities other than your job. (Alpha scale reliability 0.88)

Burnout: _____

Most people have an intuitive idea of what burnout is. From the research perspective, burnout is one of the elements of compassion fatigue. It is associated with feelings of hopelessness and difficulties in dealing with work or in doing your job effectively. These negative feelings usually have a gradual onset. They can reflect the feeling that your efforts make no difference, or they can be associated with a very high workload or a nonsupportive work environment. Higher scores on this scale mean that you are at higher risk for burnout.

If your score is below 23, this probably reflects positive feelings about your ability to be effective in your work. If you score above 41, you may wish to think about what at work makes you feel like you are not effective in your position. Your score may reflect your mood; perhaps you were having a "bad day" or are in need of some time off. If the high score persists or if it is reflective of other worries, it may be a cause for concern. (Alpha scale reliability 0.75)

Secondary Traumatic Stress: ______

The second component of compassion fatigue is secondary traumatic stress (STS). It is about your work-related, secondary exposure to extremely or traumatically stressful events. Developing problems due to exposure to other's trauma is somewhat rare but does happen to many people who care for those who have experienced extremely or traumatically stressful events. For example, you may repeatedly hear stories about the traumatic things that happen to other people, commonly called vicarious traumatization. If your work puts you directly in the path of danger, for example, field work in a war or area of civil violence, this is not secondary exposure; your exposure is primary. However, if you are exposed to others' traumatic events as a result of your work, for example, as a therapist or an emergency worker, this is secondary exposure. The symptoms of STS are usually rapid in onset and associated with a particular event. They may include being afraid, having difficulty sleeping, having images of the upsetting event pop into your mind, or avoiding things that remind you of the event.

If your score is above 41, you may want to take some time to think about what at work may be frightening to you or if there is some other reason for the elevated score. While higher scores do not mean that you do have a problem, they are an indication that you may want to examine how you feel about your work and your work environment. You may wish to discuss this with your supervisor, a colleague, or a healthcare professional. (Alpha scale reliability 0.81)

In this section, you will score your test so you understand the interpretation for you. To find your score on each section, total the questions listed on the left and then find your score in the table on the right of the section.

COMPASSION SATISFACTION SCALE			
Copy your rating on each of these questions on to this table and add them up. When you have added them up you can find your score on the table to the right.	3. ______ 6. ______ 12. ______ 16. ______ 18. ______ 20. ______	**The sum of my Compassion Satisfaction questions is**	**And my Compassion Satisfaction level is**
	22. ______ 24. ______	22 or less	Low
	27. ______ 30. ______	Between 23 and 41	Moderate
	Total: ______	42 or more	High

BURNOUT SCALE

On the Burnout scale you will need to take an extra step. Starred items are "reverse scored." If you scored the item 1, write a 5 beside it. The reason we ask you to reverse the scores is because scientifically the measure works better when these questions are asked in a positive way though they can tell us more about their negative form. For example, question 1. "I am happy" tells us more about the effects of helping when you are **not** happy so you reverse the score.

YOU WROTE	CHANGE TO
1	5
2	4
3	3
4	2
5	1

(Continued)

(*Continued*)

1. ______	=			
*4. ______	=	8.	**THE SUM OF MY BURNOUT QUESTIONS IS**	**AND MY BURNOUT LEVEL IS**
10. ______			22 or less	Low
*15. ______	=		Between 23 and 41	Moderate
*17. ______	=		42 or more	High
19. ______				
21. ______				
26. ______				
*29. ______	=			
			Total:	

SECONDARY TRAUMATIC STRESS SCALE			
Just like you did on Compassion Satisfaction, copy your rating on each of these questions on to this table and add them up. When you have added them up you can find your score on the table to the right.	2. ______ 5. ______ 7. ______ 9. ______ 11. ______ 13. ______ 14. ______	**The sum of my Secondary Trauma questions is**	**And my Secondary Traumatic Stress level is**
	23. ______	22 or less	Low
	25. ______ 28. ______	Between 23 and 41	Moderate
	Total ______		
		42 or more	High

Source: Beth Hudnall Stamm, "Professional Quality of Life: Compassion Satisfaction and Fatigue Version 5," pp. 1–3. Copyright © 2009 by Center for Victims of Torture (www.cvt.org). Reprinted with permission. More information about the ProQOL, its development, administration and interpretation, is available from the ProQOL website at www.proqol.org.

Intervening When Necessary

Self-monitoring and the early identification of signs of burnout, compassion fatigue, or secondary trauma are essential first steps to intervention. Gentry and Baranowsky (1999) developed a model for intervening with an experience of compassion fatigue. Their Accelerated Recovery Program for Compassion Fatigue (Gentry & Baranowsky, 1999) provides components that could prove useful in the intervention of burnout and secondary trauma.

Recognition and Acceptance

As noted, self-monitoring is an essential step in the intervention process. Early identification of symptoms and the acceptance of the reality that one is on the path toward burnout, compassion fatigue, or secondary trauma positions the counselors to identify causes and adjust accordingly.

Engage in Multidimensional Wellness Strategies

The elements identified as part of a preventive wellness program, including addressing a healthy lifestyle, mindfulness, and adjustment of work conditions, are useful as interventions. It is also useful for the counselor experiencing burnout, compassion fatigue, or secondary trauma to engage in self-soothing activities (e.g., stretching, massage, meditation, quieting response, etc.) as counters to possible employment of drugs or alcohol.

Reaching Out

The general pattern of withdrawal and disconnection often associated with these conditions needs to be addressed. The counselor needs to establish or reestablish healthy, meaningful relationships. Engaging in genuine caring interactions with colleagues and close friends will facilitate counselor self-disclosure and invite supportive responses.

Professional Assistance

Being a counselor does not preclude one from also being a client. Personal therapy and clinical supervision can help a counselor regain perspective, challenge dysfunctional beliefs, and modify stress-inducing patterns of behavior. Getting support and assistance with cognitive restructuring—targeting those negative cognitions that interfere with self-care—is especially helpful for the counselors who may know what to do but are having difficulty doing it (Lawson & Venart, 2005).

Keystones

- The experiences of burnout, compassion fatigue, and vicarious traumatization are multidimensional conditions that impact counselors physically, cognitively, emotionally, interpersonally, and can even affect core values.
- Compassion fatigue creates a state of exhaustion that negatively affects a counselor's professional identity and existential well-being.
- Burnout can result in depersonalization, emotional exhaustion, and a negative self-evaluation.
- Secondary (vicarious) trauma develops over time and can result not only in feelings of sadness, grief, irritability, and mood swings but also in profound changes in the counselor's core values and sense of self.
- Counselors must engage in self-assessment, healthy lifestyle choices, and taking time to recharge.
- To promote wellness, counselors should develop plans that integrate physical, psychological, and social wellness activities.

Additional Resources

Compassion Fatigue Self-Test: http://www.ptsdsupport.net/compassion_fatugue-selftest.html

Florida State University Traumatology Institute: https://charlesfigley.com/traumatology-institute

Harrison, R. L., & Westwood, M. J. (2009). Preventing vicarious traumatization of mental health therapists: Identifying protective practices. *Psychotherapy Theory: Research, Practice, Training, 46*(2), 203–219.

Parsons, R., Dickinson, K., & Asempapa, B. (2020). *Counselor wellness: Caring for self to care for others.* Cognella Academic Publishing.

ProQOL 5: http://proqol.org/ProQol_Test.html

Skovholt, T. M., & Trotter-Mathison, M. (2016). *The resilient practitioner: Burnout and compassion, fatigue prevention, and self-care strategies for the helping professions* (3rd ed.). Routledge.

University of Buffalo School of Social Work—Self Care Activities: http://www.socialwork.buffalo.edu/students/self-care/exercises.asp.

References

Adams, R. E., Boscarino, J. A., & Figley, C. R. (2006). Compassion fatigue and psychological distress among social workers: A validation study. *American Journal of Orthopsychiatry, 76*(1), 103–108. http://dx.doi.org/10.1037/0002-9432.76.1.103

Adams, R. E., Figley, C. R., & Boscarino, J. A. (2008). The Compassion Fatigue scale: Its use with social workers following urban disaster. *Research on Social Work Practice, 18*(3), 238–250.

Adams, T. B., Bezner, J. R., Drabbs, M. E., Zambarano, R. J., & Steinhardt, M. A. (2000). Conceptualization and measurement of the spiritual and psychological dimensions of wellness in a college population. *Journal of American College Health, 48*(4), 165–173.

American Counseling Association. (2014). *ACA code of ethics.* https://www.counseling.org/Resources/aca-code-of-ethics.pdf

American Counseling Association's Taskforce on Counseling Wellness and Impairment. (2010). http://www.counseling.org/wellness_taskforce/index.htm

Baird, K., & Kracen, A. C. (2006). Vicarious traumatization and secondary traumatic stress: A research synthesis. *Counselling Psychology Quarterly, 19,* 181–188.

Bowen, N., & Moore, J. L. (2014). Common characteristics of compassionate counselors: A qualitative study. *International Journal for the Advancement of Counseling, 36*(1), 17–29.

Bride, B. (2004). The impact of providing psychosocial services to traumatized populations. *Stress, Trauma, and Crisis, 7,* 29–64.

Bride, B. E., Radey, M., & Figley, C. R. (2007). Measuring compassion fatigue. *Clinical Social Work Journal, 35*(3), 155–163.

Butler, S. K., & Constantine, M. G. (2005). Collective self-esteem and burnout in professional school counselors. *Professional School Counseling, 9*(1), 55–62.

Campbell, A., Vance, S. R., & Dong, S. (2017). Examining the relationship between mindfulness and multicultural counseling competencies in counselor trainees. *Mindfulness. Advance online publication.* https://doi.org/10.1007/s12671-017-0746-6

Catanese, S. A. (2010). *Traumatized by association: The risk of working sex crimes.* https://heinonline.org/HOL/LandingPage?handle=hein.journals/fedpro74&div=24&id=&page

Centers for Disease Control and Prevention. (2019). *Chronic diseases in America.* https://www.cdc.gov/chronicdisease/resources/infographic/chronic-diseases.htm

Cohen, J. S., & Miller, L. (2009). Interpersonal mindfulness training for well-being: A pilot study with psychology graduate students. *Teachers College Record, 111,* 2760–2774.

Craig, C. D., & Sprang, G. (2010). Compassion satisfaction, compassion fatigue, and burnout in a national sample of trauma treatment therapists. *Anxiety, Stress, and Coping, 23*(3), 319–339.

Cramer, T., & Liddle, B. (2005). Secondary traumatic stress among disaster mental health workers responding to the September 11 attacks. *Journal of Traumatic Stress, 18*(1), 8–96.

Danieli, Y. (1996). Who takes care of the caregiver? In R. J. Apfel & B. Simon (Eds.), *Minefields in their hearts* (pp. 189–205). Yale University Press.

Dunkley, J., & Whelan, T. A. (2006). Vicarious traumatization: Current status and future directions. *British Journal of Guidance & Counselling, 34*(1), 107–116.

Escuriex, B. F., & Labbe, E. E. (2011). Health care providers' mindfulness and treatment outcomes: A critical review of the research literature. *Mindfulness, 2*(4), 242–253.

Evans, T. D., & Villavisanis, R. (1997). Encouragement exchange: Avoiding therapist Burnout. *The Family Journal, 5*(4), 342–345. http://dx.doi.org/10.1177/1066480797054013

Fanzo, J. C., Graziose, M. M., Kraemer, K., Gillespie, S., Johnston, J. L., de Pee, S., Monterrosa, E., Badham, J., Bloem, M. W., Dangour, A. D., Deckelbaum, R., Dobermann, A., Fracassi, P., Moazzem Hossain, S., Ingram, J., Jerling, J. C., Jones, C. J., Indrayana Jap, S., Kiess, L., Marshall, Q., Martin, K., Narayan, A., Amuyunzu-Nayamongo, M., Pepping, F., & West, K. P. (2015). Educating and training a workforce for nutrition in a post-2015 world. *Advanced Nutrition, 6*(6), 639–647.

Figley, C. R. (Ed.). (1995). *Compassion fatigue: Coping with secondary traumatic stress disorder.* Brunner/Mazel.

Figley, C. R. (2002). Compassion fatigue: Psychotherapists' chronic lack of self-care. *Journal of Clinical Psychology, 58*(11), 1433-1441. http://dx.doi.org/10.1002/jclp.10090

Figley, C. R., & Stamm, B. H. (1996). Psychometric review of compassion fatigue self-test. In B. H. Stamm (Ed.), *Measurement of stress, trauma, and adaptation.* Sidran Press.

Fothergill, A., Edwards, D., & Burnard, P. (2004). Stress, burnout, coping and stress management in psychiatrists: Findings from a systematic review. *International Journal of Social Psychiatry, 50,* 54–65.

Freudenberger, H. J. (1974). Staff burnout. *Journal of Social Issues, 30*(1), 159–165.

Gentry, J. E., & Baranowsky, A. (1999, November). *Accelerated Recovery Program for Compassion Fatigue.* Pre-conference workshop presented at the 15th Annual meeting of the International Society for Traumatic Stress Studies, Miami, FL.

Goodman, M. J., & Schorling, J. B. (2012). A mindfulness course decreases Burnout and improves well-being among healthcare providers. *International Journal of Psychiatry in Medicine*, *43*(2), 119–128. https://doi.org/10.2190/PM.43.2

Grafanaki, S., Pearson, D., Cini F., Godula, D., Mckenzie, B., Nason, S., & Anderegg, M. (2005). Sources of renewal: A qualitative study on the experience and role of leisure in the life of counselors and psychologists. *Counselling Psychology Quarterly*, *18*, 31–40.

Hamann, D. L., & Gordon, D. G. (2000). Burnout: An occupational hazard. *Music Educators Journal*, *87*, 34–39.

Han, B., Compton, W. M., Blanco, C., & Colpe, L. J. (2017). Prevalence, treatment, and unmet treatment needs of U.S. adults with mental health and substance use disorders. *Health Affairs*, *36*(10), 1739–1747.

Harr, C., & Moore, B. (2011). Compassion fatigue among social work students in field placements. *Journal of Teaching in Social Work*, *31*, 350–363.

Health Resources and Services Administration (HRSA), U.S. Department of Health & Human Services. (2019). *Designated health professional shortage areas statistics: Designated HPSA quarterly summary.* https://data.hrsa.gov/topics/health-workforce/shortage-areas

Hoge, M. A., Stuart, G. W., Morris, J., Flaherty, M. T., Paris, M., & Goplerud, E. (2013). Mental health and addiction workforce development: Federal leadership is needed to address the growing crisis. *Health Affairs*, *32*(11). https://doi.org/10.1377/hlthaff.2013.0541

Jacob, C. J., & Holczer, R. (2016). The role of mindfulness in reducing trauma counselors' vicarious trauma. *Journal of the Pennsylvania Counseling Association*, *15*, 31–38.

Jenkins, S. R., & Baird, S. (2002). Secondary traumatic stress and vicarious trauma: A validational study. *Journal of Traumatic Stress*, *15*(5), 423–432.

Lawson, G., & Myers, J. E. (2011). Wellness, professional quality of life, and career-sustaining behaviors: What keeps us well? *Journal of Counseling and Development*, *89*(2), 163–171.

Lawson, G., & Venart, B. (2005). *Preventing counselor impairment: Vulnerability, wellness and resiliency.* Vistas Online, Article 53. https://www.counseling.org/Resources/Library/VISTAS/vistas05/Vistas05.art53.pdf

Lawson, G., Venart, E., Hazler, R. J., & Kottler, J. A. (2007). Toward a culture of counselor wellness. *Journal of Humanistic Counseling, Education and Development*, *46*, 5–19.

Lee, S. M., Cho, S. H., Kissinger, D., & Ogle, N. T. (2010). A typology of burnout in professional counselors. *Journal of Counseling & Development*, *40*, 142–154.

Maslach, C. (1982). *Burnout: The cost of caring.* Prentice Hall.

Maslach, C., Leiter, M. P., & Schaufeli, W. B. (2009). Measuring burnout. In C. L. Cooper & S. Cartwright (Eds.), *The Oxford handbook of organizational well-being* (pp. 86–108). Oxford University Press.

Maslach, C., Schaufeli, W. B., & Leiter, M. P. (2001). Job burnout. *Annual Review of Psychology*, *52*, 397–422.

McCann, I. L., & Pearlman, L. A. (1990). Vicarious traumatization: A framework for understanding the psychological effects of working with victims. *Journal of Traumatic Stress*, *3*(1), 131–149.

Meadors, P., & Lamson, A. (2008). Compassion fatigue and secondary traumatization: Provider self-care on the intensive care units for children. *Journal of Pediatric Health*, *22*(1), 24–34.

Morse, G., Salyers, M., Rollins, A., Monroe-DeVita, M., & Pfahler, C. (2012). Burnout in mental health services: A review of the problem and its remediation. *Administrative Policy in Mental Health and Mental Health Services Research*, *39*(5), 241–352.

National Alliance on Mental Health. (2019). *Prevalence of mental illness.* https://www.nami.org/learn-more/mental-health-by-the-numbers

Oddie, S., & Ousley, L. (2007). Assessing burnout and occupational stressors in a medium secure service. *British Journal of Forensic Practice*, *9*(2), 32–48.

Parsons, R., Dickinson, K., &, Asempapa, B. (2020). *Counselor wellness: Caring for self to care for others.* Cognella Academic Publishing.

Pearlman, L. A., & McKay, L. (n.d.). *Understanding and addressing vicarious trauma.* https://headington-institute.org/files/vtmoduletemplate2_ready_v2_85791.pdf

Pearlman, L. A., & Saakvitne, K. W. (1995). *Trauma and the therapist.* Norton.

Pines, A. M., & Aronson, E. (1988). *Career burnout.* The Free Press.

Reiner, M., Niermann, C., Jekauc, D., & Woll, A. (2013). Long-term health benefits of physical activity: A systematic review of longitudinal studies. *BMC Public Health*, *13*(1), 813.

Remen, R. N. (1996). *Kitchen table wisdom: Stories that heal.* Riverhead Books.

Rohland, B. M. (2000). A survey of burnout among mental health center directors in a rural state. *Administration & Policy in Mental Health*, *27*(4), 221–237.

Roscoe, L. J. (2009). Wellness: A review of theory and measurement for counselors. *Journal of Counseling & Development*, *87*, 216–226.

Rothaupt, J. W., & Morgan, M. M. (2007). Counselors' and counselor educators' practice of mindfulness: A qualitative inquiry. *Counseling and Values*, *52*, 40–54.

Rudolph, J. M., Stamm, B. H., & Stamm, H. E. (1997). *Compassion fatigue: A concern for mental health policy, providers, and administration.* Poster presentation at the Annual Meeting of the International Society for Traumatic Stress Studies, Montreal, Canada.

Sabin-Farrell, R., & Turpin, G. (2003). Vicarious traumatization: Implications for the mental health of health workers? *Clinical Psychology Review*, *23*(3), 449–480. http://dx.doi.org/10.1016/S0272-7358(03)00030-8

Salston, M. D., & Figley, C. R. (2003). Secondary traumatic stress effects of working with survivors of criminal victimization. *Journal of Traumatic Stress, 16*(2), 167–174. http://dx.doi.org/10.1023/A:1022899207206
Schaufeli, W. B. (2003). Past performance and future perspectives of burnout research. *South African Journal of Industrial Psychology, 29*, 1–15.
Shapiro, S. L., Brown, K. W., & Biegel, G. M. (2007). Teaching self-care to caregivers: Effects of mindfulness-based stress reduction on the mental health of therapists in training. *Training and Education in Professional Psychology, 1*, 105–115.
Siebert, D. C. (2005). Personal and occupational factors in burnout among practicing social workers: Implications for research, practitioners, and managers. *Journal of Social Service Research, 32*(2), 25–44.
Skovholt, T. M., & Trotter-Mathison, M. (2011). *The resilient practitioner: Burnout prevention and self-care strategies for therapists, counselors, teachers and health professionals* (2nd ed.). Routledge.
Smart, D., English, A., James, J., Wilson, M., Daratha, K. B., Childers, B., & Magera, C. (2014). Compassion fatigue and satisfaction: A cross-sectional survey among U.S. healthcare workers. *Nursing and Health Sciences, 16*(1), 3–10. http://dx.doi.org/10.1111/nhs.12068
Sprang, G., Clark, J. J., & Whitt-Woosley, A. (2007). Compassion fatigue, compassion satisfaction, and burnout: Factors impacting a professional's quality of life. *Journal of Loss and Trauma, 12*(3), 259–280.
Stamm, B. H. (2002). Measuring compassion satisfaction as well as fatigue: Developmental history of the Compassion Fatigue and Satisfaction Test (CFST). In C. R. Figley (Ed.), *Treating compassion fatigue* (pp. 107–119). Brunner/Routledge.
Stamm, B. H. (2012a). *Professional Quality of Life Scale (ProQOL 5).* http://proqol.org/ProQol_Test.html
Stamm, B. H. (2012b). *Professional Quality of Life: Compassion Satisfaction and Fatigue Version 5 (ProQOL).* www.proqol.org
Stevanovic, P., & Rupert, P. A. (2004). Career-sustaining behaviors, satisfactions, and stresses of professional psychologists. *Psychotherapy: Theory, Research, Practice, Training, 41*(3), 301–309. https://doi.org/10.1037/0033-3204.41.3.301
Trippany, R. L., Kress, V. E., & Wilcoxon, S. A. (2004). Preventing vicarious trauma: What counselors should know when working with trauma survivors. *Journal of Counseling and Development, 82*, 31–37.
Tyssen, R., Vaglum, P., Grønvold, N. T., & Ekeberg, Ø. (2001). Suicidal ideation among medical students and young physicians: A nationwide and prospective study of prevalence and predictors. *Journal of Affective Disorders, 64*(1), 69–79.
Warburton, D., Nicol, C., & Bredin, S. (2006). Health benefits of physical activity: The evidence. *Canadian Medical Association Journal, 174*(6), 801–809.
Webb, K. M. (2011). Care of others and self: A suicidal patient's impact on the psychologist. *Professional Psychology: Research and Practice, 42*, 215.
White, R. L., Babic, M. J., Parker, P. D., Lubans, D. R., Astell-Burt, T., & Lonsdale, C. (2017). Domain-specific physical activity and mental health: A meta-analysis. *American Journal of Preventive Medicine, 52*(5), 653–666.

CHAPTER 15

The Future of Clinical Mental Health Counseling

Challenges and Opportunities

It's tough to make predictions, especially about the future.

—Yogi Berra (1925–2015)

Lawrence Peter "Yogi" Berra was a professional Baseball Hall of Fame player (catcher) from the mid-1940s to mid-1960s (16 seasons). Although noted for his baseball prowess, Yogi is also known for his "yogi-isms," such as the one referenced above.

The truth to his commentary is often overshadowed by the humor found within. In the case of predicting the future, Yogi is right on. Making predictions is tough and is often seen as a fool's game.

Defining the future role and function of mental health counselors is not within my power. However, reviewing contemporary trends, as they may foreshadow our profession's future, is of value, especially if we are to not only prepare for our future but to actively craft it. This chapter highlights the emerging trends that are defining and challenging our profession.

After completing this chapter, the reader will be able to:

- Explain the factors that are important to the advancing of professionalization of mental health counseling.
- Describe the role of research and science in mental health counseling.
- Describe the benefits and potential costs to the expanding inclusion of technology within mental health counseling practice.
- Explain why counselors will need to be more knowledgeable and skilled in strategies of social change.

Advancing Professionalization of Mental Health Counseling

As described in Chapter 12, a profession is often defined as having the following characteristics: (1) it is composed of a disciplined group of individuals, (2) members possess specialized knowledge and skills, (3) practice is governed by ethical standards, and (4) the profession has gained public recognition. By all accounts, mental health counseling has met these criteria.

As we look at the elements presented in this definition, we can project a future wherein membership grows, specialized knowledge and skills continue to unfold, and ethics will evolve. The one area of challenge for the profession is expanding the recognition received not only by the public and those we serve but also by state and national authorities and other professionals and professional organizations.

The future for the profession will include continued movement toward professionalization as assisted by the articulation of training standards and the emergence of the credentialing of professional counselors (see Chapter 14). This professionalization, which is well underway, is far from complete and will continue with a strengthening of each mental health counselor's professional identity.

Strengthening of Professional Identity

Professional identity refers to both the development of each counselor's view of self as a professional and the establishment of a collective and unified identity of all who claim to be mental health counselors. These two areas mutually inform one another with a professional identity (Lile, 2017).

Our profession's organizations (e.g., ACA, AMHCA) have, by of their promotion of a core mission and values, done much in support of the establishment of counselors' professional identities. Further, the increased acceptance of shared standards of competency that are deemed essential for entry into the profession (see Chapter 13) also strengthens our collective identities by providing a concrete reference to the unique knowledge and skill set that we bring to mental health services. However, an area that calls for continued efforts in service of establishing our professional identities is in the arena of gaining recognition as a coequal and valued profession among the other healthcare professions (e.g., psychiatry, clinical psychology, clinical social work).

The future will call upon counselors to embody the values and practices that make counseling unique and provide evidence of their unique value to mental health service.

Gaining Increased Public Recognition

Although all 50 states, as well as District of Columbia, Puerto Rico, and Guam, recognize licensure for counselors, the portability of licensure and credentials across state lines remains a challenge. Efforts to ensure such portability are underway (see Chapter 14), and the inclusion of counselors as service providers for the national system of TRICARE, an integrated, single-payer health service provider to military members and their families, bodes well for the increase of public recognition of counseling as a coequal and valued mental health profession.

TRICARE's recognition of professional counselors is a good step in the evolving professionalization of counseling. As of this writing, however, licensed professional counselors continue to be excluded from Medicare reimbursement. As mental health counselors continue to seek recognition and parity with other mental health providers, acceptance as Medicare providers will help to announce that parity.

Efforts are underway to rectify this injustice and slighting of professional counselors. Bipartisan legislation has been introduced in Congress that would improve access to mental health services and permit Licensed Professional Counselors (LPCs) to be reimbursed by Medicare. In the Senate, the Mental Health Access Improvement Act of 2019, S. 286, was introduced by Senators John Barrasso (R-WY) and Debbie Stabenow (D-MI). In the House of Representatives, the Mental Health Access Improvement Act, H.R. 945, was introduced by Representatives John Katko (R-NY) and Mike Thompson (D-CA).

In addition to gaining national licensure and certification and inclusion in all third-party reimbursement programs, a third measure of the recognition that professional counseling is a valuable and coequal member of the mental health team would be the granting of clinical privilege to counselors:

"Clinical privileging is the process by which a licensed independent practitioner is granted permission by law and a health-care facility to practice independently and to provide specific services within the scope of practice defined by the practitioner's license"(National Academy of Sciences, 2010, p. 112). Clinical privileges are granted and exercised in the specific site(s) or settings(s), with requirements for qualification defined by the organization allowing privilege.

Although the specific requirements for privilege will vary setting to setting, reflecting the unique needs of the setting and the population served, most require (1) graduate training in area of mental health practice, (2) possession of licenses or certification deemed necessary for entry into specialized practice, and (3) evidence of previous supervised field work.

As mental health counselors expand their work with those with addictions and trauma, as well as those requiring residential treatment, the need for privilege as a base for the continuation of care will become much more evident.

Specialized Knowledge and Skills

The increased professionalization of counseling will be supported by further developing our professional identities and recognizing and valuing that unique identity among professionals. Another factor that will continue to contribute to the growing professionalization of mental health counseling in the future is the expansion of our specialized knowledge and skills. Like others within the mental health professions, we employ much of the same research and scientific base that supports our clinical practice. However, in addition to utilizing this knowledge in our formulation of treatment interventions, counselors will continue to move beyond intervention and program for prevention and development.

As we move into the next phase of our professional existence, mental health counselors will increase standards of practice and the training necessary to serve as a professional mental health counselor. One path that appears to be emerging for strengthening mental health counselors' professional skills and positioning them as coequals for other mental health providers is the creation of clinically oriented doctoral training.

The future may see professional investment and expansion of programs providing a Doctorate of Professional Counseling (DPC) degree. Although many mental health counselors have pursued a PhD in counseling or even counselor education, the DPC would be specifically clinically oriented, similar to psychology's PsyD degree, and is thus an alternative to research-based PhD programs. The focus of the DPC is to provide the highest level of clinical training to mental health counselors. The training and the credentialing are felt to be steps that will facilitate counselors gaining parity with other allied health professionals (Locke, 2012).

New Perspectives and Approaches to Treatment

Our understanding of the human condition continues to unfold. Research is increasingly highlighting factors that contribute not only to health and but also those factors across the biopsychosocial dimensions of the human condition that can undermine our well-being. The future will invite mental health counselors to become more mindful of these factors and employ strategies that have been proven to be effective in supporting our clients' development and well-being.

Techniques Grounded in Science

The American Counseling Association (ACA) directs its members "to use techniques/procedures/modalities that are grounded in theory and/or have an empirical or scientific foundation" (2014, C.7.a). The scientific foundation for counseling will continue to strengthen as we move into the next decades.

The future will see professional counselors not only more fully aware of the science supporting best practice but also employing those procedures that are empirically supported (see Chapter 6). The challenge will be for the profession and each mental health counselor to develop the knowledge and skills necessary to integrate the best available research with clinical expertise that reflects the client's characteristics, culture, and personal preferences.

To bridge the gap between knowing and doing, the ACA created the Center for Counseling Practice, Policy, and Research as a platform to provide clinicians with the most relevant and current practice information.

Responding to Changing Demographics

Current demographic and social trends suggest that the mental health counselors will be serving an expanded and diverse clientele. For one thing, our client base is getting older. The projection is that in the United States by 2034 there will be 77.0 million people 65 years and older as compared to 76.5 million younger than age 18 (Vespa, 2019). Older adults will outnumber children and youth. This projection highlights the fact that not only is our client base "graying" but that they will likely present with unique developmental challenges, which, in turn, require special knowledge and skills of those who serve this population.

Another trend that will impact our training and professional development is the reality that our client base is becoming much more ethnically diverse. Data from the 2020 Census will show a nation that has become more racially and ethnically diverse. The Asian American population is projected to increase by 32%, followed by the Latino population (23% increase). The non-Hispanic White population is projected to increase by just 1%, with a net gain of 1.3 million people (Mather et al., 2019). Given these projected demographics, counselors will need to exhibit multicultural competence and employ skills and techniques that reflect multicultural awareness and sensitivity.

Increasing Focus on Wellness and Prevention

The value and focus on positive psychology, wellness practices, and preventive care are increasing among healthcare providers. The recognition of the practical and financial benefits of investing in preventive care has increased and so has the emphasis on the developmental aspects of counseling, as contrasted to a strictly remedial focus.

With wellness and prevention as primary values of the counseling profession, it can be assumed that the future will see counselors increasing their efforts to integrate the preventive, developmental, wellness elements into their services. Counselors will expand their efforts in providing primary prevention services in schools and community agencies. They will find themselves in roles such as consultants, educators, providers in employee assistance programs (EAPs), and even mental health coaches.

Technology and the Mode of Service Delivery

It is undoubtedly not a futuristic prediction to state that technology will significantly impact the delivery of healthcare services, including those provided by mental health counselors. The utilization of technology in the delivery of mental health services is here and will only increase in the future. Beyond expanding our reach via distance counseling, technology will find its presence in our use of apps that support our services and even in the formation of "virtual" counselors as the first-line contact for our clients.

There are benefits and significant challenges to engaging technology in the provision of our care. Our future will be one in which mental health counselors will need to integrate the best technology into their practice while managing all the potential threats and downsides.

E-Counseling, Cybercounseling, and Telehealth

When envisioning how counselors might deliver their mental health services in the future, what might first come to mind is distance counseling through email, video conferencing, and other technologies, which is also referred to as e-counseling, cybercounseling, or telehealth. As part of a broader approach to providing healthcare services, telehealth has been described as especially beneficial to those in remote areas or who have challenges, including physical disabilities, that prohibit their ability to come to an office for a face-to-face visit (Villines, 2020).

The use of video conferencing, emails, text messages, and streaming media all show promise for those mental health counselors seeking to expand the market they serve while increasing effectiveness and cost-efficiency. Although adopting this mode of service delivery brings benefits, it also poses practical, ethical, and legal concerns (e.g., confidentiality, licensing across state lines, etc.) (Parsons & Boccone, 2020). The issues surrounding the use of technology are significant enough that the ACA devoted an entire section (i.e., Section H) in its code of ethics (ACA, 2014) to distance counseling, technology, and social media.

As with any mode of service delivered by a mental health counselor, engaging in electronic or cyberbased counseling requires the knowledge and skills essential to effective, ethical practice as applied to this platform of service delivery.

Supportive Apps

Counselors are now using mobile devices, such as cell phones, smartphones, and tablets, to access help, monitor progress, and increase understanding of their clients' mental well-being. Although such mobile devices can provide significant support for those in crisis, new technologies and applications are expanding the therapeutic utility of these devices.

Apps for smartphones or tables can be used to collect information about a client's behavior patterns or detect changes in behavior that may signify a need for intervention (National Institute of Mental Health [NIMH], 2019). Apps are available for self-management, mood tracking, passive symptom tracking, skills training, screening and assessment services, and the development of mindfulness practices. And this is just the beginning. The National Institute of Mental Health has awarded over 400 grants, totaling $445 million, for technology-enhanced mental health intervention (NIMH, 2019).

Table 15.1 provides some of the advantages and challenges of employing mobile apps as part of mental healthcare delivery.

TABLE 15.1 The Pros and Cons of Mental Health Apps

Potential Benefits
• **Convenience:** Treatment can occur anytime and anywhere (e.g., at home in the middle of the night or on a bus on the way to work) and may be ideal for those who have trouble with in-person appointments. • **Anonymity:** Clients can seek treatment options without involving other people. • **An introduction to care:** Technology may be an excellent first step for those who have avoided mental health care in the past. • **Lower cost:** Some apps are free or cost less than traditional care. • **Service to more people:** Technology can help mental health providers offer treatment to people in remote areas or many people in times of sudden need (e.g., following a natural disaster or terror attack). • **Interest:** Some technologies might be more appealing than traditional treatment methods, encouraging clients to continue therapy. • **24-hour service:** Technology can provide round-the-clock monitoring or intervention support. • **Consistency:** Technology can offer the same treatment program to all users. • **Support:** Technology can complement traditional therapy by extending an in-person session, reinforcing new skills, and providing support and monitoring. • **Objective data collection:** Technology can quantitatively collect information such as location, movement, phone use, and other information.
Challenges and Concerns
Effectiveness: The biggest concern with technological interventions is obtaining scientific evidence that they work and that they work as well as traditional methods.
For whom and what: Another concern is understanding if apps work for all people and all mental health conditions.
Privacy: Apps deal with very sensitive personal information, so app makers need to guarantee privacy for app users.
Guidance: There are no industrywide standards to help consumers know if an app or other mobile technology is proven effective.
Regulation: The question of who will or should regulate mental health technology and the data it generates needs to be answered.
Overselling: There is some concern that if an app or program promises more than it delivers, consumers may turn away from other, more effective therapies.

Source: Adapted from National Institute of Mental Health, "The Pros and Cons of Mental Health Care Apps," 2019.

It appears that apps will continue to be a part of the counselor's toolbox. At present, there is little research on the clinical utility of these apps as used in practice. Thus, the use of these apps will need to be closely monitored by the counselor and assessed for effectiveness. Several practical suggestions for the utilization of apps in counseling are presented in Table 15.2.

TABLE 15.2 Things to Consider When Utilizing Apps in Practice

Research and due diligence. With more than 10,000 mental health apps available for consumer use (Clay, 2020), it is essential that counselor's review and research specific apps before employing them. A useful resource is PsyberGuide (https://onemindpsyberguide.org).
Consider data security and client privacy. Be sure that clients understand the risks and limitations and the nature of that which perhaps should not be shared.
Therapeutic utility. All homework prescribed or materials employed should not only reflect the counselor's therapeutic approach and be in line with treatment goals but should receive client-informed consent.
Guide client in use. As part of gaining informed consent, the counselor should review the app, with its purpose and utility, and even, when appropriate, practice the use of the app with the client.

Assess and monitor effectiveness. The counselor needs to monitor client's use of the app and assess its clinical value in supporting progress and goal attainment.

Remember, apps are only tools, not treatments. As a supplement or aid to the counseling process, an app should be stopped if it harms the client or impedes progress. Apps also should be terminated if for no other reason than the client is no longer interested or engaged.

Although the counseling relationship has been seen and continues to be viewed as an essential, if not *the* essential, element within the helping process, there is some projection that the human contact may be replaced, or at least augmented, by a virtual or avatar counselor. Avatars are digital self-representations that enable individuals to interact with each other in computer-based virtual environments.

Although the concept of an avatar counselor may, on first consideration, appear silly, if not ludicrous, a virtual counselor may serve as the "first step" to a counseling relationship (Shallcross, 2012). Additionally, avatars may be useful in the application of specific therapeutic interventions.

Gorini et al. (2008), in what is seen as a seminal work on the topic, proposed two key applications of avatars in multiuser, computer-based, three-dimensional virtual worlds for delivery of online interventions for mental health problems. These authors (Gorini et al., 2008) proposed using avatars to deliver exposure-based therapy for anxiety disorders and substance abuse problems and secondly as a tool to facilitate anonymous online peer support communities. Since their work, others have studied the utility of avatars not only with anxiety disorders (Powers et al., 2013) but also when working with clients experiencing persecutory delusions (Freeman et al., 2016). The current use of avatars has just begun to scratch the service of therapeutic utility. Rehm et al. (2016) provide an excellent review of the current uses of avatars and their potential for utilization as part of e-mental health interventions.

Counselors as Advocates

Our expanding understanding of the influence of systems and ecology in the development of human behavior and the promotion of wellness and mental health has set the stage for mental health counselors to move beyond lip service of valuing prevention to engaging as advocates and agents of system change. Multicultural competence and social justice commitment will become an increasingly integral part of the practice of mental health counseling.

The evidence is too clear to ignore. We cannot help repair the psychosocial damage created by oppressive systems only to return our clients to those same systems. Counselors must view "client problems more contextually and use advocacy to remove oppressive environmental barriers" (Lewis et al., 2011, p. 7).

The forces of oppression, disenfranchisement, and devaluing that damage our clients must be addressed as part of our treatment plans. The use of social advocacy as a means of addressing conditions that impede the academic, career, and personal/social development of individuals, families, and communities must be integrated into the services we provide (Ratts, 2009).

Counselors will increasingly resist being complicit with maintaining the status quo, which means engaging in efforts to adjust clients to the context, even when it is the context that needs adjusting. We will engage with strategies that result in system change. As we move into the next phase of our profession's development, we will give greater voice to our prevention values by engaging in social advocacy—targeting those systemic factors that cause and maintain the suffering encountered by our culturally diverse clients.

Keystones

- One trend projected to grow in the future is the advancement in mental health counseling professionalization through expanded membership, increased employment of practice rooted in science, and increased public recognition.
- In gaining public recognition and professional equity with others in the mental health field, mental health counselors will continue to work for the portability of licensure; expansion of third-party payers, including Medicare; and clinical privilege acquisition.
- Trends suggest that mental health counselors will increase their engagement with best practices and the employment of empirically supported treatments.
- The utilization and integration of technology into practice will continue with the expansion of cybercounseling, clinical apps, and the employment of avatars.
- As counselors employ an ecological perspective to client wellness, increased emphasis will be given to counselors as advocates for social change.

Additional Resources

American Counseling Association. (2020). *Advocacy competencies: A social justice framework for counselors.* https://www.counseling.org/docs/default-source/competencies/aca-advocacy-competencies-updated-may-2020.pdf?sfvrsn=f410212c_4

American Psychological Association. (2015). *What you need to know before choosing online therapy.* https://www.apa.org/topics/online-therapy

One Mind PsyberGuide. (n.d.). *Apps and digital health resources reviewed by experts.* https://onemindpsyberguide.org

Substance Abuse and Mental Health Services Administration. (2015). *Using technology-based therapeutic tools in behavioral health services.* Treatment Improvement Protocol (TIP) Series 60. HHS Publication No. (SMA) 15-4924. https://www.ncbi.nlm.nih.gov/books/NBK344045/

References

American Counseling Association. (2014). *ACA code of ethics.* https://www.counseling.org/Resources/aca-code-of-ethics.pdf

Clay, R. (2020). *Using apps with your patients.* American Psychological Association. https://www.apa.org/monitor/2020/04/career-using-apps

Freeman, D., Bradley, J., Antley, A., Bourke, E., DeWeever, N., Evans, N., Černis, E., Sheaves, B., Waite, F., Dunn, G., Slater, M., & Clark, D. M. (2016). Virtual reality in the treatment of persecutory delusions: Randomized controlled experimental study testing how to reduce delusional conviction. *British Journal of Psychiatry, 209*(1), 62–67.

Gorini, A., Gaggioli, A., Vigna, C., & Riva, G. (2008). A second life for eHealth: Prospects for the use of 3-D virtual worlds in clinical psychology. *Journal of Medical Internet Research, 10*(3), e.21.

Lewis, J. A., Ratts, M. J., Paladino, D. A., & Toporek, R. L. (2011). Social justice counseling and advocacy: Developing new leadership roles and competencies. *Journal of Social Action in Counseling and Psychology, 69*, 222–227.

Lile, J. J. (2017). Forming a professional counselor identity: The impact of identity processing style. *Journal of Counselor Preparation and Supervision, 9*(2). http://dx.doi.org/10.7729/92.1163

Locke, D. W. (2012). DPC—The next step. *Counseling Today.* https://ct.counseling.org/2012/02/dpc-the-next-step/

Mather, M., Jacobsen, L. A., Jarosz, B., Kilduff, L., Lee, A., Pollard, K. M., Scommegna, P., & Vanorman, A. (2019). *Population Bulletin, 74*(1), 1–21. https://www.prb.org/wp-content/uploads/2019/06/PRB-PopBulletin-2020-Census.pdf

National Academy of Sciences, Committee on the Qualifications of Professionals Providing Mental Health Counseling Services Under TRICARE, Board on the Health of Select Populations, Institute of Medicine. (2010). *Provision of mental health counseling services under TRICARE.* National Academies Press.

National Institute of Mental Health. (2019). *Technology and the future of mental health treatment.* https://www.nimh.nih.gov/health/topics/technology-and-the-future-of-mental-health-treatment/index.shtml

Parsons, R. D., & Boccone, P. (2020). *Ethical decision making: A guide for the 21st century counselor.* Cognella Academic Press.

Powers, M. B., Briceno, N. F., Gresham, R., Jouriles, E. N., Emmelkamp, P. M., & Smits, J. A. (2013). Do conversations with virtual avatars increase feelings of social anxiety? *Journal of Anxiety Disorders, 27*(4), 398–403.

Ratts, M. J. (2009). Social justice counseling: Toward the development of a "fifth force" among counseling paradigms. *Journal of Humanistic Counseling, Education and Development, 48,* 160–172.

Rehm, I. C., Foenander, E., Wallace, K., Abbott, J. M., Kyrios, M., & Thomas, N. (2016). What role can avatars play in e-mental health interventions? Exploring new models of client–therapist interaction. *Frontiers in Psychiatry, 7,* 186. https://doi.org/10.3389/fpsyt.2016.00186

Shallcross, L. (2012). What the future holds for the counseling profession. *Counseling Today.* https://ct.counseling.org/2012/03/what-the-future-holds-for-the-counseling-profession/

Vespa, J. (2019). *The U.S. joins other countries with large aging populations.* https://www.census.gov/library/stories/2018/03/graying-america.html

Villines, Z. (2020). *Telemedicine benefits: For patients and professionals.* https://www.medicalnewstoday.com/articles/telemedicine-benefits

INDEX

ABOUT THE AUTHOR

Richard D. Parsons, PhD, is a full professor in the Counselor Education Department at West Chester University. He has more than 40 years of university teaching in counselor preparation programs. Before his university teaching, Dr. Parsons spent 9 years as a school counselor in an inner-city high school. He has had a private clinical practice for over 40 years and serves as a consultant to educational institutions and mental health service organizations throughout the tri-state area of Pennsylvania, New Jersey, and Delaware. He has been the recipient of many awards and honors, including the Pennsylvania Counselor of the Year award.

Dr. Parsons has authored or co-authored more than 80 professional articles and books. His most recent books include the co-authored texts *Counselor Wellness: Caring for Self to Care for Others* (Cognella Academic Publishing), *The School Counselor as Consultant: Expanding Impact From Intervention to Prevention* (Cognella Academic Publishing), *Intentional Counseling, and Ethical Practices in the Human Services* (Sage). Dr. Parsons also serves as co-editor for a 24-book series, *Counseling and Professional Identity*, published by Sage Publications, and as editor of a 10-book series titled *The Cognella Series on Student Success*, published by Cognella Academic Publishing.

www.ingramcontent.com/pod-product-compliance
Lightning Source LLC
Chambersburg PA
CBHW080618051126
54393CB00005B/511
9781793548078